Italian Yearbook of Human Rights 2018

P.I.E. Peter Lang

Bruxelles · Bern · Berlin · New York · Oxford · Wien

Translators from the Italian version:
Rosemary Burnham, Francesca Coppola,
Demet Gümüş, Carolina Lambiase,
Elisa de Carvalho Pellegrino, Laura Andrea Duarte Reyes

The Yearbook is edited by the
University of Padova
Human Rights Centre "Antonio Papisca",
via Martiri della Libertà 2,
35137 Padova

tel. +39 049.8271817

centro.dirittiumani@unipd.it
www.italianhumanrightsyearbook.eu

Italian Yearbook of Human Rights 2018

Italian Yearbook of Human Rights
Vol. 9

Part IV. National and International Case-Law

List of Acronyms

AGCOM	The Communications Regulatory Authority (Autorità per le garanzie nelle comunicazioni)
ANCI	National Association of Italian Municipalities (Associazione Nazionale dei Comuni Italiani)
C.l.	Constitutional law (Legge costituzionale)
CAT	Convention against Torture and other Cruel, Inhuman or Degrading Treatment or Punishment
CEDAW	Convention on the Elimination of all Forms of Discrimination against Women
CFREU	Charter of Fundamental Rights of the European Union
CFSP	Common Foreign and Security Policy of the European Union
CIDU	Inter-Ministerial Committee for Human Rights (Comitato interministeriale per i diritti umani)
CIE	Identification and Expulsion Centre (Centro di identificazione ed espulsione)
CJEU	Court of Justice of the European Union
CM	Committee of Ministers of the Council of Europe
CoE	Council of Europe
CPED	International Convention for the Protection of All Persons from Enforced Disappearance
CPT	European Committee for the Prevention of Torture and Inhuman or Degrading Treatment or Punishment
CRC	Convention on the Rights of the Child
CRPD	Convention on the Rights of Persons with Disabilities
CSM	National Council of the Judiciary (Consiglio Superiore della Magistrarura)
CSDP	Common Security and Defence Policy of the European Union

Italy and Human Rights in 2017: Time to Restart

On 22 February 2018, the Italian Government presented the President of the United Nations General Assembly the country's candidacy to become a member of the Human Rights Council for the 2019-2021 term. For the third time, therefore, after 2007-2010 and 2011-2014, Italy throws its hat into the ring as a global actor for the promotion and protection of human rights, participating once again in the main multilateral platform on the subject.

Participating in such a position is now more important than ever for a country like Italy. In the first place, quality and coherence has characterised the contribution of the Italian State over the years to advance the human rights agenda on the international scene. The promotion of multilateralism, moratorium on the death penalty, women's rights and abandoning traditional practices affecting women's health, commitment against trafficking in persons, religious rights and beliefs, human rights education, protection of human rights defenders: the main themes of the Italian government international action are, in their current articulations, central for the global action to protect rights. Secondly, the Italian candidacy should be appreciated given Italy's crucial position in the rough seas of the political, economic, cultural, strategic and humanitarian dynamics of our time. From this point of view, the choice of contributing to a seat on the Human Rights Council was by no means a foregone conclusion. It also constitutes a courageous assumption of responsibility and of leadership – or so we hope.

Italy's commitments before the international community for the coming years are ambitious and strategically relevant. The document setting out its intended plan of action if elected as a member of the Council specifies the following areas:

strengthening the United Nations system for human rights (Council, UPR, special procedures, international criminal justice, response to emergencies, human rights education and support for civil society organisations); fighting against racism and xenophobia and against all forms of discrimination, including that based on sexual orientation, and against hate speech, including online; combating violence against women, abandoning traditional harmful practices and empowering women in all fields, including humanitarian action; supporting the rights of children, adolescents and young people at all levels especially through education; supporting a universal moratorium on the death penalty; promoting religious tolerance and preventing atrocities through interreligious and intercultural dialogue; fighting human trafficking; protecting and supporting people with disabilities and their rights; promoting cultural rights and protecting cultural heritage at risk; supporting human rights defenders and their protection from retaliation.

Through critically analysing and comparing this document with the previous application letters outlining Italy's commitments from 2007 and 2011, it emerges that the commitments undertaken are rather generally articulated and do not seem to stray much from the path forged in previous documents. It reiterates the traditional lines of action of the country, with some modest variations. Consistency and continuity, therefore. But perhaps, current times require something extra.

The multiple wars and humanitarian crises, the social tension that courses through our planet, the risks looming over the human and natural habitat, the widespread distrust of multilateral institutions, the attacks and retaliations that human rights defenders suffer in many countries, and the crisis of effectiveness that affects international human rights law in much of the world, would perhaps require a change of pace, or even a leap in quality from the Human Rights Council. If we want to criticise the Italian government's application letter, one limitation is this: the letter does not seem to grasp the urgency of the times. It does not seem to actively and innovatively face the multiple challenges affecting both international action for human rights beings and their protection in Italy.

A change of pace would be desirable on the part of the Human Rights Council and, more specifically, of the participating States. This is not only regarding global policies, but also with regard to the commitment to effectiveness of the rights to be implemented at home and, as far as Italy is concerned, in the European context.

In support of its application, Italy's application letter cites some of its recent successful national policies. These include adopting the National Action Plans on "Business and Human Rights" and "Women, Peace and Security"; introducing the crime of torture in the penal code; adopting legislation on civil unions between persons of the same sex. It should be noted, however, that these actions come at a considerable distance of time from the related recommendations and assumptions of commitment. The time difference between the moment in which a certain commitment is made and that in which the relative application measures are adopted is indicative not only of the complexity and delicacy of the problems involved in any action that touches the matter of fundamental rights, but also, at least in some cases, the lack of attention paid to certain issues at the political and decisional level. The consequence of this situation is a feeling of separation between the reality represented by the compressions, reductions and real violations of rights, and the answers given by the institutions. This general difficulty on the part of democratic political institutions to keep pace with the contemporary challenges and developments of the debate and of the socio-political and juridical practice on fundamental rights emerges also from the analysis conducted periodically by the Research and Editorial Board of the *Yearbook*.

Reading the previous versions of the *Italian Human Rights Agenda*, from 2012 to today, brings up a stagnant trend. The Agenda aims to map the main human rights initiatives that Italian authorities should take on regulatory, infrastructural and public policies. Every year, the Research and Editorial Board of the *Yearbook* will get rid of or move items or sub-items of the Agenda, in the light of the recommendations addressed to Italy and of the initiatives developed or implemented by the latter. Most of the Agenda items that were originally identified in 2012 have remained essentially unchanged over the past six years. In short, Italy's action for the implementation of human rights does not distinguish itself by through its dynamism and indeed, in particular area such as immigration and management of migratory flows, we are witnessing regressive human rights policies (as highlighted by the Council of Europe Commissioner for Human Rights, among others). Even the prospect of competing for access to the Human Rights Council in 2019 does not seem to have substantially changed this general trend.

On an institutional level (e.g. regarding the ratification of international instruments, adoption of action plans, active participation in dialogue with the monitoring mechanisms at regional and international level) Italy's commitment is appreciable and constant, placing the country among those that most intensely support multilateral action for the guarantee of human rights. On the level of the actual implementation of substantive commitments, however, some fundamental issues remained unresolved. This is the case, for example, of discrimination against members of the Roma, Sinti and Traveller communities, despite the adoption in 2012 of the inclusion strategy dedicated to them. The problem remains on the table, especially with reference to the housing issue and the legal recognition of the "*de facto* stateless persons" from the former Yugoslavia. As in the first edition of the *Yearbook* (2011), also in this edition (2018), as in all the intermediate ones, the situation of those belonging to these minorities remains a concern for international monitoring bodies. Another example is the question of overcrowding of prisons: despite the promising reduction of the phenomenon found in the two-year period 2014-2015, due to the introduction of a multiplicity of measures, including sometimes limiting the use of criminal detention tout-court, the relationship between prisoners and prisoners' capacities has returned to growth, as has been pointed out, among others, by the Council of Europe's Committee for the Prevention of Torture in its most recent report on Italy. It is almost cloying to mention the failure to create independent national institutions for human rights, a structural and lasting gap, the subject of dozens of recommendations addressed to the Italian authorities in the last decade (see *Yearbook 2017*, p. 20-23). Compared to the previous application letters to the Human Rights Council, the one presented in 2018 omits mentioning the establishment of a national Commission among the voluntary commitments of the Government for the next three years.

It is particularly alarming to note that a decline in dynamism seems to also characterise the sub-national human rights infrastructure. The effervescence of innovative and advanced initiatives, developed on the net with international and transnational subjects, has in fact traditionally hit Italy on the international scene, making it a living and dynamic actor. Thanks to this infrastructure, Italy has managed to compensate for the lack of public bodies for human rights at the national level. In recent years, however, there is also a gradual decline in operations in this area. This conclusion appears to be fattening, as well as in the light of some empirical observations, also from the consideration of a significant indicator: the presence on the Internet of institutional pages of sub-national bodies dedicated to the themes of peace and human rights. This presence has generally become more rarefied, concentrating in some territorial realities where the theme is particularly rooted. Alongside the unravelling of initiatives and opposites of network and media presence, there is also less visibility and operational capacity of national structures. This trend also involves the more or less formalised networks of ombudsmen, guarantors of children, guarantors of the rights of prisoners, etc. to activate a regional or local level, the ability to connect and represent, advocate and influence on national politics is certainly weakened.

The above-mentioned regulatory and institutional achievements, in particular the adoption of important policy documents and action plans on key themes for the promotion and guarantee of rights, such as the fight against discrimination or violence against women, are often referred to by national authorities as evidence of the country's active commitment to fundamental rights. In reality, however, the approval and implementation of an action plan on matters that have an impact on rights is not enough, if these actions do not link results, duly documented, on the material level. In particular, the likelihood of positive results for the enjoyment of rights from the adoption of the action plans and their implementation is also a function of the quality of the action plans themselves. And the technical quality of these programming tools is sometimes questionable. The deficiencies concern, for example, the generic way in which objectives and priorities for action are formulated, and the existence of significant gaps in the periodic monitoring and evaluation of the results achieved. The in-depth analysis contained in this edition of the *Yearbook*, dedicated to the *Implementation of the National Action Plan on Violence against Women*, clearly shows the nature and extent of these continuing difficulties.

Alongside these weaknesses and weaknesses, some promising ideas can be observed. On the issue of Human Rights Defenders, for example, the Government has shown growing interest and willingness to cooperate with the recent proposals of civil society, in particular the advocacy action promoted by the "In Defense of" (*In Difesa di*) network. A commitment that seems to be particularly reflected in the work of the OSCE, of which Italy will have the Presidency during 2018. Another pilot experience of great value is the initiative of the "humanitarian corridors", a synergy between civil society organisations and community and voluntary realities, accompanied by the institutions of the State, aimed at making possible the arrival in Italy under conditions of legality and security of individuals and families from areas of conflict that will benefit, once in Italy, of international protection (see Part II, National Bodies with Jurisdiction over Human Rights, VIII).

2018 marks numerous important recurrences for human rights and for the country's commitment to this field. Firstly, the 70th anniversary of the Universal Declaration of Human Rights, and the 20th anniversary of the United Nations Declaration on Human Rights Defenders. In the domestic sphere, 2018 is also the 70th anniversary of the entry into force of the Republican Constitution and the 30th anniversary of the first regional law on human rights and the culture of peace (r.l. 18/1988 of Veneto). From the point of view of the general commitment proclaimed in view of the probable election of Italy to the Human Rights Council, all of these recurrences could help provide an incentive for the country to emerge from its relative "immobility", and to foster reflection on human rights at national and sub-national levels leading to greater generative capacity with regard to human rights and peace norms and policies.

In addition to presenting itself as a model for the international community, Italy's commitment to the development and implementation of human rights must be coherently reflected in action within its borders and within the framework of the European Union. The spaces for improvement are many and wide, and a courageous and far-sighted action would be the right answer to the many voices that feed, mostly in bad faith, scepticism and hostility on the enduring value of human rights.

Italian Human Rights Agenda 2018

In the following pages, the Research and Editorial Board of the *Italian Yearbook of Human Rights* at the University of Padova Human Rights Centre "Antonio Papisca" presents the updated version of the *Italian Human Rights Agenda*. This work was originally started to better analyse the recommendations received from Italy in the international sphere and of the most critical issues identified in the various editions of the same Yearbook.

The Agenda is an orientation tool concerning the main initiatives to be implemented on the legislative, infrastructural and policy level in order to strengthen the national system of promotion and protection of human rights.

In line with the stagnant trend of human rights highlighted in the Introduction, this year the Research and Editorial Board has not found significant progress on the action of Italy in this area. If the previous edition of the Agenda saw the elimination of only one item and the reformulation of another four, the variations contained in the 2018 edition are reduced to a minimum. These concern moving the sub-items related to two national action plans (Strategic Plan on Male Violence against Women and the Second Biennial Action Programme for the Promotion of the Rights and Integration of Persons with Disabilities) from the part of the Agenda which recommended its adoption, which took place during 2017, to the part where the Agenda is emphasised the need to provide information on the implementation and impact of the various plans adopted and being implemented.

Italian Agenda of Human Rights 2018

Normative Level	1) Ratify the following legal instruments at the United Nations and Council of Europe: a. International Convention on the Protection of the Rights of All Migrant Workers and the Members of their Families; b. Protocol XII to the Convention for the Protection of Human Rights and Fundamental Freedoms; c. Protocol XV to the Convention for the Protection of Human Rights and Fundamental Freedoms; d. Protocol XVI to the Convention for the Protection of Human Rights and Fundamental Freedoms; e. European Convention on Nationality; f. Additional Protocol to the Criminal Convention on Corruption.
	2) Deposit the instruments of ratification for the following legal instruments for which Parliament has already approved the relative ratification and implementation laws a. Convention on Human Rights and Biomedicine (Oviedo Convention); b. Additional Protocol to the Convention on Human Rights and Biomedicine concerning Transplantation of Organs and Tissue of Human Origin.
	3) Promote awareness of and application of the Declaration on the right to peace adopted by the United Nations General Assembly on 19 December 2016.
	4) Accept article 25 of the European Social Charter (revised) on the right of workers to protection of their claims in the event of insolvency of their employer.
	5) Withdraw the declaration that excludes the application for Italy of Chapter C of the European Convention on the Participation of Foreigners in Public Life at Local Level and, accordingly, provide for the introduction of active and passive voting rights in local elections for foreigners who have been residing in Italy for a certain number of years.
	6) Include hate motivation as an aggravating circumstance in article 61 of the Italian criminal code.
	7) Align the crime of torture, introduced as article 613-*bis* of the criminal code, so that it is in conformity with article 1 of the UN Convention against Torture.
	8) Expressly recognise representative non-governmental organisations within Italian jurisdiction having particular competence in issues regulated by the European Social Charter (revised) the right to present collective complaints pursuant to the 1995 Protocol.
	9) Complete the adoption process of the parliamentary bill on defamation in light of the UN, Council of Europe and OCSE standards.
	10) Continue efforts to reform the system of prevention and repression of corruption both in the public and private sector, with special reference to the most recent recommendations by GRECO on the following issues: pressing charges of corruption, transparency of party funding and prevention of corruption of members of parliament, magistrates and public prosecutors.

Infrastructural Level	11) Complete as promptly as possible the system of independent national human rights institutions, in line with the Paris Principles adopted by the United Nations: a. Establish the National Human Rights Commission; b. Establish the National Ombudsperson.
	12) Ensure the existence of a permanent parliamentary Human Rights Commission, in one or both Chambers.
	13) Assign all Ministries an *ad hoc* human rights office.
	14) Provide independent authorities operating in areas directly related to human rights with necessary human resources and funds.
Implementation of international obligations and commitments	15) Complete the legislative process for the implementation of the Statute of the International Criminal Court concerning substantive law.
	16) Increase the timeliness and full execution of the European Court of Human Rights rulings, including paying out compensation awarded, and improve Italy's capacity to conform to the standards defined by the same Court.
	17) Address as a matter of urgency the issue of excessive duration of legal proceedings, including those initiated to seek remedy for their excess duration.
Policy Adoption	18) Hold an annual debate on human rights in Parliament.
	19) Adopt the following National Action Plans, providing them with suitable tools for monitoring and assessment: a. National Action Plan on the human rights situation within detention structures; b. National Programme related to education about democratic citizenship and to the education and training about human rights;
	20) Provide information about the fulfilment and impact of the following National Action Plans: a. National Strategy for the inclusion of Roma, Sinti and Travellers (2012-2020); b. National Strategy for preventing and combating discrimination on grounds of sexual orientation or gender identity; c. National Plan against racism, xenophobia and intolerance for the three-year period 2013-2015; d. National Act Plan against human trafficking and serious exploitation (2016-2018); e. National Action Plan for business and human rights (2016-2021); f. National Action Plan on "Women, Peace and Security" (2016-2019); g. Fourth National Plan of Action and interventions to protect the rights and development of children and adolescents (2016-2017); h. National Strategic Plan on Male Violence against Women (2017-2020). i. Second two-year Action Programme for the promotion of the rights and integration of persons with disabilities (2018-2020).
	21) Formally extend the remit of UNAR to include all forms of discrimination, including those based on language, religion, nation of origin, disabilities, sexual orientation and gender identity.
	22) Allocate sufficient public social expenditure for various categories (health, disability, family support, unemployment, social housing and combating social exclusion).
	23) Reinforce efforts to resolve the problem of overcrowding in prisons, making further progress on the structural measures and deflation mechanisms introduced.

Initiatives in specific areas	
Women's rights	24) Promote real equality between men and women in all aspects of public and private life, specifically through adopting policies and actions directed at: a. Reducing the under-representation of women in highest roles of political organisms, including Parliament and Regional Councils, public administration, including the diplomatic service, and in the private sector; b. Reducing the salary gap between men and women; c. Fostering a more balanced share of family duties between men and women, both domestic work and care-giving; d. Eliminating stereotyped attitudes towards the roles and responsibilities of men and women within the family, society and workplace; e. Supporting the integration process for foreign women; f. Tackling and resolving the issue of dismissal without just cause or excuse ("blank resignation letters") for pregnant women and working mothers.
Children's rights	25) Adopt general legislative provisions that enshrine the right to be listened to in court, in administrative bodies, in the institutions, at school and in the family on any issue that directly regards them and to establish suitable mechanisms and procedures to this end, to ensure that the participation of children really takes place.
	26) Amend the criminal code so as to expressly prohibit and criminalise the recruitment and deployment, either by the armed forces or armed groups, of young people under the age of 18 in course of armed conflicts.
	27) Adopt legislation prohibiting and criminalising the sale of light and small calibre arms to States which deploy child soldiers.
Citizenship rights, the rights of migrants, refugees and asylum seekers	28) Address migratory flows as a structural phenomenon, systematic planning for which must be assigned to instruments of an ordinary nature (rather than to emergency measures linked to a purely security-orientated viewpoint), and to multi-level governance with the involvement of the relevant Ministries, Regions, local administrations and NGOs.
	29) Respect the principle of *non-refoulement*, the right of asylum seekers to an individual examination of their cases, as well as immediate access to asylum procedures and other forms of national and international protection, including where there are bilateral deals for return and for cooperation in the management of migration flows.
	30) Give substance to the initiatives designed to remedy the inflexibility of the parameters of the Dublin III Regulations in order to satisfy the expectations of both those requesting international protect and the needs of the communities in Europe which are most heavily impacted the influx of migrants who are potential asylum seekers.
	31) Support the activities of the "Roundtable on the Legal Status of Roma", established on 30 January 2013 as part of the National Strategy of Inclusion for Roma, Sinti and Travellers, with the objective of finding solutions to the situation of statelessness large numbers of these communities originally from former Yugoslavia, and of their children born in Italy (the so-called "*de facto* stateless people").

	32) Develop a more expeditious identification system, in order to reduce as far as possible the period that migrants are detained while waiting for the identification procedure to be completed and ensuring the full respect of human rights for people detained in repatriation centres.
	33) Re-examine laws on citizenship in light of the principle *ius humanae dignitatis*, continuing with the direction taken by the simplification of acquiring citizenship status pursuant to article 33 of l.d. 21 June 2013, No. 69.

Structure of the Yearbook 2018

As it was for its previous editions, the *Italian Yearbook of Human Rights 2018* aims at presenting a snapshot of the human rights situation in Italy, both from a legislative and "infrastructural" point of view, and from that of the practical implementation of policies and initiatives to promote and protect them. This version of the Yearbook looks specifically at the calendar year 2017. The level of detail and background analysis provided in the various sections allows for crosscutting and targeted readings, which can also be developed by consulting the analytical indexes.

The information presented in the first three Parts of the *Yearbook* comes from public records, normally consultable via the official websites of each body examined. For Part IV, the databases of the aforementioned Courts were used (for Italian case-law, most data was taken from the Giuffrè *"De Iure"* database). The Archive is managed by the University of Padova Human Rights Centre pursuant to article 2 r.l. Veneto 55/1999.

Part I of the *Yearbook* illustrates the main developments in Italy's incorporation of international and regional standards into its domestic legislation. The overview starts from international level (United Nations) and moves on to regional level, comprising legislation drawn up by the Council of Europe and the European Union, before presenting domestic legislation that transposes international obligations into national and regional laws.

Part II illustrates the human rights infrastructure in Italy and is divided into three chapters. The first describes the structure, functions and activities of State bodies (Parliament, Government, the Judiciary, independent authorities) and also presents the activities of civil society organisations and academic institutions operating at State level. The second chapter considers the sub-national level of the Italian legal order and illustrates the variegated local and regional human rights infrastructure and the relative coordinating bodies. The third chapter is devoted to the "peace human rights" infrastructure and to initiatives developed in this area by the Region of Veneto. The specific focus on this Region is explained by the pioneering commitment shown by Veneto, dating back to its 1998 r.l. 18, in promoting a culture of human rights, peace and international solidarity.

Part III deals with Italy's position with reference to the international and regional bodies and mechanisms for monitoring the implementation of human rights. It includes the assessments and recommendations that these bodies have addressed to Italy following specific missions to the

State and periodic monitoring activities. The role of Italy within these organisations and the contribution of its diplomatic representatives for the promotion of human rights at regional and global level are highlighted. This Part is subdivided into five chapters. The first focuses on the United Nations system, focusing in particular on the activities of the General Assembly, the Human Rights Council, the Treaty Bodies and the specialist Agencies. The second chapter is devoted to the Council of Europe, while the third to the European Union. These two chapters complement the information presented in Part I (concerning legislation) and in Part IV (concerning case-law), relative to Council of Europe and EU activities in 2016. The fourth chapter deals with the Organisation for Security and Cooperation in Europe (OSCE) and its bodies for the promotion of the human dimension of security. The fifth and final chapter is on international humanitarian and criminal law. In this area, in addition to providing updates on Italy's level of conformity, there is a list of all international peace missions to which Italian troops contributed in 2017.

Finally, *Part IV* presents a selection of domestic and international case-law concerning Italy over the reference period. It comprises three chapters, into which the cases are subdivided according to the subjects to which the various judgements refer. The chapters address domestic case-law (mainly of the Constitutional Court, the Court of Cassation and the Council of State), case-law of the European Court of Human Rights and case-law of the Court of Justice of the European Union; in the latter only cases directly concerning Italy are recorded. A targeted reading of the case-law is also possible using the index of the referred case-law at the end of the book.

Considering the updated information provided in these four Parts of the *Yearbook*, this year, the Research and Editorial Board presents a new section of the Introduction aimed at elaborating on specific aspects of Italy's action regarding human rights. In this part, the design and implementation of the special action plan against sexual and gender-based violence will be analysed. The section is edited by Dr. Claudia Pividori.

In-depth Analysis. The Special Action Plan against Sexual and Gender-based Violence 2015: Implementation and Feasibility of a National Action Plan

This in-depth analysis will present a bilateral evaluation of the special action plan against sexual and gender-based violence (2015-2017), provided for by l. 119/2013 and adopted via the bill of 7 July 2015.

Firstly, an analysis of the compliance of the Italian National Action Plan (NAP) is presented with respect to international standards, primarily those established by the Istanbul Convention on preventing and combating violence against women and domestic violence.

The content and structure of the Plan will be investigated and analysed to discover whether those characteristics make it an effective operative tool for the prevention of and fight against male violence against women in Italy. To assess the NAP in terms of conformity to international standards, the following dimensions were used: a) the guiding principles and the fundamental juridical premises; b) the elaboration phase of the NAP; c) the central and territorial governance system; d) the definition of public policies in the areas of preventing, protecting against and combatting violence; e) the implementation phase; f) the evaluation and monitoring phase.

The second part of this study aims to paint as complete and precise a picture as possible of the implementation process of the NAP, the provisions in the plan and any other activities that were not expressly foreseen but have been implemented nevertheless. For each of the lines of action elaborated in the NAP (prevention, protection, punishment), as well as the corresponding intervention axes, the objectives and actions envisaged were compared with the actions actually carried out and the resources allocated. Before analysing fully the NAP, there follows a summary of the phenomenon of male violence on women in Italy.

I. Male Violence against Women in Italy

According to the latest survey conducted by ISTAT on violence against women (Survey on women's safety – 2014), 31.5% of 16-70 year-olds (6,788,000) have suffered some form of physical or sexual violence during their lifetime: 20.2% physical violence; 21% sexual violence; 5.4% rape or attempted rape. The same survey reveals that 26.4% of women have suffered psychological or economic violence from their current partner and 46.1% from a former partner. 16.1% of women are victims of stalking. Regarding the most severe forms of violence, the perpetrators are mainly either the woman's current or former partner.

With respect to the similar 2006 ISTAT survey, there are some positive signs of development. Comparing data on violence that occurred in the 5 years preceding the two surveys (2006 and 2014), physical and sexual violence fell by current partners and by former partners, as well as sexual violence perpetrated by men other than partners and psychological violence committed by the current partner (from 42.3% to 26.4%). However, much violence remains in its most serious forms (rape and attempted rape) and there has been an increase in the severity of the violence. Compared to 2006, injuries caused by violence increased in 2014 (those committed by partners rose from 26.3% to 40.2%) and the number of women reported to have feared for their lives saw an increase from 18.8% in 2006 to 34.5% in 2014.

Moreover, considering data from the 5 years preceding the 2006 and 2014 surveys, there is an emerging trend of a greater awareness of violence. More women consider violence as a crime (up from 14.3% to 29.6% for partner violence) and report it more frequently to law enforcement (from 6.7% to 11.8%). They are more likely to talk about it with someone (from 67.8% to 75.9%) and to seek help from specialised services, including anti-violence centres as their first call (from 2.4% to 4.9%).

These trends are substantially confirmed by the data provided by the Ministry of the Interior on the total number of complaints submitted (male and female victims). There is a growing tendency to report the crime of stalking (from 9,027 in 2011 to 13,177 in 2016, + 31%) and maltreatment in the family (from 9,294 cases in 2011 to over 14,000 cases in 2016, + 33%), with the exception of sexual violence crimes, of which complaints have decreased by about 12% in the last six years. The percentage incidence of the number of female victims for the three types of crime is respectively: 88%; 77-74%; 80%, confirming a gender dimension of this phenomenon.

While in the last 25 years in Italy, on the whole the number of murders has decreased, male homicide has decreased the (from 4 per 100,000 males in 1992 to 0.9 in 2015). On the other hand, the number of female victims remained overall stable (falling from 0.6 to 0.4 per 100,000 women). From 2011-2016, the number of women killed was on average 160 per year. Women, however, unlike men, are killed mainly by family or someone known to the victim. According to the ISTAT and the ıistry of the Interior data, in the last ten years, the murder of women by a partner or former partner accounts for between 39% and 55%. When these statistics are put together with the number of murders committed by other relatives, it shows that three quarters of murders of women take place within the family.

Therefore, male violence against women is a structural phenomenon, not merely episodic or emergency, and is closely linked to inequality and therefore to the difference in power relation between men and women. Consequently, surveys on the social and cultural context in which these differences develop are crucial to complete the cognitive framework on the phenomenon of violence against women in Italy, in particular those related to gender roles and stereotypes. According to the 2011 ISTAT survey "Stereotypes, Renunciations and Gender Discrimination", while some stereotypes about traditional gender roles appear to have been overcome in Italy, others remain, such as the balance and distribution of household chores.

The 2016 Eurobarometer provides some interesting data on gender-based violence, indicating that a large majority of Italians (90%) think that violence against women in Italy is a common phenomenon, but to a much higher degree than in other European countries declare that they are not aware of women victims of violence in their family or friend circles. Moreover, while 88% of respondents say they consider violence against women to be unacceptable and always punishable by law, 11% think domestic violence is a private matter and therefore should be solved within the family. 18% of respondents think it is wrong but not illegal to force their partner to have sexual intercourse. Finally, although 78% of Italians think that violence against women occurs mainly in the home, 30% believe that a woman is more likely to be raped by a stranger.

Equality between men and women can be considered using composite indicators developed by EIGE (European Institute for Gender Equality) – the Gender Equality Index. Italy made significant progress towards gender equality in most of the core domains assessed (Work, Money, Knowledge, Time, Power and Health), however it remains below the EU average (66.2) and has significant gender inequalities.

	2005	**2010**	**2012**	**2015**
Gender Equality Index	**49.2**	**53.3**	**56.5**	**62.1**
Work	60.8	61.3	62.4	62.4
Money	76.2	78.9	78.7	78.6

	2005	2010	2012	2015
Knowledge	54.1	53.8	56.7	61.4
Time	60.1	55.1	61.4	59.3
Power	16.1	25.2	29.4	45.3
Health	85.8	86.3	86.5	86.3

Source: EIGE

The most significant improvement since 2005 has been made within "power" domain, although it continues have the lowest score. Although women have made progress in decision-making positions in the political and economic sphere, they are still vastly under-represented. There are also critical issues related to the "time" domain, showing an unequal distribution between women and men of time dedicated to domestic activities, welfare and free time. The "work" domain is also characterised by significant gender inequalities, Italy boasting the lowest female employment rate among EU countries.

II. Analysis of the Italian Action Plan in the Light of International Standards

A. *The Guiding Principles and the Fundamental Juridical Premises*

A first observation linking the Special Action Plan against Sexual and Gender violence 2015-2017 (NAP) and the basic legal preconditions for violence against women concerns the title of the document itself. While the title of the plan refers to sexual violence and gender-based violence, the contents of the NAP essentially address the phenomenon of male violence against women. Although based on gender, the latter is not synonymous with gender-based violence, as the title of the plan erroneously suggests.

Overall, the NAP consistently adopts a human rights approach. It appropriately refers to international instruments in this area and recognises male violence as a violation of women's human rights and a form of gender discrimination that negatively affects society structurally and not merely episodically.

It must be noted that in its introduction, the NAP does not provide a definition of violence that recognises the multiple and interconnected manifestations. Instead, the importance of raising awareness of the various forms of violence against women (physical, sexual, psychological, economic) is emphasised in the part devoted to the Integrated Data

Collection System. There is also no reference to the concepts of multiple discrimination and inter-sectionality, or to perspectives that do not consider gender as an isolated category, but rather look at its interconnections with other social categories such as ethnicity, disability and sexual orientation.

Compared to the multi-agency work methodology, the NAP recognises the need to coordinate in synergy with all the actors, both institutional and non-institutional, who are involved in different ways at combating the phenomenon of male violence against women. The recognition of the role of anti-violence centres is less coherent. In the *Objectives part*, the anti-violence centres are highlighted for their social relevance and knowledge of the sector, in connection with the feminist political experience. However, in the remaining parts of the NAP, they stop being cited as central to the plan, considered on a par with others private social sector subjects.

B. Development Phase of the Plan

The Special Plan, issued pursuant to article 5 of l. 119/2013, was approved two years later with parliamentary bill 7 July 2015. One of the most critical aspects of the NAP compared to the international recommendations concerns its overall structure. The NAP does not establish an organic, coherent and multi-sectoral activity programme based on current data and knowledge of male violence against women. In particular, even though the 2006 and 2014 ISTAT findings were already available, the NAP does not present any quantitative or qualitative data on the causes, incidences and impact of male violence against women in Italy. Therefore, the plan misses the possibility to link identified actions to a strategy that clearly addresses the problems identified by the statistical surveys and therefore to carry out a monitoring action. Concerning the latter, although there are some references to monitoring and evaluation, the NAP does not provide an analytical description of objectives and result indicators (see below, point F.).

The participation of women's civil society organisations in the *preparation phase* is required by article 7 Istanbul Convention, and therefore article 5(1) of l. 119/2013. The articles provide that the Minister for Equal Opportunities should utilise the "contribution of the administrations concerned, the women's associations involved in the fight against violence and anti-violence centres".

An inter-ministerial task force was set up on 22 July 2013 to this end, organised into seven sub-groups. In addition to the Department for Equal Opportunities, the task force included representatives of the Ministries of

Justice, the Interior and Health, of Education, Foreign Affairs, Defence, Economy and Finance, Labour and Economic Development, as well as the territorial associations who are engaged in combating the phenomenon (*UDI, Pink Telephone, "DIRE"*, *Pangea*, "*Masculine Plural*" and "*Counselling Centre for Abusive Men*"). From the information available, it is not clear how much of the seven sub-groups' work actually found its way into the text, as with the contribution of civil society. Civil Society members were called to participate in the online consultation on the draft of the Plan open on the website of the Presidency of the Council of Ministers and the Department for Equal Opportunities from 10 December 2014 – 10 January 2015.

C. Central and Territorial Governance System

Article 10 Istanbul Convention provides that the Parties designate or establish one or more official bodies responsible for coordinating, implementing, monitoring and evaluating policies and measures aimed at preventing and combating all forms of violence covered by this Convention.

The National Plan governance is presented as a multi-level strategy potentially suitable for coordinating action between central and local government. Pursuant to the Plan, the Prime Minister's Office, through the Department for Equal Opportunities, is responsible for managing the central roles, coordinating the system and planning actions "in synergy with the central administrations, Regions, local authorities and private social and non-governmental organisations engaged in the fight against violence and the protection of victims (anti-violence centres)". It is managed by two collegiate bodies: an inter-institutional committee with political duties, comprising representatives of the State administrations, Regions and local authorities; and a National Observatory on Gender Violence. The latter supports with technical tasks and in which the same institutional subjects that comprise the Committee also participate. This also includes the representatives of organisations working on the issue of violence against women and experts appointed by the delegated political authority in equal opportunities.

Both bodies were formally established by Prime Ministerial Decree of 25 July 2016, one year after the NAP was adopted. This inevitably led to a delay in activities and the allocation of resources. The governance structure of the NAP has also suffered from a political-institutional weakness of the Department of Equal Opportunities. The Department depends on the Presidency of the Council of Ministers and was directed by Ministers "without portfolio" who were specifically appointed for this task, by ministers who simultaneously held other positions (work, welfare) or by Undersecretaries. Since the entry into force of l. 119/2013 which provided for the adoption of the NAP, the strength of the Department's action was compromised due to changing four delegates (the Ministers and Undersecretaries *Idem*, Guerra, Martelli, Boschi) and many months of political absence pending the delegation of power by the President of the Council of Ministers.

Regarding territorial governance, the Plan requires Coordination Tables to be set up at the headquarters of territorial areas. These Tables are assigned the task of "facilitating the planning of guidelines, monitoring and evaluation of the territorial policies to combat violence against women". The Department of Equal Opportunities has demanded confirmation of the establishment of these bodies and of their activities at the end of June 2016 from each Region (Court of Auditors, Resolution 5 September 2016, No. 9/2016/G).

D. Definition of Public Policies in Preventing, Protecting against and Combatting the Phenomenon of Violence

The Istanbul Convention lays out the implementation of "global and coordinated policies aimed at preventing and combating the phenomenon of violence against women, as well as the protection of victims and the criminalisation of the perpetrators of violence". This is reiterated by international recommendations.

Prevention

The Plan dictates the need to promote a change in attitudes, gender roles and stereotypes that make male violence against women acceptable. This objective is based on three pillars: communication, education, training. In the area of communication, the scope of the media is identified as a privileged area. In the education area, there is no mention of non-formal education, nor significant environments such as the family, workplaces, sports or religious associations. Finally, there are no actions or lines of action dedicated to specific categories of persons (men and boys, parents, minors or adolescents at risk) and none that identify and intervene on risk factors associated with violence.

Protection

As opposed to the definition of policies aimed at protecting and aiding women victims of violence, the NAP identifies "risk assessment", "rescue" and the "social-work reintegration" as the pillars of intervention. Special emphasis is given to hospital-medical reception for the integrated treatment of the physical and psychological consequences of violence on women's health. However, the NAP does not deal with emergency reception, access to specialised support services, the free anti-violence phone number, legal support services or the protection of minors involved in situations of violence. Finally, although the NAP mentions them, it does not consider shelters and anti-violence centres as fundamental elements for the specialised support for women involved in situations of violence.

Punishment

Despite the strategic importance of law enforcement and the judiciary to violence, the only action identified by the Plan within the "Punishment" action line is the one concerning the recovery of abusive men. In this sense, while respecting the competences of the bodies assigned to the judicial and public security functions, no reference is made to actions to protect victims of violence in criminal investigations and proceedings, or the subject of secondary victimisation, of protective measures and the need for coordination between civil and criminal action.

Data collection system

In the NAP, data collection and research assume a central role, as referred to in article 11 of the Istanbul Convention. A substantial subsection of the central governance part is dedicated to data collection on violence (indicated as one of the objectives in l. 119/2013). In line with international recommendations, the NAP envisaged the establishment of an integrated data collection and processing system at the Department of Equal Opportunities. It would aim at strengthening awareness of the phenomenon and building a monitoring system for implementing the NAP and its related policies. To fulfil this objective, a group of experts was appointed, through presidential decree 19 October 2015, to propose designs and means of development of the information system of the database. On 25 November 2016, a protocol was signed between the Department of Equal Opportunities and ISTAT, and on 24 March 2017, the two signed an institutional agreement.

E. Implementation of the Plan

The Plan does not include a detailed description of objectives, priorities, and short, medium or long-term actions. Moreover, apart from the validity period (2015-2017), in the NAP there are no indications about the timing of the planned activities, nor to those in charge of implementing any given action. The objectives are often vaguely defined and, in some cases, specific activities are not clearly linked to the aims expressed.

Give that among the fundament elements for implementing this Action Plan there is an adequate governance system, the political-institutional "weakness" of the central government authority in charge of its management has affected the way and timing of implementation of the NAP. Among other things, this mis-management has resulted in the late appointment of the bodies providing political guidance (Committee) and technical support (Observatory).

As a consequence of the delays in the procedures for setting up the Committee and the Observatory, established one year after the entry into force of the NAP, the first initiative attributable to the NAP was launched at the beginning of 2016. It was the publication of a Public Call for Application aimed at financing projects for the strengthening of territorial services and anti-violence centres. The call was published in the Official Gazette on 8 March 2016.

Regarding the budget, article 4 of the NAP states the resources allocated for the years 2013-2015 (for a total of about €30 million), recalling an additional €10 million allocated for 2016. Based on the data provided by the Department of Equal Opportunities, all the resources envisaged by the NAP have been allocated, for a total of over €43 million. In addition to this total, €10 million was allocated to finance projects aimed at preventing and combating violence against women, published in a Public Call for Applications on 24 July 2017.

Furthermore, although para. 4 of the NAP identifies four different destinations for the resources allocated, there are no clear indications as to the destination of resources with respect to each of the lines of action, prevention, protection, punishment, and of the related intervention pillars identified in article 5 NAP. As emphasised by the Court of Auditors (Resolution 5 September 2016, No. 9/2016/G) the Plan does not specify the basis of the criteria for allocating resources. The lines of action in Chapter 5 of the NAP are not accompanied by financial analysis and, making the chapter lack any link between the lines of action and the allocation of the available funds.

F. Evaluation and Monitoring of the Plan

With regard to evaluation and monitoring, in para. 3.1 dedicated to central governance, the NAP assigns the task of monitoring its implementation and assessing the impact of policies on the fight against male violence against women to the National Observatory on Violence. Moreover, the Observatory is tasked with monitoring the positive implementation of actions in compliance with the Guidelines drawn up by the Expert Group on language, as well as the use of paid leave for women included under protection. Finally, in article 7, the NAP required that, by 31 December 2015 and subsequently each year, the central level of government must report the state of implementation of the actions indicated to the Italian Parliament.

The choice to entrust monitoring and evaluation to the Observatory, a body represented in many institutional sectors in which participate a number of civil society associations working in the area of violence against women, and the choice to instruct the Department of Equal Opportunities to report annually to Parliament progress made, is in line with international guidelines. However, the NAP does not identify any performance or result indicators (final or intermediate) for the objectives and actions envisaged. In short, there are no benchmarks on which to evaluate the efficiency and effectiveness of the measures taken to achieve the objectives pursued.

In any case, based on the information available, it does not appear that the Observatory has carried out any monitoring or evaluation activities of the Plan, nor that the Department of Equal Opportunities has submitted reports to Parliament on the state of implementation of the NAP. On 16 June 2017, the Equal Opportunities Department signed an Agreement with the Department of the National Research Council (CNR), which in addition to the evaluation of the next three-year NAP, aims to evaluate the results of the interventions implemented by the NAP 2015-17.

III. Conclusion: is the Italian NAP a Good Plan?

Based on the analysis carried out, there are many dimensions in which NAP conforms inadequately with international standards. Regarding the contents of public policies on preventing and combating violence against women, the set of identified lines of actions responds unsatisfactorily to the obligation to develop a global and coordinated response. Key sectors such as non-formal education, specialised services and the justice system have not been considered, and the mechanisms for linking the relevant actions to the sectors identified are just as weak. However, the aspects of the overall structure of the NAP are even more inadequate compared to international standards. As already highlighted, the Italian NAP does not present a detailed description of aims, priorities, or short, medium or long-term actions; it does not suggest a timeline of envisaged activities or the actors involved; it does not provide reference parameters to evaluate the efficiency and effectiveness of the interventions adopted. These characteristics, and their evident absence, render the Italian NAP a complex tool to monitor and evaluate, and does not allow for a learning process to define of future policies. The

Italian NAP therefore appears to be both inadequate for the purposes of a national action plan and as an effective tool for guiding a country in a global and coordinated way to implement actions to prevent and combat violence against women.

Despite the limitations of its overall structure, the following section aims to demonstrate the implementation status of the NAP over the period 2015-2017. The tables below present and compare the objectives and actions envisaged with the actions undertaken and the resources allocated for each line of action of the NAP. The summary of the implementation status of the emerging NAP is varied: for some lines of action, the objectives and actions envisaged were followed punctually; in other cases, the actions undertaken correspond only partially or do not correspond to the provisions made in the NAP; in other cases, no activities or resources were found that meet the stated objectives.

Summary of the state of the NAP

1. Prevention

Communication

Objectives

- Media Awareness
- Promoting gender language in public administration

Actions Envisaged

- Publication of guidelines for promotion and awareness of gender language

Resources Allocated

- 11.7 million via public fund
- 613 thousand annually for 1522

Actions Undertaken

- Protocol with State Railways and Italian Post for awareness programmes
- Communication Campaign and 1522 promotion for 25 November (2015, 2016, 2017)
- l gs d 70/2017 redefining rules on direct contributors to editors
- DPCM 28 April 2017 on public services

Education

Objectives

- Education for teachers on equality and respect
- Gender approach in educational practice

Actions Envisaged

- Guiding document per schools
- Reflecting on use of language in textbooks
- Technical table with editors for the revision of code of self-regulation

Action Undertaken

- L. 107/2015 *"Buona Scuola"* "Good Schools"
- National Educational Plan for Respect and MIUR Guidelines 2017

Resources Allocated

- 5 million via public fund

Training

Objectives

- Specific training for all professional figures

Actions Envisaged

- Integrated and multi-disciplinary training for all operators in the territory

Actions Undertaken

- Protocol and collaboration deal between DPO/*Carabinieri* corps and DPO/Ministry of the Interior
- Training of social-health personnel indicated among the objectives for the division of regional funds

Resources Allocated

- 260 thousand (deal with *Carabinieri* corps)
- Quota of divided funds for regions

2. Protection

Risk assessment

Objectives

- Promote protective and supportive action for women at risk of violence

Actions Envisaged

- Make risk assessment guidelines available (attached to plan)

Actions Undertaken

- No specific actions undertaken

Resources Allocated

- No specific resources

Assistance Pillar

Objectives

- Integrated treatments for the physical and psychological consequences of violence
- Reinforcing public and private social-health services

Actions Envisaged

- Recognition code to access emergency health services
- Dedicated treatment courses in A&E
- Memorandum of Understanding at territorial level for the realisation of treatment courses

Actions Undertaken

- Adopting guidelines for health system and hospital system for the social-health aid and assistance to women victims of violence

Resources Allocated

- 12 million for anti-violence centres, assistance services, territorial services network
- 1 million public call for application for migrant women + 1 million for detained women

Social-work Reinsertion Pillar

Objectives

- Empowerment (support, protection, assistance and social integration)
- Economic autonomy

Actions Envisaged

- Support courses to reach work and economic autonomy
- Monitoring of discharge access ex article 24, lgs.d. 80/2015

Actions Undertaken

- Objective for the division of regional funds
- INPS applicative circular on retributed discharge (No. 65/2016)

Resources Allocated

- 4.4 million via public fund
- 250 thousand via public fund on economic violence
- Quota fund assigned to regions (focus on work insertion and living autonomy)

3. Punishment

Intervention programmes for perpetrators

Objectives

- Prevent violent behaviour and re-offense
- Fight denial of male responsibility

Actions Envisaged

- Launch of integrated psychological, criminological interventions for perpetrators

Action Undertaken

- No specific action undertaken

Resources Allocated

- 1.25 million via public funds

4. Other Actions

Integrated database

Objectives

- Measuring and understanding gender violence against women

Actions Envisaged

- Founding a national database dedicated to violence

Actions Undertaken

- Creating an expert group
- Signing protocol + DPO/ISTAT institutional deal
- Integrated framework on violence against women

Resources Allocated

- 2 million (deal DPO/ISTAT)

Part I

The Reception Of International Rules On Human Rights In Italy

International Human Rights Law*

The first Part of the *Yearbook* is divided into two chapters. The first is devoted to updates concerning the major international human rights instruments that Italy has ratified, as well as to the identification of both those international instruments signed but not ratified by the Country and those adopted in 2017 that have not been subjected to any initiative of acceptance yet.

The framework of Italy's international obligations takes into consideration the universal conventions adopted within the system of the United Nations, the conventions of the Council of Europe, and also the European Union treaties and secondary law. Accordingly, the information provided are preliminary to the presentation of the national normative apparatus – the Constitution, national and regional laws – which is the subject of the following chapter.

I. Legal Instruments of the United Nations

During 2017, Italy did not file new instruments of ratification.

II. Legal Instruments on Disarmament and Non-proliferation

In 2017, the United Nations adopted the Treaty on the Prohibition of Nuclear Weapons, which was still yet to enter into force on 31 December 2017.

III. Legal Instruments of the Council of Europe

On 21 February 2017, Italy ratified the 2005 Council of Europe Convention on the Prevention of Terrorism and the respective Additional Protocol of 2015. On the same date, Italy also proceeded with the deposit of the instrument of ratification of the Protocol of Amendment to the Convention on the Suppression of Terrorism, adopted in 2003.

* Andrea Cofelice, Pietro de Perini, Claudia Pividori

On 19 May 2017, the Council of Europe opened to the signatures the Convention on Offences relating to Cultural Property. Italy signed it on 14 October 2017.

IV. European Union Law

A. *Treaties*

As envisaged by the Treaty of Lisbon, since 1 December 2009, the EU legal framework has consisted of two fundamental instruments: the Treaty on the European Union (TEU) and the Treaty on the Functioning of the European Union (TFEU). Article 6 TEU attributes the status of primary law to the Charter of Fundamental Rights of the EU, and also refers specifically to the rights guaranteed by the European Convention for the Protection of Human Rights and Fundamental Freedoms (ECHR) and those deriving from the constitutional traditions common to the Member States, which are part of EU law as general principles.

Furthermore, in the Preamble of the TEU, explicit reference is made to the 1989 Community Charter of Fundamental Social Rights of Workers and the 1961 European Social Charter of the Council of Europe (revised in 1996). Both these instruments are also mentioned in the TFEU in the context of Title X on Social Policy (article 151).

B. *EU Law in 2017*

During 2017, the European Parliament and the Council of the EU adopted directives, regulations and decisions with particular relevance for human rights. For its part, the European Commission presented significant communications and legislative proposals.

In 2017, the following directives were adopted: on combating terrorism and replacing Council Framework Decision 2002/475/JHA and amending Council Decision 2005/671/JHA (2017/541 of 15 March 2017); on the protection of workers from the risks related to exposure to carcinogens or mutagens at work (2017/2398 of 12 December 2017).

Among the regulations adopted in 2017 with relevance to human rights, the following are of note: Regulation 2017/1601 of 26 September 2017 establishing the European Fund for Sustainable Development; Regulation 2017/1563 of 13 September 2017 on the cross-border exchange between the Union and third countries of accessible format copies of certain works and other subject matter protected by copyright and related rights for the benefit of persons who are blind, visually impaired or otherwise print-disabled.

Some decisions particularly relevant to the topic considered were taken: Decision 2017/866 of 11 May 2017 on the signature, on behalf of the European Union, of the Council of Europe Convention on Prevention and Combating Violence against Women and Domestic Violence with regard to asylum and non-refoulement; Decision 2017/865 of 11 May 2017 on the signature, on behalf of the European Union, of the Council of Europe Convention on preventing and combating violence against women and domestic violence with regard to the judicial cooperation in criminal matters; Decision (CFSP) 2017/346 of 27 February 2017 extending the mandate of the European Union's Special Representative for Human Rights; Decision 2017/2269 of 7 December 2017 establishing a Multiannual Framework for the European Union Agency for Fundamental Rights for 2018-2022.

As regards the communications adopted by the Commission in 2017, the following are worth mentioning: follow-up to the EU strategy for the Eradication of trafficking in human beings and the identification of further concrete actions (COM/2017/0728); EU Action Plan for 2017-2019 on tackling the gender pay gap (COM/2017/0678); Communication on the Delivery of the European Agenda on Migration (COM/2017/0558); Midterm review of the EU framework for national Roma integration strategies (COM/2017/0458); Agenda for a socially fair transition towards clean, competitive and connected mobility for all (COM/2017/0283); Establishment of a European Pillar of Social Rights (COM/2017/0250); Protection of children in migration (COM/2017/0211); Renewed action plan for a more effective return policy in the European Union (COM/2017/0200); First Annual Report on the Facility for Refugees in Turkey (COM/2017/0130); Safer and healthier work for all – Modernisation of the EU Occupational Safety and Health Legislation and Policy (COM/2017/012); Exchange and Protection of Personal Data in a Globalised World (COM/2017/07).

From the adoption of l. 24 December 2012, No. 234, the adaptation of the Italian legal system to the European one is achieved through two legislative instruments: the European Law and the Law of European delegation. While the former contains regulations for the direct implementation of EU law aimed at remedying cases of incorrect transposition of EU legislation, the latter contains the delegation provisions required for the transposition of directives and other Union acts.

On 25 October 2017, the Parliament adopted the 2016-2017 law of European delegation. With particular reference to the protection of fundamental rights, the provision confers the Government delegation to implement regulation 2016/679 of 27 April 2016 concerning the protection of natural persons with regard to the processing of personal data, while adopting principles and criteria for the implementation of Directive 2016/681 of 27 April 2016 on the use of passenger name record (PNR) data for the purposes of prevention, detection, investigation and prosecution of terrorist offences and serious crime.

On 20 November, l. 167/2017 was adopted containing provisions for the fulfillment of the obligations deriving from Italy's membership of the European Union (European Law 2017). As part of this provision, interventions regarding the protection of fundamental rights concerned: provisions for the full implementation of the Framework Decision 2008/913/JHA on combating certain forms and expressions of racism and xenophobia by means of criminal law (EU Pilot case 8184/15/JUST); access to Fund benefits for compensation for victims of violent intentional crimes (infringement proceedings 2011/4147); provisions on the protection of water: monitoring of chemicals (EU Pilot case 7304/15/ENVI); changes to the code regarding the protection of personal data, pursuant to lgs.d 30 June 2003, No. 196 and provisions concerning the functioning of the Guarantor for the protection of personal data.

Finally, as regards the evolution of some infringement procedures launched in previous years, it ought to be noted that as regards the infringement procedure No. 2011/2215 related to the violation of article 14 of Directive 1999/31/EC on the subject of landfills, on 17 May 2017 the Commission appealed to the Court of Justice of the EU pursuant to article 258 TFEU. With respect to infringement procedure No. 2014/2059, on 15 May 2017 the Commission presented an additional opinion pursuant to article 258 TFEU for incorrect application of Directive 91/271/EEC on treatment of urban waste water, whereas on 27 April an additional opinion was submitted for infringement of Directive 2008/50/EC on air quality and, in particular, on not respecting the limits of NO^2 and PM_{10}.

In 2017, the following infringement procedures were closed: Infringement Procedure No. 2013/0276 on the failure to transpose Directive 2011/51/EU 11 May 2011 which extends the scope to beneficiaries of international protection; No. 2014/0135 on the failure to transpose Directive 2011/95/EU on the assignment of the quality of beneficiary of international protection; No. 2014/2126 on the alleged violation of Regulation 604/2013 (Dublin Regulation) and Directive 2005/85/EC (Procedures Directive); No. 2014/2235 on incorrect transposition of Directive 2008/115/EC (Return Directive) and the alleged violation of Directive 2003/9/EC (Reception Directive); No. 2014/4253 on the fee for the issue of the long-term EU residence permit.

Italian Law*

I. Constitution of the Italian Republic

"The Republic recognises and guarantees the inviolable rights of the persons, both as an individual and in the social group where the human personality is expressed. The Republic expects that the fundamental duties of political, economic and social solidarity be fulfilled" (article 2).

"All citizens have equal social dignity and are equal before the law, without distinction of sex, race, language, religion, political opinion, personal and social conditions. It is the duty of the Republic to remove those obstacles of an economic or social nature which constrain the freedom and equality of citizens, thereby impeding the full development of the human person and the effective participation of all workers in the political, economic and social organisation of the Country" (article 3).

"The Italian legal system conforms to the generally recognised principles of international law. The legal status of foreigners is regulated by law in conformity with international provisions and treaties. A foreigner who, in his home Country, is denied the actual exercise of the democratic freedoms guaranteed by the Italian Constitution shall be entitled to the right of asylum under the conditions established by law. A foreigner may not be extradited for a political offence" (article 10).

"Italy rejects war as an instrument of aggression against the freedom of other peoples and as a means for the settlement of international disputes. Italy agrees, on conditions of equality with other States, to the limitations of sovereignty that may be necessary to a world order ensuring peace and justice among the Nations. Italy promotes and encourages international organisations furthering such ends" (article 11).

The whole of Fundamental Principles and Part I of the Constitution (articles 1-54) is devoted to the fundamental rights and duties of citizens, which are grouped into four areas: civil relations, ethical and social relations, economic relations and political relations.

II. National Legislation

During 2017, the Parliament and the Government adopted legislative acts (laws, decree-laws, legislative decrees) that are directly and indirectly

* Pietro de Perini, Claudia Pividori

related to the protection and promotion of internationally recognised human rights. Below are listed the legislative acts on the basis of the following typologies:

a) general legislative acts;

b) legislative acts concerning specific subjects;

c) legislative acts concerning the protection of particular groups.

a) General Legislative Acts

Civil unions

Lgs.d. 19 January 2017, No. 5 (Adapting the the civil status provisions regarding recording, transcripts and annotations, as well as normative amendments and additions to the regulations of civil unions, pursuant to article 1, paragraph 28, letters a) and c), of l. 20 May 2016, No. 76).

Lgs.d. 19 January 2017, No. 6 (Normative modifications and additions to regulations in criminal matters for the necessary coordination with the discipline of civil unions, pursuant to article 1, paragraph 28, letter c), of l. 20 May 2016, No. 76).

Lgs.d. 19 January 2017, No. 7 (Changing and reorganising the norms of private international law for civil unions regulation, pursuant to article 1, paragraph 28, letter b) of l. 20 May 2016, No. 76).

Elections

L. 3 November 2017, No. 165 (Changing the election system of the Chamber of Deputies and the Senate of the Republic. Delegating the Government to establish single-member and plurinominal constituencies).

Security

L. 18 April 2017, No. 48 (Conversion into law, with amendments, of the Lgs.d. 20 February 2017, No. 14, containing urgent provisions on the security of cities).

b) Legislative Acts concerning Specific Subjects

Crime, criminal procedure

Lgs.d. 15 March 2017, No. 38 (Implementing Council Framework Decision 22 July 2003, 2003/568/JHA (combating corruption in the private sector)).

L. 23 June 2017, No. 103 (Modifying the penal code, the criminal procedure code and the penitentiary system).

L. 14 July 2017, No. 110 (Introducing torture as an offense in the Italian legal system).

L. 30 November 2017, No. 179 (Provisions to protect those reporting crimes or irregularities that have come to light in the context of a public or private employment relationship).

Civil service

Lgs.d. 6 March 2017, No. 40 (Establishing and regulating the universal civil service, in accordance with article 8 of l. 6 June 2016, No. 106).

Education, culture

L. 8 March 2017, No. 44 (Amending l. 20 February 2006, No. 77, concerning the protection and enhancement of intangible cultural heritage).

Lgs.d. 15 March 2017, No. 35 (Implementing Directive 2014/26/EU on the collective management of copyright and related rights and on multi-territorial licensing of rights to musical works for online use in the internal market).

Lgs.d. 13 April 2017, No. 60 (Regulations promoting humanistic culture, enhance heritage and cultural productions and support creativity, in accordance with article 1, paragraphs 180 and 181, letter g), of l. 12 July 2015, No. 107).

Lgs.d. 13 April 2017, No. 63 (Effectiveness of the right to education in terms of defining benefits related to personal services, conditions of hardship and to support services, and to strengthening of the 'student card', in accordance with article 1, paragraphs 180 and 181, letter f), of l. 13 July 2015, No. 107).

Health

L. 8 March 2017, No. 24 (Provisions on the safety of treatments and the person being assisted, as well as on the professional responsibility of health care professionals).

L. 31 July 2017, No. 119 (Conversion into law, with amendments, of lgs.d. 7 June 2017, No. 7 containing urgent provisions concerning prevention of vaccine-preventable diseases).

L. 22 December 2017, No. 219 (Regulations on informed consent and advance treatment provisions).

Poverty

L. 15 March 2017, No. 33 (Delegation containing Regulations on the fight against poverty, the reorganisation of services and the system of social interventions and services).

Lgs.d. 15 September 2017, No. 147 (Provisions to introduce a national measure to combat poverty).

c) Legislative Acts Devoted to the Protection of Special Groups

Migrants

L. 13 April 2017, No. 46 (Converting into law, with amendments, l.d. 17 February 2017, No. 13, containing urgent provisions to speed up proceedings in the field of international protection and for the fight against illegal immigration).

Children and adolescents

L.d. 7 April 2017, No. 47 (Provisions concerning measures to protect unaccompanied foreign minors).

Lgs.d 13 April 2017, No. 65 (Establishing an integrated education system from birth to six years, pursuant to article 1, paragraphs 180 and 181, letter e) of l. 13 July 2015, No. 107).

L. 29 May 2017, No. 71 (Provisions to protect minors and to prevent and tackle cyber-bullying).

Lgs.d. 7 December 2017, No. 203 (Reforming legislative provisions regarding the protection of minors in the cinematographic and audiovisual sector, pursuant to article 33 of l. 14 November 2016, No. 220).

Persons with disabilities

Lgs.d. 13 April 2017, No. 66 (Regulations promoting the inclusion of students with disabilities, pursuant to article 1, paragraphs 180 and 181, letter c) of l. 13 July 2015, No. 107).

Linguistic minorities

C.l. 4 December 2017, No. 1 (Amending the special statute for Trentino-Alto Adige/South Tyrol on the protection of the Ladin linguistic minority).

Victims of disasters / crime

L. 25 January 2017, No. 9 (Establishing the National Day of Civil Victims of Wars and Conflicts in the World).

L. 8 March 2017, No. 20 (Establishing the National Day of Memory and Commitment in Remembrance of the Victims of Mafias).

L. 20 December 2017, No. 212 (Establishing the Day in Memory of the Righteous of Humanity).

L. 29 December 2017, n. 227 (Establishing the National Day in Memory of Road Traffic Victims).

III. Municipal, Provincial and Regional Statutes

Starting from 1991, following the adoption of l. 8 June, 1990, No. 142 (Arrangement of local autonomies), the so-called "peace human rights" norm, originally contained in article 1 of the Veneto Regional Law of 30 March 1988, No. 18 (now updated by L. 55/1999) on "Regional interventions for the promotion of a culture of peace", has been included in the statutes of numerous Italian Municipalities, Provinces and Regions.

The standard text reads:

"The Municipality … (the Province … the Region …), in accordance with constitutional principles and international norms that recognise the innate rights of human persons, sanction the rejection of war as a means of resolving international disputes and promote cooperation between the peoples, peacefully recognises a fundamental right of the person and of the peoples.

For this reason, the Municipality … (the Province … the Region …) promotes the culture of peace and human rights through cultural initiatives and research, education, cooperation and information that tend to transform the City into a land of peace.

The Municipality … (the Province … the Region …) will take direct initiatives and will favour those of cultural and scholastic institutions, associations, voluntary groups and international cooperation".

There are also numerous statutes of local and regional authorities that contain a specific reference to international human rights norms and principles, in particular the UN Charter, the Universal Declaration of Human Rights, the International Covenant on Civil and Political Rights, the International Covenant on Social and Cultural Economic Rights, the International Convention on the Rights of the Child, the Charter of Fundamental Rights of the EU (see *Yearbook 2011*, p. 65-69).

In 2017, no changes were made to the regional statutes with reference to the "peace human rights" norm. There are 14 Italian Regions that contain this provision within their statutory laws, either in its standard formulation or in alternative formulations (Apulia, Basilicata, Calabria, Campania, Emilia-Romagna, Lazio, Liguria, Lombardy, Marche, Molise, Piedmont, Tuscany, Umbria and Veneto).

IV. Regional Laws

This section lists the laws on human rights, equal opportunities, development cooperation, fair trade, minorities, migration, Ombudspersons, and the protection of children's rights, workers' rights, the rights of persons with disabilities, solidarity, social advancement, family assistance, and citizenship and legality education adopted by the Councils of the Italian Regions and Autonomous Provinces in 2017. The laws are divided according to topics and listed, for each authority, in chronological order.

Peace, human rights, development cooperation, fair trade

R.l. Friuli-Venezia Giulia 23 March 2017, No. 4 (Provisions to develop and promote the solidarity economy).

R.l. Veneto 12 September 2017, No. 29 (Withdrawal from the Interregional Observatory on Development Cooperation: Repealing article 18 of r.l. 16 December 1999, No. 55 (Regional Interventions for the Promotion of Human Rights, Culture of Peace, Development Cooperation and Solidarity)).

Equal opportunities, gender issues

R.l. Campania 1 December 2017, No. 34 (Interventions to favour the personal, social, and economic autonomy of women victims of gender violence and their children and recovery actions aimed at men who are the perpetrators of violence).

R.l. Friuli-Venezia Giulia 17 November 2017, No. 38 (Amending l. 17/2000 (Implementing anti-violence projects and establishing centres for women in difficulty)).

R.l. Umbria 11 April 2017, No. 3 (Regulations against discrimination and violence determined by sexual orientation and gender identity).

Ombudspersons, children's Ombudspersons

R.l. Calabria 1 February 2017, No. 2 (Establishing the Regional Observatory for Children).

R.l. Campania 7 August 2017, No. 25 (Establishing the Regional Ombudsperson for the Rights of Persons with Disabilities).

P.l. Trent 20 June 2017, No. 5 (Amending the Ombudsman 1982: Establishing the Ombudsperson for the rights of prisoners and the Guarantor of the rights of minors).

People with disabilities

R.l. Basilicata 20 November 2017, No. 30 (Provisions to recognise Italian Sign Language and the full accessibility of deaf people to collective life).

R.l. Campania 7 August 2017, No. 2 – see: *Ombudspersons, child sponsors, personal guarantors*

R.l. Campania 6 October 2017, No. 26 (Organising services for people of developmental age with neurodevelopmental disorders and neuropsychiatric pathologies and of people with autism spectrum disorders).

R.l. Lombardy 22 February 2017, No. 2 (Regional contributions to install video surveillance systems in the homes for the elderly and people with disabilities in Lombardy).

R.l. Molise 24 October 2017, No. 16 (Regional provisions for autism spectrum disorders and pervasive developmental disorders).

R.l. Molise 18 December 2017, No. 22 (Establishing the Regional Fund for non self-sufficiency).

R.l. Sicily 1 March 2017, No. 4 (Extending the provisional exercise for 2017 and establishing the Regional Disability Fund – Urgent regulations for appointment procedures in the regional health sector).

R.l. Tuscany 18 October 2017, No. 60 (General provisions on rights and policies for persons with disabilities).

R.l. Tuscany 28 December 2017, No. 81 (Interventions to promote individual mobility and personal autonomy of people with disabilities).

R.l. Veneto 17 October 2017, No. 38 (Regulations for the support for families and elderly people, people with disabilities, and people in conditions of vulnerability or non self-sufficiency, for the qualification and support for family assistants).

Workers' rights

R.l. Abruzzo 21 April 2017, No. 27 (Provisions on the protection of employment levels in the regional territory and further urgent provisions).

R.l. Calabria 5 July 2017, No. 31 (Provisions to promote access for young people to the primary sector and to combat the abandonment and consumption of agricultural land).

R.l. Campania 9 October 2017, No. 29 (Regulations for the protection of psychological health in the workplace and for the prevention of bullying and work-related inconveniences).

R.l. Campania 20 November 2017 No. 31 (Provisions on the prevention and protection against the risk of falls from height during building work. Modifying r.l. 27 February 2007, No. 3 (Discipline at public works, services and supplies in Campania)).

R.l. Emilia-Romagna 10 February 2017, No. 1 (Participation of the Emilia-Romagna Region in the "Vanguard initiative for new growth through smart specialization" association).

R.l. Friuli-Venezia Giulia 12 April 2017, No. 7 (Provisions to support the employability of young people – AttivaGiovani –, to support recruitment of ancillary employment contracts and experimental measures of intensive support for relocation).

R.l. Lombardy 24 November 2017, No. 26 (Provisions to promote worker stability by adopting social clauses in regional calls for tenders).

R.l. Lombardy 12 December 2017, No. 35 (Provisions on social farming).

R.l. Molise 5 July 2017, No. 6 (Measure for the income support of employees in the sector of the Molise poultry supply chain).

Solidarity, social promotion, assistance to families

R.l. Abruzzo 30 August 2017, No. 49 (Regulations to support small businesses operating in the territories of the region affected by the earthquakes of 2016 and 2017).

R.l. Abruzzo 30 November 2017, No. 57 (Amending r.l. 30 August 2017, No. 49 (Regulations to support small businesses operating in the territories of the region affected by the earthquakes of 2016 and 2017) and other financial provisions).

R.l. Abruzzo 15 December 2017, No. 63 (Amending r.l. 26 April 1978, No. 21 (Establishing family, infancy, maternity, and responsible parenthood care services) and further social provisions).

R.l. Apulia 13 July 2017, No. 28 (Law on participation).

R.l. Apulia 22 November 2017, No. 45 (Interventions in support of separated or divorced spouses who are in particular conditions of economic hardship).

R.l. Basilicata 20 November 2017, No. 29 (Promotion and enhancement of active aging and solidarity across generations).

R.l. Calabria 22 December 2017, No. 50 (Interventions for educational-therapeutic stays in the Calabria region for children, adolescents and young people with diabetes mellitus).

R.l. Campania 22 May 2017, No. 11 (Provisions to tackle and prevent bullying and cyberbullying in Campania).

R.l. Campania 9 October 2017, No. 29 – see: *Workers' rights*

R.l. Friuli-Venezia Giulia 12 April 2017, No. 8 (Establishing municipal councils of young people) by modifying r.l. 22 March 2012, No. 5 (Law for the autonomy of young people and the Guarantee Fund for their opportunities)).

R.l. Friuli-Venezia Giulia 9 May 2017, No. 12 (Regulations on culture, sport and solidarity).

R.l. Friuli-Venezia Giulia 24 May 2017, No. 17 (Changes to r.l. 22 March 2012, No. 5 (Law for the autonomy of young people and the Guarantee Fund for their opportunities), concerning interventions to tackle and prevent bullying).

R.l. Friuli-Venezia Giulia 6 October 2017, No. 33 (Regulations promoting the right to play and ludic motor recreational activities).

R.l. Friuli-Venezia Giulia 6 November 2017, No. 35 (Provisions on expansion of the survival wage and its coordination with the active measure of income support).

R.l. Friuli-Venezia Giulia 1 December 2017, No. 40 (Provisions to support scholastic paths for action in the event of the disappearance of minors).

R.l. Lazio 14 June 2017, No. 5 (Establishing Regional Civil Service).

R.l. Lombardy 7 February 2017, No. 1 (Framework of regional interventions to tackle and prevent bullying and cyberbullying).

R.l. Lombardy 6 November 2017, No. 24 (Regional assistance and assistance to victims of terrorism and information, training and research to learn about and prevent violent radicalisation processes).

R.l. Marche 19 April 2017, No. 14 (Provisions to protect children and adolescents and to develop projects to support the "Sustainable and Friendly Cities of Children and Adolescents" in the Marche region).

R.l. Marche 15 May 2017, No. 16 (Amending r.l. 10 August 1998, No. 30 (Interventions in favour of the family)).

R.l. Marche 2 August 2017, No. 25 (Urgent provisions to simplify and accelerate reconstruction interventions following the 2016 earthquakes).

R.l. Piedmont 19 June 2017, No. 8 (Regional interventions to tackle and prevent usury, extortion and over indebtedness).

P.l. Trent 22 September 2017, No. 10 (Reducing waste, recovering and distributing food and non-food surpluses and pharmaceutical products and amending related provincial laws).

P.l. Trent 16 November 2017, No. 14 (Reforming elderly persons welfare: modifying p.l. 28 May 1998, No. 6, p.l. 24 July 2012, No. 15 (relating to the elderly and the non self-sufficient), p.l. on social policies 2007 and p.l. on health protection 2010).

R.l. Tuscany 29 September 2017, No. 53 (Urgent actions to face the consequences of the exceptional meteorological events of 9 and 10 September 2017 that occurred in the territories of the Municipalities of Livorno, Rosignano Marittimo, and Collesalvetti).

R.l. Umbria 17 January 2017, No. 1 (Regulations completing the reconstruction of the areas affected by the 1997 and earlier earthquakes).

R.l. Umbria 14 November 2017, No. 16 (Regional interventions to promote donation and distribution activities of food, non-food, and pharmaceutical products for purposes of social solidarity).

R.l. Veneto 14 April 2017, No. 10 (Regulations to enhance the support administrator to protect vulnerable individuals).

R.l. Veneto 8 August 2017, No. 23 (Promotion and enhancement active aging).

R.l. Veneto 17 October 2017, No. 38 – see: *People with disabilities*

Education for citizenship and legality

R.l. Abruzzo 12 June 2017, No. 36 (Amending and supplementing r.l. 12 November 2004, No. 40 (Regional measures to promote education of legality and to guarantee the right of citizens' safety). Establishing the Regional Legality Observatory).

R.l. Friuli-Venezia Giulia 24 May 2017, No. 16 (Changes to r.l. 22 March 2012, No. 5 (Law for the autonomy of young people and the Guarantee Fund for their opportunities), concerning the promotion of school projects for the study of the principles of citizenship education).

R.l. Friuli-Venezia Giulia 9 June 2017, No. 21 (Regulations on the prevention and contrast of organised crime and mafia and for the promotion of the culture of legality).

R.l. Liguria 8 February 2017, No. 2 (Amending r.l. 5 March 2012, No. 7 (Regional initiatives to prevent organised and mafia crime and promote a culture of legality).

R.l. Marche 7 August 2017, No. 27 (Regulations promoting a culture of legality and responsible citizenship).

R.l. Umbria 3 August 2017, No. 13 (Further amending r.l. 19 October 2012, No. 16 (Measures for the coordinated implementation of regional policies tackling and preventing organised crime and mafia, as well as promoting a culture of legality and responsible citizenship. Integrating r.l. 14 October 2008, No. 13 (provisions to promote an integrated urban security system and policies to ensure the right to the security of citizens) – repealing r.l. 19 June 2002, No. 12)).

Part II

The Human Rights Infrastructure in Italy

National Bodies with Jurisdiction over Human Rights*

International human rights law requires States to set up structures that are adequately specialised in promoting and protecting fundamental rights. In this regard, a distinction shall be made between, on one hand, strictly governmental bodies, and on the other, independent structures directly emanating from civil society. The latter in particular, through channels different from those classically used by governmental powers, aim to participate in policy-making and to promote and develop a human rights culture, as well as to prevent violations.

In this chapter, the composition, mandate and activities of the following institutions will be illustrated:

Parliamentary bodies: The Special Commission for the Promotion and Protection of Human Rights of the Italian Senate; the Permanent Committee on Human Rights instituted within the Foreign Affairs Commission (III) of the Italian Chamber of Deputies; the Parliamentary Commission for Children and Adolescents;

Governmental bodies: Bodies established within the Prime Minister's Office: Department for Equal Opportunities; Commission for International Adoptions; National Committee on Bioethics. Bodies established within the Ministry of Foreign Affairs: Inter-Ministerial Committee for Human Rights; National Commission for UNESCO. Bodies established within the Ministry of Labour and Social Policy: National Observatory for Children and Adolescents; National Observatory Monitoring the Condition of Persons with Disabilities; and other departments and bureaus of the Ministry of Justice which work specifically on human rights matters.

The Constitutional Court.

Judicial authorities: The Court of Cassation, acting as the supreme judge of legitimacy.

Independent authorities: The Communications Regulatory Authority; the Data Protection Authority; the Committee Guaranteeing the Implementation of the Law on Strikes Affecting Essential Public Services; the National Ombudsperson for Children and Adolescents; National Ombudsperson for the Rights of Persons in Prison or Deprived of Liberty.

---

* Andrea Cofelice

Italy's national human rights infrastructure is completed by academic institutions promoting not only research, but also education and training in human rights issues, and by several non-governmental organisations, some of which function through networking.

I. Parliamentary Bodies

A. Senate of the Republic: Special Commission for the Protection and Promotion of Human Rights

The Senate's Special Commission for the Protection and Promotion of Human Rights was first set up during the 14th legislature (motion 20, 1 August 2001) and is the fruit of long experience by the Committee against Capital Punishment (1996–2001). Since the Commission is not permanent, it must be instituted formally at the beginning of each legislature and the Senate did so during the 15th legislature (motion 20, 12 July 2006), the 16th legislature (motion 13, 26 June 2008) and the 17th legislature (motion 7, 26 March 2013). In the latter motion, the Senate decided to commence the proceedings for the establishment of a permanent human rights commission.

The Commission has the task of studying, observing and taking initiatives on issues concerning the protection and promotion of internationally recognised human rights. To this end, it can establish relations with institutions of other countries and with international bodies; carry out missions in or outside Italy, in particular with foreign Parliaments, even – if necessary – in order to establish agreements fostering human rights or to facilitate other forms of collaboration; it can carry out informational procedures and formulate proposals and Assembly reports; and provide its advisory opinions on proposed legislation as well as on matters deferred to other Commissions.

The Commission is made up of 25 members, present in proportion to the size of the parliamentary groups to which they belong. Among these members, the Commission elects the bureau, made up of the Chair, two Vice Chairs and two Secretaries.

In 2017, the Commission was composed as follows: Chair: Luigi Manconi; Vice Chairs: Riccardo Mazzoni, Daniela Donno; Secretaries: Giovanni Bilardi, Paola De Pin; Members: Silvana Amati, Anna Maria Bernini, Federica Chiavaroli, Franco Conte, Peppe De Cristofaro, Aldo Di Biagio, Enzo Fasano, Emma Fattorini, Elena Ferrara, Miguel Gotor, Sergio Lo Giudice, Emanuela Munerato, Venera Padua, Francesco Palermo, Maria Rizzotti, Lucio Romano, Manuela Serra, Ivana Simeoni, Daniela Valentini, Guido Viceconte.

In the ambit of the survey of the various levels and systems of human rights protection currently in place in Italy and abroad, in 2017, the Commission held 12 hearings of representatives from associations, organisations and institutional bodies, and of individual experts, as reported below.

- 15 February: Fabrizio Petri, Chair of the Interministerial Committee on Human Rights, on the activity of the CIDU.
- 21 February: Marco Minniti, Minister of the Interior, on migration.
- 23 February: Ismail Mohammed, representative of the *Sudan Liberation Movement* and Antonella Napoli, Chair of *Italians for Darfur Association,* on the 2017 annual report.
- 28 February: Davide Faraone, Undersecretary of State for Health, on use of restraint.
- 1 March: Stephane Jaquemet, UNHCR delegate for Southern Europe, and Andrea De Bonis, UNHCR official, on the UNHCR's proposals for better refugee protection in the European Union and in the world.
- 8 March: Franco Gabrielli, head of police, on immigration.
- 3 May: Carlo Stasolla and Marco Zanne, from *Associazione 21 luglio*, on the 2016 annual report on the condition of Roma and Sinti in housing emergency in Italy.
- 9 May: Michel Forst, UN Special Rapporteur on the situation of human rights defenders, and Francesco Martone, advocacy officer of *Un ponte per…!*, ("A Bridge For…!") on the protection of human rights defenders.
- 26 September: Roberto Mignone, UNHCR representative for Libya, on the issue of respecting human rights and conditions of migrants in Libya.
- 27 September: Santi Consolo, head of the Prison Administration Department, on prison conditions in Italy.
- 11 October: Rezan Kader, High representative of the regional government of Kurdistan in Italy and the Holy See, on the future of the Kurdistan region after the referendum.
- 5 December: Laura Baldassare, councilor for citizens, schools and supportive communities, and Michela Micheli, head of the Social Policies, Subsidiarity and Health Department of the Municipality of Rome, on the reception system for asylum seekers and refugees and on Roma camps and gathering centres in the capital.

Furthermore, in 2017, the Commission adopted two reports: the Report on Identification and Expulsion Centres (January), and the Report on Detention Centres for Repatriation in Italy (December).

B. Chamber of Deputies: Permanent Committee on Human Rights

The international protection of human rights is one of the focal points of the activities performed by the Commission for Foreign and European Union Affairs (Third Commission) of the Chamber of Deputies. As from the 10th legislature (1987-1992), the Commission set up within it the Permanent Committee on Human Rights, which, especially through hearings, ensures that Parliament is kept continually informed and up-to-date with regard to the status of international human rights. The Committee also has the task of following the course of individual human rights measures, performing preliminary tasks pertinent to the activities of the Commission. The Committee for the current legislature (17th) was set up on 16 July 2013.

In 2017, the Committee was composed as follows: Chair: Pia Elda Locatelli; Vice Chair: Gianna Farina; Secretary: Marta Grande; Members: Maria Rosaria Carfagna, Franco Cassano, Khalid Chaouki, Edmondo Cirielli, Fucsia Fitzgerald Nissoli, Michele Nicoletti, Erasmo Palazzotto, Gianluca Pini, Lia Quartapelle Procopio, Mariano Rabino, Carlo Sibilia (until 23 January 2017), Maria Edera Spadoni, Sandra Zampa.

In the ambit of the survey on the protection of minority rights to maintain peace and security at the international level, in 2017, the Committee held ten hearings of representatives from associations and organisations, institutions and individuals, as reported below.

- 23 February: Fabrizio Petri, President of the Interministerial Committee for Human Rights and Cristiana Carletti, legal expert at the CIDU, on the third Italian National Action Plan implementing the United Nations Security Council Resolution 1325 (2000).
- 7 March: Francesca Tardioli, central director for the United Nations and human rights in the Directorate General for political and security affairs of the Ministry of Foreign Affairs and International Cooperation, on the strategy and action of Italy on "Women, Peace and Security" after the Security Council mandate.
- 3 May: Ramy Salhi, director of the Maghreb regional office of the *Euro-Mediterranean Human Rights Network*, Naïma Hammami, assistant Secretary General of the *Union Générale Tunisienne du Travail*, Jamel M'Sallem, President of the *Ligue Tunisienne des Droits de l'Homme*, Malek Kfif, member of the *Bureau National du Forum Tunisie des Droits Économiques et Sociaux*, and Lilia Rebai, coordinator of the *Tunisia programs for the Euro-Mediterranean Human Rights Network*, on the activities of the *EuroMed Rights* network.

- 28 June: Safak Pavey, member of the Great National Assembly of Turkey, and Gloria Muñoz Ramirez, human rights activist in Mexico.
- 19 July: Igor Kochetkov, director of the *Russian LGBT Network*, and Yuri Guaiana, coordinator of transnational issues of the *Radical Rights Association*, on the human rights situation of LGBTI people in Russia.
- 12 October: Sam Rainsy and Saumura Tioulong, members of the *Cambodia National Rescue Party* at the National Assembly of Cambodia, as well as Elisabetta Zamparutti and Matteo Angioli, presidency members of the *Radical Party*, on human rights violations in the context of intense political clashes related to the electoral campaign for the 2018 elections in Cambodia.
- 19 October: Federico Soda, director of the coordination office for the Mediterranean of the International Organization for Migration, on the activities of the organisation in the Mediterranean, with particular reference to Libya.
- 25 October: Abdirahman Mahdi, vice president of the *Unrepresented Nations and Peoples Organization*, on the human rights situation in Ethiopia.
- 21 November: Rajja Altallu, co-director of the *Center for Civil Society and Democracy*, and Federico Calabrese Martuscelli, adviser of the Ministry of Foreign Affairs, on the human rights situation in Syria.
- 5 December: Armando Armas, member of the National Assembly of Venezuela, on the human rights situation in Venezuela.

C. Bicameral Bodies: Parliamentary Commission for Children and Adolescents

The Parliamentary Commission for Children and Adolescents was set up by l. 23 December 1997, No. 451, although its name and responsibilities were modified by l. 3 August 2009, No. 112.

Essentially, the Commission is entrusted with a supervisory and policymaking role related to the enforcement of international obligations and domestic law on children's rights. It may also present to the two Houses of Parliament observations and proposals concerning the effects and limitations of current legislation, and the possible need to amend it to ensure compliance with international law concerning the rights of the child.

The Commission is composed of 20 Senators and 20 Representatives appointed, respectively, by the Chair of the Italian Senate and the Chair of the Italian Chamber of Deputies, proportionately to the total number of members in the various parliamentary groups. In 2016 the Commission was composed as follows: Chair: Michela Vittoria Brambilla; Vice Chairs: Rosetta Enza Blundo, Sandra Zampa; Secretary: Maria Antezza; Members from the Chamber of Deputies: Maurizio Baradello (prematurely passed away in May

that acts as an observatory of the phenomenon of the "fashion of disorders" of children.

- 18 July: Vincenza Palmieri and Pierluigi Bonici, respectively president and vice president of the National Institute of Family Pedagogy; Elisabetta Scala, vice president of *Movimento italiano genitori*, and Virginia Ciaravolo and Iolanda Ippolito, respectively president and councilor of the association *Mai più violanza infinita*, on the subject of gender violence and violence against minors.
- 19 September: Alberto Villani, president of the Italian Society of Paediatrics, and Maria Luisa Scattoni, researcher at the Higher Institute of Health, on the paediatric area in Italy.
- 26 September: Rita Potena, director of the Operational Unit for the protection of mental health and rehabilitation at developmental age of the ASL (Local Health Service) Roma2, Mental Health Department, and Gianluigi Scannapieco, general director of the *"Burlo Garofalo"* Institute of Hospitalisation and Treatment of Trieste, on the issue of disability.
- 10 October: Mario Melazzini, general director of the *Italian Pharmaceutics Agency*; Nicola Pinelli, director of the *Italian Federation of Health and Hospital Organisations*, and Massimiliano Raponi, representative of the *Italian Paediatric Hospitals Association*, on issue of psychophysical development of minors.
- 17 October: Andrea Vania, head of the Centre for paediatric dietetics and nutrition at the Department of Paediatrics at University of Rome "La Sapienza", and Teresa di Fiandra, from the General Directorate for Health Prevention, office for addiction prevention, doping and mental health, of the Ministry of Health, on nutritional problems in paediatric age.
- 24 October: Antonella Della Pina, representative of the *Nidi Violati* ("Violated Nests") national campaign, and Stefano Boschi, representative of the *Aiutiamo le Famiglie* ("Helping Families") association, on children's physical and mental health as a result of forced expulsion from the family unit.
- 7 November: Laura Dalla Ragione, president of the Italian Society of rehabilitation, eating behaviour and weight disorders.

Furthermore, in 2017, the Commission adopted two conclusive documents regarding the cognitive survey on the right of minors to use artistic and cultural heritage (April) and the cognitive survey on the protection of the psychophysical health of minors, with reference to the section entitled *The right to health of minors with disabilities* (June).

D. Parliamentary Initiatives Concerning Human Rights

Presented below is a brief overview of the main human rights legislation produced by the Italian Parliament in 2017, subdivided into bills and guidelines and watchdog initiatives (motions, interpellations, questions for an oral or written answer, resolutions, agenda proposals). The proposer or first signer, the code (the letter "C" indicating that the initiative was presented in the Chamber of Deputies and the letter "S" that it was presented in the Senate), the title, the date of presentation and the most recent update are listed for each initiative.

In 2017, Parliament adopted a total of 166 human rights initiatives, including 14 bills, 17 motions, 8 interpellations, 17 questions for an oral answer, 54 questions for a written answer, 21 questions submitted to Commissions, 5 Assembly resolutions, 8 Commission resolutions and 22 Assembly agenda proposals.

Acronym List of Parliamentary Groups employed in the following tables

ALA-PRI: *Alleanza Liberal Popolare – Partito Repubblicano Italiano* ("Liberal-Popular Alliance-Italian Republican Party")
Art. 1-MDP-LeU: *Articolo 1 – Movimento Democratico e Progressista – Liberi e Uguali* ("Article 1- Progressive and Democratic Movement – Free and Equal)
Aut(SVP-UV-PATT-UPT)-PSI: *Per le Autonomie-Partito Socialista Italiano* ("In Support of Autonomies – Italian Socialist Party")
FI-PdL: *Forza Italia – Il Popolo delle Libertà* ("Forza Italia – The People of Freedom")
FL(Id-PL): *Federazione della Libertà* ("Federation of Freedom")
Lega: *Lega Nord* ("Northern League")
M5S: *Movimento 5 Stelle* ("Five Star Movement")
Mixed: *Gruppo Misto* ("Mixed Group")
NcI: *Noi con l'Italia* ("We together with Italy")
PD: *Partito Democratico* ("Democratic Party")
PLI: *Partito Liberale Italiano* ("Italian Liberal Party")
SC-ALA CLP-MAIE: *Scelta Civica-Alleanza Liberal Popolare per la Costituente Liberale e Popolare- Movimento Associativo Italiani all'Estero* ("Civic Choice- Liberal-Popular Alliance for the Liberal-Popular Costituent – Associative Movement of Italians Living Abroad")
SI-SEL-POS: *Sinistra Italiana-Sinistra Ecologia e Libertà-Possibile* ("Italian Left-Left, Environment and Freedom-Possible")

Bills

The 14 bills presented concerned the following issues: the right to vote (5); the right to privacy and to be forgotten (3); the right to freedom of religion (2); ratification of international instruments (1); freedom of opinion and expression (1); bioethics (1); economic, social and cultural rights (1).

Date	Initiative	Latest update
10/01/2017	Daniele Gaetano BORIOLI (PD) – S. 2638 Extension of the right to vote for the election of the Senate of the Republic to citizens who are eighteen years old.	16/02/2017 assigned (examination not yet begun)
23/01/2017	Lucrezia RICCHIUTI (Art. 1-MDP-LeU) and others – S. 2659 Provisions on temerarious government initiatives against journalists.	31/01/2017 assigned (examination not yet begun)
08/03/2017	Massimo PARISI (SC-ALA CLP-MAIE) and others – C.4356 Amendment of article 57 and abrogation of the first paragraph of article 58 of the Constitution concerning the composition and election of the Senate of the Republic.	19/03/2017 assigned (examination not yet begun)
04/04/2017	Giulio MARCON (SI-SEL-POS) – C.4404 Amendments to articles 81, 97 and 119 of the Constitution, concerning the elimination of the balanced budget principle and the safeguarding of people's fundamental rights in financial decisions and in the organisation of public offices	03/05/2017 assigned (examination not yet begun)
21/04/2017	Matteo MANTERO (M5S) – S. 2801 [Bill biological testament] Regulations on informed consent and instructions for future treatment and living wills	14/12/2017 definitively approved. Law
29/05/2017	Ricardo Antonio MERLO (SC-ALA CLP-MAIE) and others – C.4518 Introduction of article 21-*bis* of the Constitution, on the right of access to information and protection of confidentiality	19/06/2017 assigned (examination not yet begun)
20/09/2017	Fausto Guilherme LONGO (Aut(SVP-UV-PATT-UPT)-PSI) – S. 2907 Provisions for facilitate the right to vote of Italian citizens residing abroad through the introduction of electronic voting	30/10/2017 assigned (examination not yet begun)
20/09/2017	Luigi LACQUANITI (Art. 1-MDP-LeU) and others – C.4650 Regulations on religious freedom and abrogation of legislation on permitted cults	13/12/2017 assigned (examination not yet begun)

Date	Initiative	Latest update
27/09/2017	Paolo GENTILONI SILVERI and others – S. 2921 Ratification and implementation of the following protocols: a) Protocol No. 15 on the amendment to the Convention for the Protection of Human Rights and Fundamental Freedoms (Strasbourg, 24 June 2013); b) Protocol No. 16 on the amendment to the Convention for the Protection of Human Rights and Fundamental Freedoms (Strasbourg, 2 October 2013)	17/10/2017 currently under examination by the Commission
28/09/2017	Ernesto PREZIOSI (PD) – C.4667 Rules on religious freedom and abrogation of legislation on permitted cults	28/09/2017 still to be assigned
10/10/2017	Nunzia DE GIROLAMO (FI-PdL) and others – C.4692 Introduction of the ban on the anonymous use of the internet and provisions on the protection of the right to be forgotten	10/11/2017 assigned (examination not yet begun)
25/10/2017	Gian Marco CENTINAIO (Lega) and others – S. 2953 Provisions to guarantee voting secrecy	12/12/2017 assigned (examination not yet begun)
29/11/2017	Giovanni ENDRIZZI (M5S) – S. 2991 Provisions to facilitate the exercise of the vote of citizens who are temporarily in a place other than that of residence for reasons of work, study or medical treatment	29/11/2017 still to be assigned
18/12/2017	Stefano QUINTARELLI (Mixed) and others – C.4791 Provisions for the protection of the identity of the users of the Internet and delegation to the Government for the regulation of the supply and use of protected digital identities.	18/12/2017 still to be assigned

Source: openparlamento (search criteria: "human rights", "rights of the person")

Motions

Of the 17 motions presented, 6 concern bioethics; 4 the right of migrants, refugees and asylum seekers; 3 the protection of human rights at an international level (with particular reference to Venezuela and Yemen); 2 disarmament; 1 the right to education; and 1 women's rights.

Interpellations

Date	Initiative	Latest update
17/01/2017	Giovanna MARTELLI (Art. 1-MDP-LeU) and others – C.2/01589 Milagro Sala, founder and leader of the Argentine social organisation Tupac Amaru, as well as deputy of the Parlasur, is illegally detained together with other members of the social movement…	09/05/2017 concluded
01/02/2017	Carlo GIOVANARDI (FL(Id-PL, PLI)) and others – S. 2/00443 To the Minister of Health – it is asked: what do you intend to do to put an end to medical experiments on Italian (or residents in Italy) transgender people…	01/02/2017 presented
28/02/2017	Renato BRUNETTA (FI-PdL) – C.2/01685 On the question of infringement of the right of defense …	10/03/2017 concluded
12/04/2017	Sergio LO GIUDICE (PD) – S. 2/00461 Whereas: the Chechen Republic is part of the Russian Federation…	12/04/2017 presented
19/04/2017	Renato BRUNETTA (FI-PdL) – C.2/01765 On the question of infringement of the right of defense …	19/04/2017 presented
20/11/2017	Roberto GIACHETTI (PD) – C.2/02025 To urgently convene a new National Conference on the problems associated with the spread of narcotic and psychotropic substances…	20/11/2017 presented
27/11/2017	Lia QUARTAPELLE PROCOPIO (PD) – C.2/02034 Whereas: hundreds of migrants died a few miles away from the port of Lampedusa on 3 October 2013…	27/11/2017 presented
28/11/2017	Roberto RAMPI (PD) – C.2/02043 Whereas: on the 26 and 27 October 2017, the prisons of Turin and Asti…	28/11/2017 presented

Source: *openparlamento* (search criteria: "human rights", "rights of the person")

Questions for an oral answer

The 17 questions for an oral answer presented concerned the following issues: protection of human rights on an international level (with particular reference to Venezuela, Russia, Mediterranean, Congo and Iraq) (5); the rights of migrants, refugees and asylum seekers (4); prison conditions and prisoners' rights (2); the right to sexual and reproductive health (1);

the freedom of expression (1); the right to adequate accommodation (1); the rights of persons with disabilities (1); business and human rights (1); and discrimination based on gender identity and sexual orientation (1).

Date	**Initiative**	**Latest update**
11/01/2017	Laura FASIOLO (PD) – S. 3/03385 Whereas: in the past years the great migratory flow, through sea and land, to our country…	11/01/2017 presented
24/01/2017	Stefano VACCARI (PD) – S. 3/03421 On 31 December 2015, the prison population was…	25/01/2017 concluded
26/01/2017	Ivana SIMEONI (Mixed) and others – S. 3/03444 On 28 December 2016, the Court of Audit, central control section on the management of state's administrations, filed Resolution No. 18/2016/G, concerning the "Fund for non self-sufficiency"…	30/03/2017 concluded
16/03/2017	Roberto COTTI (M5S) – S. 3/03590 The non-governmental organisation "Facing Finance" presented the report "Dirty profits 5" which highlights how the voluntary commitments undertaken by companies…	16/03/2017 assigned to a commission
28/03/2017	Luis Alberto ORELLANA (Aut(SVP-UV-PATT-UPT)-PSI) and others – S. 3/03622 According to what was reported by the Transsexual Identity Movement…	28/03/2017 presented
04/04/2017	Luis Alberto ORELLANA (Aut(SVP-UV-PATT-UPT)-PSI) and others – S. 3/03640 To the Minister of Foreign Affairs and International Cooperation – Whereas: Venezuela…	19/04/2017 concluded
18/04/2017	Giovanna MARTELLI (Art. 1-MDP-LeU) and others – C.3/02961 In relation to the application of the l. No. 194 of 1978…	19/04/2017 concluded
19/04/2017	Loredana DE PETRIS (Mixed) – S. 3/03673 The concerns of civil rights and liberties in Russia…	19/04/2017 presented
02/05/2017	Giulio MARCON (SI-SEL-POS) – C.3/02992 On 27 April 2017 the public prosecutor of Catania, Carmelo Zuccaro…	03/05/2017 concluded

Date	Initiative	Latest update
12/09/2017	Pia LOCATELLI (Mixed) – C.3/03213 On 20 and 21 May, a working meeting organised by Euromed Rights was held in Rome on…	12/09/2017 presented
16/10/2017	Lia QUARTAPELLE PROCOPIO (PD) – C.3/03302 Since the end of the Second Congo War, in 2003…	17/10/2017 concluded
18/10/2017	Riccardo MAZZONI (ALA-PRI) and others – S. 3/04060 Whereas: the extraordinary result of the Kurdish independence referendum…	18/10/2017 presented
15/11/2017	Francesco CAMPANELLA (Art. 1-MDP-LeU) and others – S. 3/04100 On the economic agreement between the Libyan armed militias and the Italian government to prevent the boats from leaving…	15/11/2017 presented
17/11/2017	Giuditta PINI (PD) – C.3/03368 The Office of the United Nations High Commissioner for Human Rights has defined the European policy on migratory flows from Africa as follows…	17/11/2017 presented
28/11/2017	Michela ROSTAN (Art. 1-MDP-LeU) and others – C.3/03391 In the north of Naples, in the municipalities of Scampia, Casoria and Giugliano, an emergency situation affects 360 families who are living in a forgotten hell and unsettling conditions…	29/11/2017 concluded
05/12/2017	Enrico BUEMI (Aut(SVP-UV-PATT-UPT)-PSI) and others – S. 3/04136 Whereas: the prohibition of displaying Nazi symbols…	05/12/2017 presented
14/12/2017	Ornella BERTOROTTA (M5S) – S. 3/04158 To the Ministers of Foreign Affairs and International Cooperation and Justice – a request to provide information on the detention of an Italian citizen, Tiziana Gamannossi, in Libya…	20/12/2017 concluded

Source: *openparlamento* (search criteria: "human rights", "rights of the person")

Questions for a Written Answer

The 54 questions for a written answer concerned the following issues: the protection of human rights at the international level (with particular reference to Brazil, Pakistan, Iran, Venezuela, Eritrea, Libya, Iraq, Congo, Egypt, Israel/Palestine, Gambia, Azerbaijan) (17); the rights of migrants, refugees and asylum seekers (10); human rights defenders (5); bioethics and right to health (4); disarmament and arms trade (3); women's rights (3); prison conditions and prisoners' rights (3); racial discrimination (2); discrimination based on gender identity and sexual orientation (2); children's rights (1); cultural rights (1); business and human rights (1); right to adequate accommodation (1); civil rights (1).

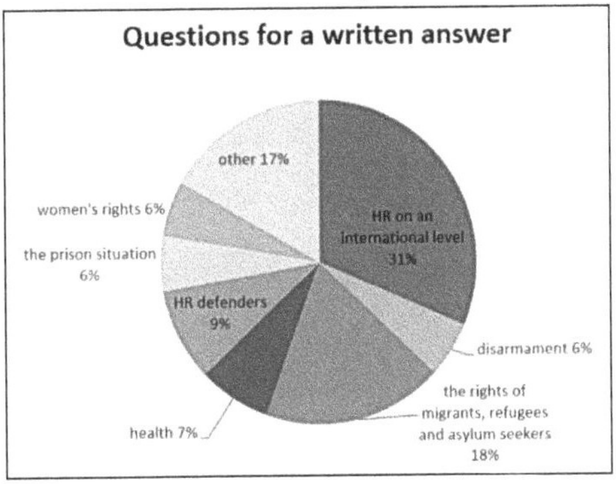

Source: *openparlamento* (search criteria: "human rights", "rights of the person")

Questions submitted to Commissions

The 21 questions submitted to commissions concerned the following issues: the protection of human rights at the international level (with particular reference to Israel/Palestine, North Korea, Iraq, Russia, Turkey, Egypt, Congo, Myanmar, Morocco, Cambodia) (12); the rights of migrants, refugees and asylum seekers (2); prison conditions and prisoners' rights (2); disarmament and arms trade (1); the rights of persons with disabilities (1); the right to sexual and reproductive health (1); women's rights (1); development cooperation (1).

Date	Initiative	Latest update
01/02/2017	Maria Edera SPADONI (M5S) – C.5/10444 Effective authorisation of transit and export of weaponry from Italy to Saudi Arabia...	02/02/2017 concluded
28/02/2017	Lia QUARTAPELLE PROCOPIO (PD) – C.5/10701 On 25 May 2016, a question was asked in response to the Commission, No. 5-08784, which reported the case of the 18-year-old North Korean footballer...	25/05/2017 concluded

Date	Initiative	Latest update
09/03/2017	Eleonora CIMBRO (Art. 1-MDP-LeU) and others – C.5/10802 It is well known that the Israeli Government is proceeding rapidly and in a worrying way with plans for the forced transfer of 46 Bedouin communities…	22/03/2017 concluded
30/03/2017	Donatella DURANTI (Art. 1-MDP-LeU) and others – C.5/11002 On 17 March 2017, as recorded by a detailed complaint from Amnesty International, an air attack by the US-led anti-Isis coalition caused the death of…	30/03/2017 presented
10/04/2017	Giovanna MARTELLI (Art. 1-MDP-LeU) and others – C.5/11092 On the application of the l. No. 194 of 1978…	10/04/2017 presented
12/04/2017	Lia QUARTAPELLE PROCOPIO (PD) – C.5/11129 According to reports by influential newspapers in the Russian press such as «Novaya Gazeta», on the weekend of April 2, there were raids in Chechnya…	11/07/2017 concluded
27/04/2017	Arturo SCOTTO (Art. 1-MDP-LeU) and others – C.5/11233 While the Council of Europe decided to start monitoring respect for human rights, democracy and the rule of law in the aftermath of the referendum in Turkey…	19/07/2017 concluded
10/05/2017	Maria Edera SPADONI (M5S) – C.5/11318 On 29 August 2014, the new law "General Discipline on International Development Cooperation" came into force…	10/05/2017 presented
26/05/2017	Marietta TIDEI (PD) – C.5/11458 On 17 April 2017, about 1,500 Palestinian prisoners, on the initiative of the leaders of Fatah…	26/05/2017 change of commission to respond
11/07/2017	Lia QUARTAPELLE PROCOPIO (PD) – C.5/11787 According to reports from Russian and international newspapers such as «Novaya Gazeta», as well as non-governmental organisations involved in the defense of human rights…	19/07/2017 concluded
26/07/2017	Andrea MAESTRI (SI-SEL-POS) and others – C.5/11984 On 17 March 2017, from the prison house San Michele in Alessandria, a convict contravened his parole…	28/07/2017 concluded

Date	Initiative	Latest update
20/09/2017	Gianna MALISANI (PD) – C.5/12225 The lawyer Ibrahim Metwaly was picked up at the Cairo airport…	20/09/2017 change of commission to respond
21/09/2017	Cristian IANNUZZI (Mixed) and others – C.5/12253 Violence against women, as reported by the press…	21/09/2017 change of commission to respond
21/09/2017	Lia QUARTAPELLE PROCOPIO (PD) – C.5/12245 Since the end of the Second Congo War, in 2003…	16/10/2017 concluded
27/09/2017	Lia QUARTAPELLE PROCOPIO (PD) – C.5/12289 In Myanmar there are many ethnic groups and religions…	28/09/2017 concluded
28/09/2017	Cristian IANNUZZI (Mixed) and others – C.5/12332 In recent months, there has been a significant decrease in migrant arrivals by sea from the Libyan coast…	28/09/2017 change of commission to respond
06/10/2017	Ernesto PREZIOSI (PD) – C.5/12377 The important result achieved by actions promoted by the Government regarding the collapse of refugees landings coming from North Africa…	06/10/2017 change of commission to respond
20/10/2017	Beatrice BRIGNONE (SI-SEL-POS) and others – C.5/12508 Elena, aged twenty-one, and Maria Chiara P., aged twenty-six, are two disabled sisters from Senegal…	20/11/2017 change of minister responsible
15/11/2017	Cristian IANNUZZI (Mixed) and others – C.5/12723 Morocco is often considered the most stable country in North Africa…	19/12/2017 change of minister responsible
20/12/2017	Andrea MAESTRI (SI-SEL-POS) and others – C.5/12957 La Cassa delle ammende (Register of Judgments, Orders and Fines) is an Italian public body established in the prison administration department…	20/12/2017 concluded
20/12/2017	Filippo GALLINELLA (M5S) – C.5/12952 Human rights violations reported in Cambodia…	20/12/2017 concluded

Source: *openparlamento* (search criteria: "human rights", "rights of the person")

Assembly Resolutions

Date	Initiative	Latest update
02/08/2017	Eleonora CIMBRO (Art. 1-MDP-LeU) and others – C.6/00343 On the Deliberation of the Council of Ministers on the participation of Italy in the mission in support of the Libyan Coast Guard…	02/08/2017 not accepted
02/08/2017	Luca FRUSONE (M5S) – C.6/00340 Whereas: the Libyan Government of National Accord led by al Sarraj…	02/08/2017 not accepted
02/08/2017	Erasmo PALAZZOTTO (SI-SEL-POS) – C.6/00339 Whereas: l. 21 July 2016, No. 145, laying down provisions concerning the participation of Italy in international missions…	02/08/2017 not accepted
18/10/2017	Michela MONTEVECCHI (M5S) – S. 6/00267 On 13 September the President of the European Commission, Jean Claude Juncker, presented the "State of the Union 2017" to the European Parliament, devoting much of his speech to migration…	18/10/2017 not accepted
18/10/2017	Ettore ROSATO (PD) – C.6/00359 Whereas: at the European Council, which will take place on 19-20 October, some of the most urgent issues concerning migration will be examined…	18/10/2017 accepted

Source: *openparlamento* (search criteria: "human rights", "rights of the person")

Commission Resolutions

Date	Initiative	Latest update
22/02/2017	Roberto COTTI (M5S) – S. 7/00302 At the conclusion of the examination, in accordance with article 50 of the rules of procedure, the deal assigned on the deliberation of the Council of Ministers on the participation of Italy in international missions…	22/02/2017 declared foreclosed
17/05/2017	Marietta TIDEI (PD) – C.7/01261 Whereas: since 2011, the Syrian people live dramatic and unspeakable suffering…	17/05/2017 presented
18/05/2017	Maria Edera SPADONI (M5S) – C.7/01263 Whereas: in April 2017, a raid took place in 82 provinces across Turkey…	18/05/2017 presented

Date	Initiative	Latest update
31/05/2017	Francesco VERDUCCI (PD) – S. 7/00333 A renewed partnership with the countries of Africa, the Caribbean and the Pacific (ACP)...	31/05/2017 approved
01/08/2017	Peppe DE CRISTOFARO (Mixed) – S. 7/00349 At the conclusion of the examination, in accordance with article 50 of the rules of procedure, the deal assigned on the deliberation of the Council of Ministers on the participation of Italy in international missions...	01/08/2017 not accepted
01/08/2017	Vincenzo SANTANGELO (M5S) – S. 7/00348 On recent developments in the situation in Libya...	01/08/2017 not accepted
06/10/2017	Pia LOCATELLI (Mixed) – C.7/01359 After two independence wars fought against the Russian Federation, Chechnya...	06/10/2017 presented
12/12/2017	Pia LOCATELLI (Mixed) – C.7/01419 The Cambodian Supreme Court ordered the dissolution of the main opposition party...	19/12/2017 accepted

Source: openparlamento (search criteria: "human rights", "rights of the person")

Assembly Agenda Points

The 22 agenda points presented to the Assembly concerned the following issues: the rights of migrants, refugees and asylum seekers (5); bioethics (5); the protection of human rights at the international level (with particular reference to Syria, Israel/Palestine and Libya) (3); the right to freedom of expression (3); the crime of torture (2); and 1 of each of the following themes: Italy's participation in international peacekeeping missions; children's rights; ratification of international instruments; human rights and business.

Date	Initiative	Latest update
08/03/2017	Bruno MARTON (M5S) – S. 9/DOC. XXIV,N At the conclusion of the examination, in accordance with article 50 of the rules of procedure, the deal assigned on the deliberation of the Council of Ministers on the participation of Italy in international missions...	08/03/2017 not accepted
15/03/2017	Erika STEFANI (Lega) – S. 9/02067/005 Introduction of a new crime (child brides) of forced marriage or civil union and deceit of victims to travel with the aim of marriage...	15/03/2017 declared foreclosed

Date	Initiative	Latest update
29/03/2017	Michela MONTEVECCHI (M5S) – S. 9/02705/014 In the examination of the d.l. 17 February 2017, No. 13 on urgent provisions for the acceleration of proceedings concerning international protection…	29/03/2017 declared foreclosed
29/03/2017	Loredana DE PETRIS (Mixed) – S. 9/02705/011 Whereas: providing additional recruitment of specialised officers assigned to the tasks of recognising international protection is to be appreciated…	29/03/2017 declared foreclosed
11/04/2017	Paola BINETTI (Mixed) and others – C.9/04394/058 Whereas: the international situation in Syria…	11/04/2017 accepted as recommendation
11/04/2017	Lara RICCIATTI (Art. 1-MDP-LeU) and others – C.9/04394/019 Whereas: Article 19 of the provision, entitled "Urgent provisions to ensure the effectiveness of expulsions and the strengthening of the centres of…	11/04/2017 not accepted
11/04/2017	Stefano QUARANTA (Art. 1-MDP-LeU) and others – C.9/04394/011 Whereas: the nature and the extent of the migration phenomenon require a radical change of the policies on the topic, beyond the emergency…	11/04/2017 not accepted
20/04/2017	Guido GUIDESI (Lega) – C.9/01142-A/038 On nutrition and hydration treatments…	20/04/2017 accepted as recommendation
20/04/2017	Stefano ALLASIA (Lega) – C.9/01142-A/035 Whereas: on 4 April 1997, the "Convention for Human Rights and Dignity of the Human Being" was signed in Oviedo…	20/04/2017 accepted as recommendation
20/04/2017	Barbara SALTAMARTINI (Lega) and others – C.9/01142-A/034 Whereas: on 4 April 1997, the "Convention for Human Rights and Dignity of the Human Being" was signed in Oviedo…	20/04/2017 accepted as recommendation
20/04/2017	Matteo MANTERO (M5S) – C.9/01142-A/016 Whereas: the examination provision regulates the anticipated treatment provisions…	20/04/2017 accepted as recommendation

C. National Committee on Bioethics

The National Committee on Bioethics performs an advisory role vis-à-vis the Government, Parliament and other institutions, with a view to providing guidelines on legislative and administrative instruments designed to define the criteria to use in medical and biological practice in order to protect human rights. It also has a role in informing the public and in raising awareness with regard to ethical problems arising in connection with progress in scientific research and in technological applications in the life sciences and in healthcare.

The Committee was established by the d.p.c.m. 28 March 1990. It is made up of the following bodies: Chair (Lorenzo d'Avack, Professor in Philosophy of Law); Vice Chairs (Riccardo Di Segni, Chief Rabbi of Rome; Laura Palazzani, Professor in Philosophy of Law); Office of the President (made up of the Chair and the Vice Chairs); Assembly.

One of the tasks of the Committee is to produce studies and make recommendations that can also be used for legislative purposes. The Committee's documents offer in-depth focus and reflection on ethical and legal issues that arise as knowledge in the field of the life sciences advances. According to their nature and purpose, the documents are classified as: opinions (approved in the Committee's assembly on the basis of inquiries conducted by working groups); motions (urgent documents approved with a two-thirds majority of those present in the assembly); responses (documents in which the Committee makes recommendations on issues about which its opinion has been sought by other bodies or by physical persons).

The following opinions and motions were approved in 2017:

Opinions:

- In defence of the national health service (26 January);
- Genetic editing and CRISPR-CAS9 technique: ethics considerations (23 February);
- Ethics committees in the clinic (31 March);
- Immigration and health (23 June);
- Caring for people with mental illness: bioethical problems (23 June).

Motions:

- Motion for a fair access policy to innovative drugs with high efficacy for serious diseases: price reduction and containment of costs for the National Health Service and Citizens (23 February);

- Declaration on the labelling of homeopathic preparations and information transparency (28 April);
- Motion on non-optimal packaging of medications (23 June).

III. Ministry of Foreign Affairs and International Cooperation

The Ministry of Foreign Affairs has a number of directorate-generals and offices that deal specifically with human rights, disarmament and cooperation. Since March 2016, responsibility for issues dealt with in the United Nations ambit have been entrusted to Undersecretary Vincenzo Amendola.

Particularly worthy of note is Office II – Human rights advocacy and international humanitarian law, Council of Europe, which falls within the directorate-general for Political Affairs and Security. Other offices in the same directorate are: Office I – The United Nations system and the institutional reform process, peacekeeping operations and preventive diplomacy; Office V – Disarmament, arms control and nuclear, biological and chemical non proliferation, Office of the national authority for the banning of chemical weapons; Office VI – Organisation for Security and Cooperation in Europe. The theme of human rights also relates across the board to the directorate-general for Global Affairs (Office IV – Energy, environmental protection and sustainable global development policies), the directorate-general for the European Union (Office III – European space of freedom, security and justice, the free movement of people and migratory flows towards the European Union) and the directorate-general for Development Cooperation (Office I – Development of cooperation policies within the European Union; Office II – Multilateral development cooperation; Office VI – Emergency and humanitarian aid; Office VIII – Planning and monitoring of the cooperation budget; gender issues, the rights of children and people with disabilities).

A. *Inter-Ministerial Committee for Human Rights (CIDU)*

The Inter-Ministerial Committee for Human Rights (CIDU) was established by decree of the Minister of Foreign Affairs on 15 February 1978, No. 519; its composition was updated by d.c.p.m. on 11 May 2007. Over 2012–2013 the CIDU was involved in a restructuring process: initially phased out as a result of the spending review, it was re-established on 5 September 2013. It maintained its functional competences because it was regarded as indispensable, both for its advice and its strategic guidance regarding the promotion and protection of human rights and in ensuring correct compliance with the obligations that Italy assumed following the signature and ratification of conventions and international agreements in this field.

CIDU is chaired by a functionary of the diplomatic service appointed by the Minister of Foreign Affairs: Fabrizio Petri in 2017. Committee members include representatives of the Prime Minister's Office, of various Ministries and of many different institutions (such as the Association of Italian Municipalities (ANCI); the Conference of Presidents of the Regions and Autonomous Provinces; the Union of Italian Provinces (UPI); the National Commission for UNESCO; the Italian Committee for UNICEF; the Italian Society for International Organisation (SIOI); as well as three eminent personalities in the field of human rights.

CIDU has the following tasks: to promote measures necessary for ensuring full compliance with international obligations assumed by Italy; to facilitate the implementation of international conventions in Italy; to draft the reports Italy is required to submit to the pertinent international organisations; to maintain and develop appropriate relations with civil society organisations engaged in promoting and protecting human rights.

In September 2017, the report on the activities carried out by the CIDU for the year 2016 was sent to the Chamber of Deputies. The report provides Parliament with the results of collaborative activities with the bodies of the United Nations, the Council of Europe and the European Union on the submission of the periodic reports provided by the international human rights instruments of which Italy is a part; as well as visits prepared by the aforementioned organisations in order to obtain specific elements or to identify concrete situations in areas deemed to be particularly sensitive to human rights. In this regard, in 2016 the CIDU carried out the following activities.

United Nations

- Discussing the first periodic report presented by Italy on the implementation of the Convention on the Rights of Persons with Disabilities (Geneva, 24-25 August 2016);
- Preparing the response to the *list of issues* related to the International Covenant on Civil and Political Rights;
- Preparing the First Report to the Convention for the Protection of All Persons from Enforced Disappearance;
- Discussing the 19th and 20th periodic report on the implementation of the International Convention on the Elimination of All Forms of Racial Discrimination (Geneva, 1-2 December 2016);
- Second cycle of the Universal Periodic Review by the UN Human Rights Council;

- Visit to Italy of the delegation of experts of the Office of the United Nations High Commissioner for Human Rights (27 June – 1 July 2016);
- Follow-up to the visit to Italy of the UN Subcommittee on Prevention of Torture, which took place from 16-22 September 2015.

Council of Europe

- Follow-up to the visit to Italy of the delegation of the Advisory Committee on the framework of the Convention for the Protection of National Minorities of the Council of Europe, held from 29 June – 3 July 2015;
- Follow-up to the visit to Italy of the European Commission delegation against racism and intolerance of the Council of Europe, which took place from 14-18 September 2015;
- Visit to Italy of the Council of Europe's Committee for the Prevention of Torture (7-21 April 2016).

European Union

- Visit to Italy of the director of the Fundamental Rights Agency (FRA) (4-5 July 2016).

B. Italian National Commission for UNESCO

The Commission was established by inter-ministerial decree on 11 February 1959, at the Ministry of Foreign Affairs, two years after Italy entered the Organisation, and pursuant to article 7 of the UNESCO Charter.

> Members of the Commission include representatives from Parliament, the Prime Minister's Office, various Ministries, public and private agencies, local authorities and civil society.
>
> The Commission's mission is to promote the implementation of UNESCO programmes in Italy; to spread the ideals of the Organisation, especially among the younger generations; to disseminate information on its principles, goals and activities, thus stimulating action by institutions, civil society and the world of culture, education and science. The Commission also advises the Government regarding its dealings with UNESCO.

In 2017, the Ministry of Foreign Affairs nominated Franco Bernabè as president, while the post of Secretary General was held by Enrico Vicenti.

The National Commission receives funding for institutional activities and its functioning through chapter 2471/10 of the budget forecast of the Ministry of Foreign Affairs. In 2017, this funding was around €7,000 which covers no more than the basic functioning of the Commission, making it extremely difficult to perform its public activities.

Despite these shortages, in 2017, the National Commission carried out many activities (seminars, conferences, meetings in schools, competitions, exhibitions, workshops, shows) in various Italian cities, especially regarding the different UN International Days, including International Mother Language Day (21 February), World Poetry Day (21 March), World Book and Copyright Day (23 April) and International Jazz Day (30 April).

IV. Ministry of Labour and Social Policies

Many departments and offices within the Ministry of Labour and Social Policies deal specifically with human rights.

The following are particularly worthy of note:

- Directorate-General for Inclusion and Social Policies. Functions: promoting policies to combat poverty, social exclusion and severe marginalisation; promoting and monitoring policies for children and adolescents, and the protection of minors; coordination policies for the social inclusion, protection and promotion of the rights and opportunities of persons with disabilities; managing the National Fund for Social Policies, the National Fund for the Non Self-Sufficient, the National Fund for Childhood and Adolescence and other funds for financing social policies and monitoring transferred resources; study, research and investigations concerning social policies; participation in all the pertinent internationally significant activities, and managing relations with the European Union, the Council of Europe, the International Labour Organisation, the United Nations and the Organisation for Economic Cooperation and Development.
- Directorate-general for the third sector and social groups. Functions: promoting and supporting the activities carried out by third sector subjects, especially initiatives relating to social promotion and voluntary associations, in order to facilitate the growth of an active society welfare to support policies of social inclusion and integration; promotion, development and coordination of policies, initiatives and activities to support the spread of corporate social responsibility.
- Directorate-general for immigration and integration policies. Functions: programming migratory flows, and managing and monitoring entry quotas of foreign workers as well as bilateral cooperation agreements with countries of origin; coordinating policies for social and job integration of foreign immigrants and initiatives designed to prevent and combat discrimination, xenophobia and racism; developing international cooperation for activities to prevent and study social and employment emergencies, and for initiatives regarding work-related migratory flows.

In 2012, the Directorate-General for immigration and integration policies took over the functions of the Committee for foreign minors, which was abolished in accordance with the decree on the so-called spending review (article 12, para. 20 of l.d. 95/2012, converted into law, with amendments, in l. 135/2012). Consequently, the Directorate-General is now responsible for monitoring the presence of foreign minors temporarily present on Italian territory, whether they be unaccompanied minors present on Italian territory or admitted minors.

As regards unaccompanied minors, the Directorate-General may adopt two kinds of measures: the first is "no repatriation", which amounts to activating the procedures for integrating the person into Italy; the second is "assisted repatriation", designed to reunite the child with his or her family in their Country of origin. As regards the first option, responsibility for managing and monitoring the measures is placed in the hands of local authorities. The most frequent choice made for unaccompanied minors in Italy is to place them in residential care facilities for children.

As regards admitted minors, the Directorate-General makes decisions, following due appraisal and according to predetermined criteria, at the request of organisations, associations or Italian families, regarding the temporary admission of children into the framework of humanitarian programmes. The Committee then makes decisions on temporary fostering and repatriation. It keeps a register of minors already admitted into the framework of humanitarian programmes and defines criteria for assessing requests for the admission of temporarily admitted minors.

By 31 December 2017, 18,303 unaccompanied foreign minors were registered with the Committee, about a thousand more than 31 December 2016. Once again, the vast majority of these (93.2% of the total) were boys. The main countries of origin are Gambia (12%), Egypt (9.9%), Guinea (9.6%), Albania (9.2%) and Eritrea (8%): together, these five represent just under half of unaccompanied foreign minors in Italy (48.7%). The region with the highest number of minors (about 43% of the total) in reception centres is still Sicily, in line with a trend which has consolidated over many years, followed by: Calabria (7.9%), Lombardy (6.6%), Lazio (5.7%), Emilia Romagna (5.6%) and Apulia (5%).

A. National Observatory for Children and Adolescents

The Observatory performs a role of coordination among central administrations, local and regional bodies, associations, professional groups and non-governmental organisations dedicated to children's issues.

It was instituted by l. 23 December 1997, No. 451, and is currently regulated by decree of the President of the Republic (d.p.r.), 14 May 2007, No. 103, which assigns it joint chairmanship by the Ministry of Labour and Social Policies and the Undersecretary of State to the Prime Minister's Office mandated with family policies. It is made up of representatives from national and local public administrations, associations and professional orders, voluntary and third sector organisations as well as experts in the field of children's rights.

Presidential decree 103/2007 assigns the Observatory the task of preparing three documents about the condition of childhood and adolescence in Italy:

– The *National Plan of Action and of Measures to Safeguard the Rights and Development of Children and Adolescents*. Drawn up every two years, the plan contains the fundamental strategic guidelines and concrete commitments that the Government intends to pursue in order to develop a satisfactory policy for children and adolescents in Italy. The last National Plan adopted by the Observatory refers to the years 2016/2017.

– The *Report on the Condition of Children and Adolescents in Italy*. It aims to provide an updated picture of the aspects that characterise the condition of children and adolescents in Italy, and of the social services system and measures for promoting and protecting the rights of children and adolescents. In October 2017, the Observatory published the *Report on the Condition of Childhood and Adolescence in Italy 2012-2015*, divided into five thematic areas: an overview of childhood and adolescence in Italy (with particular reference to births, family relationships in evolution and in crisis, resources for children and adolescents); poverty of children and families and measures to combat social exclusion; educational services system for children in Italy; integration and social inclusion from a socio-juridical point of view (with particular attention to children and adolescents with foreign citizenship, Roma and Sinti children and adolescents, unaccompanied foreign minors, children and adolescents with disabilities and special educational needs and adolescents involved in the juvenile criminal circuit); support for parenting and reception system.

– The *Periodic Report of the Government to the UN Committee on the Rights of the Child regarding the application of the 1989 International Convention on the Rights of the Child*, pursuant to article 44 of the Convention. The latest report (combining the 3rd and 4th reports) was sent by Italy in January 2009, and discussed in October 2011 (see *Yearbook 2012*, p. 194-199).

In carrying out its functions, the National Observatory uses the National Centre of Documentation and Analysis for Children and Adolescents, which performs documentation, analysis, research, monitoring and training tasks.

More specifically, the National Centre of Documentation deals with:

– collecting and disseminating regional, national, European, and international norms and regulations, as well as statistical data and scientific studies;

– creating an annually updated map, based on information provided by regional authorities, of public, private and non-governmental services, including social and health care services, and of financial resources dedicated to children at the national, regional and local level;

– analysing the situation of childhood and adolescence in Italy, including the conditions of foreign minors;

– preparing an outline, based on National Observatory directives, of the biennial report on the condition of children in Italy, and of the Government report to the United Nations Committee on the Rights of the Child on the domestic implementation of the Convention on the Rights of the Child;

– formulating proposals, also at the request of local authorities, for the creation of pilot projects designed to improve children's living conditions as well as to assist mothers during the prenatal period.

B. National Observatory Monitoring the Conditions of Persons with Disabilities

The Observatory is an advisory body offering technical and scientific support in defining national policies regarding disabilities.

It was instituted by l. 3 March 2009, No. 18, at the Ministry of Labour, Health and Social Policies. It is chaired by the Ministry of Labour and includes a maximum of 40 members, who are appointed by ministerial decree and represent central administrations involved in defining and implementing disability-related policies; regional and local authorities; social security institutions; the National Statistics Institute; trade unions; and most representative associations and organisations of persons with disabilities, joined by a maximum of five experts of proven experience in the field of disabilities. Within the Observatory there is also a technical-scientific Committee, with the purpose of analysis and scientific direction in relation to the activities and tasks of the organism.

The Observatory's tasks include the following: to promote the implementation of the United Nations Convention on the Rights of Persons with Disabilities and to prepare, together with CIDU, the national report for the monitoring procedure established by that Convention; to prepare a biennial Plan of Action on disability implementing national and international laws; promotes the realisation of studies and research that can help to identify priority areas in which to direct actions and actions for the promotion of the rights of persons with disabilities.

With the Presidential Decree of the Council of Ministers of 5 December 2016, the duration of the Observatory has been extended for the three-year period 2017-2020. The new Observatory took office on 11 October 2017.

V. Ministry of Justice

Within the Ministry of Justice there are various departments and bureaus specifically involved with human rights. The most relevant are:

- Office II: (Directorate-General for litigation and human rights – Department of legal affairs): it is actively involved in examining cases pending before the European Court of Human Rights. In addition, it is responsible for drafting the reports requested by international human rights bodies, mainly by the Council of Europe and UN bodies and committees.
- Department for Juvenile Justice and Community: the office deals with promoting and protecting the rights of unaccompanied foreign minors and of persons at risk of social exclusion.

The "National Plan for the Prevention of Suicidal Conduct in the Adult Penitentiary System", approved by the Ministry of Justice and the State-Regions Conference, was published in the Official Gazette of 14 August 2014, No. 189. The National Plan includes the risk assessment tools, the monitoring of potentially critical situations, the operational protocols for the management of cases at risk and the management of urgencies, as well as the monitoring and evaluation of the actions undertaken.

VI. Judicial Authorities

The judiciary, that is to say the various organs of justice – ordinary, administrative and auditing – constituting judicial power, is the fundamental guarantee of rights and legality in a State that respects the principles of democracy, the division of powers and the rule of law. The Italian courts – the Constitutional Court, which delivers judgments regarding the constitutionality of laws, the Supreme Court, which is the court of last resort, the penal and civil tribunals and trial courts, and those concerned with administrative, audit and military matters – deal in a contentious manner with cases which often affect human rights in the most various ways and according to the most disparate perspectives. Access to a judge to obtain a ruling on a right that a plaintiff claims has been breached is a fundamental human right, linked to which are the many other procedural rights that distinguish the fair trial.

Besides ruling on individual cases, the justice system contributes to building and to the evolution of applicable law, through its own case-law. In recent years, and in relation to the theme of fundamental rights in particular, Italian rulings have been strongly influenced by that of international courts, especially the European Court of Human Rights and the

Court of Justice of the European Union. The interaction between national judicial organs and international courts with jurisdiction over human rights stresses the universal nature of the latter. The dialogue with international courts and with those of other countries called upon to apply the same standards regarding individual human rights does not just concern the State supreme courts, but all judges, who can draw on rulings made in foreign or international courts to improve existing guarantees regarding fundamental rights, fully respecting the Constitution and the law.

Part IV of this *Yearbook* is specifically devoted to a summary presentation of cases in the Italian courts on which rulings were delivered in 2017 (with particular reference to the judgments of the Constitutional Court and the Supreme Court), and of case-law elaborated by the European Court of Human Rights or the Court of Justice of the European Union which directly concerns Italy, either because the Italian State was the "defendant" or because the intervention of the European judge regarded pleas presented by Italian citizens or related to Italian legal norms.

VII. Independent Authorities

There are ten independent authorities in Italy: the Communications Regulatory Authority (AGCOM); the Data Protection Authority; the Committee Guaranteeing the Implementation of the Law on Strikes Affecting Essential Public Services; the Authority Protecting Free Competition and the Market (Antitrust Authority); the Italian Companies and Stock Exchange Commission (CONSOB); the Institute for Vigilance on Private Insurance and Insurances of Collective Interest (ISVAP); the Regulatory Authority for Electricity and Gas; the Authority for Vigilance on Contracts for Public Works, Services and Supplies; the National Ombudsperson for Children and Adolescents; the National Ombudsperson for the Rights of Persons in Prison or Deprived of Liberty.

The five authorities that relate more pertinently to human rights are described below.

A. Communications Regulatory Authority (AGCOM)

AGCOM was set up by l. 31 July 1997, No. 249. It has a dual mandate: to ensure correct competition among market actors and to guarantee the fundamental freedoms of citizens in the area of communications, particularly as regards the protection of minors.

The composition of the Authority is disciplined by decree 6 December 2011, No. 201 (the so-called "Save Italy" decree), and its conversion into law

(22 December 2011, No. 214). In 2017, the Authority was made up as follows: Chair: Angelo Marcello Cardani; members of the *Services and Products Commission*: Antonio Martusciello and Francesco Posteraro; members of the *Commission for Infrastructure and Networks*: Antonio Nicita and Mario Morcellini (from 15 March 2017). The Council consists of the Chair and all the Commissioners.

According to the 2017 annual report of its activities and work programmes (reference period: May 2016 – April 2017), the Authority paid particular attention to the supervision of the protection of minors and persons with disabilities. In particular, at the regulatory level, general measures have been adopted to guarantee the provision of universal service and the accessibility of services to users with disabilities. With regard to content surveillance activities, the Authority, in monitoring of national television programmes, initiated a series of investigative proceedings for violations of provisions to protect minors, 57% of which ended with an injunction.

B. Data Protection Authority

The Data Protection Authority was instituted by l. 31 December 1996, No. 675, later substituted by lgs.d. 30 June 2003, No. 196 (Personal data protection code), with the aim to ensure protection of the fundamental rights and freedoms and respect for the dignity of persons, in the processing of personal data.

The Data Protection Authority is a collegial body made up of four members elected by Parliament, who remain in office for a seven-year non-renewable mandate. The current body is made up of Antonello Soro (Chair), Augusta Iannini (Vice Chair), Giovanna Bianchi Clerici and Licia Califano.

During 2017, the Authority issued 533 *provisions* to protect the fundamental rights of individuals with regard to the processing and circulation of personal data, with particular reference to the following issues (among others): freedom of the press; right to education, work, health and scientific research; rights of minors; handling of sensitive data; and internet and social media.

C. Commission Guaranteeing the Implementation of the Law on Strikes Affecting Essential Public Services

The Commission was instituted by l. 12 June 1990, No. 146, and subsequent modifications. It comprises five members designated by the Chairs of the Chamber of Deputies and the Senate among experts in matters of constitutional law, labour law and industrial relations, and appointed by decree of the President of the Republic. In 2017, the members of the Commission were: Giuseppe Santoro Passarelli (Chair), Lauralba Bellardi, Alessandro Bellavista, Domenico Carrieri, Orsola Razzolini.

Some of the Commission's main tasks are:

- assessing the capacity of essential services to guarantee protection of both the right to strike and the enjoyment of constitutionally guaranteed human rights;
- requesting that those calling the strike delay the date of abstention from work if the Commission intends to attempt conciliation, or if it finds that the abstention violates legal and/or contractual obligations for strikes in essential public services;
- pointing out to those calling the strike any violations of norms concerning advance notice or any other requirements relative to the phase preceding collective abstention;
- notifying the appropriate authority which can order strikers back to work of situations where the strike or collective abstention could give rise to an imminent, probable risk of infringing constitutionally protected human rights;
- taking note of behaviour by administrations or enterprises which provide essential public services in clear violation of the law;
- assessing behaviour of both parties and if any non-compliance or violation of legal or contractual obligations relative to essential services emerges, inflicting penalties pursuant to article 4 of l. 146/1990 as amended by article 3 of l. 83/2000, ordering the employer to apply the disciplinary actions.

The annual report on the activity carried out in 2016 was presented in June 2017. According to data contained in the report, strikes in the essential public services sector remain at rather high levels. In the year in review, a slightly increasing trend was noted compared to previous year. The overall number of strikes (national, local, sectoral, refusal of overtime, etc.) called in essential public services was 2,352, compared to 2,261 in 2015. The days affected by the strike actions fell to 840, distributed in the various sectors of essential public services. In particular, the conflict remains strong in the following sectors: local public transport (368 strikes called), environmental hygiene (340), cleaning and multi-service (243), air transport (215), regions and local self-government (179), rail transport (145).

The majority of strike actions were called in full compliance with the law: indeed, the Commission only intervened with 466 preventative actions to highlight potential breaches of legislation, which led to adjustments in almost all of the cases (over 96%). Consequently, only 23 assessments of behaviours of trade unions, individual workers, or employers were made.

Analysing the causes of the conflict, in its report the Commission aims to draw the attention of public institutions to the need to identify the resources available for the conclusion and renewal of national collective agreements; given that a persistent situation of uncertainty (due to the agreements natural expiration) contributes to nurture the conflict, and often pushes it out of the control of trade unions. Furthermore, the Commission hopes that collective bargaining, even in its decentralised dimension, will be: less fragmented and will not give rise to unjustified inequality, in terms of treatments, within the same service; where possible, assisted by clauses aimed at safeguarding employment levels, often already below the minimum thresholds set by national reference collective agreements.

D. National Ombudsperson for Children and Adolescents

The National Ombudsperson for Children and Adolescents was established with l. 12 July 2011, No. 112. It is a single presiding organ, and the holder of the post is appointed by the Presidents of the Chamber of Deputies and of the Senate, who choose a figure of unquestioned morality, independence and professional competence in the field of children's rights. The term of office is four years. From March 2016, Filomena Albano has held the post of Ombudsperson.

The Ombudsperson has, amongst others, the following responsibilities:

- to promote the implementation of the UN Convention on the Rights of the Child, and of other pertinent international and European instruments, and to ensure appropriate forms of collaboration with all the national and international bodies and organisations engaged in promoting and protecting children and adolescents;
- to express opinions on legislative initiatives concerning the protection of the rights of children and adolescents, and the report that the Government presents periodically to the UN Committee on the Rights of the Child;
- to inform the Government, Regions and other local or territorial bodies involved, in relation to their respective responsibilities, of all appropriate measures to ensure full promotion and protection of the rights of children and adolescents;
- to inform judicial authorities and bodies concerned of problem cases or risks of minors' rights being infringed, as well as serious cases of neglect of minors, so that they can be taken into care by the appropriate authorities;

- to enhance knowledge of the rights of children and adolescents, organising, to this end, awareness-raising activities, studies, and research.

Article 6 of l. 112 also allows anyone to address the Ombudsperson to report violation of rights or the risk thereof. Finally, article 3 states that the Ombudsperson is to establish appropriate forms of cooperation with the regional Ombudspersons or similar figures. The National Conference for the Rights of Children and Adolescents was set up for this purpose; coordinated by the National Ombudsperson, it brings together all the other Ombudspersons, where these have been established (see this Part, Sub-national Human Rights Structures, IV).

In June 2017, the Ombudsperson presented the report to Parliament on the actions undertaken on 2016. During the year, the Ombudsperson continued examining the pertinent bills, with particular attention to the proposals aimed at guaranteeing the protection of minors in the digital environment, equal opportunities for children and adolescents, implementation of a child-friendly justice system. Among these, Senate bill 2583, approved 29 March 2017 (l. 7 April 2017, No. 47), containing an organic reform of the discipline of unaccompanied foreign minors. The bill establishes a list of voluntary guardians at the juvenile court and attributes the Ombudsperson with the responsibility of electing and training such tutors, as well as stipulating special memoranda of understanding together with the presidents of the courts to promote and facilitate their appointment in regions that do not have regional guarantors.

In 2016, the Ombudsperson held three hearings in Parliament. On 28 June, it was heard in the Parliamentary Commission for children and adolescents, as part of the fact-finding survey on minors outside the family. This meeting was an opportunity to point out that the removal of a child from the family of origin must constitute the last possible course of action, only feasible if all the measures of supporting the family have not given the expected results. The open questions are: the problem of the data regarding minors placed outside the family, currently fragmented and out of date; the issue of control on children's placement, due to some flaws in cooperation among the institutional organs concerned; the absence of national regulatory standards relating to residential communities hosting minors outside the family.

On 30 June 2017, the Ombudsperson was audited by the Justice Commission of the Chamber of Deputies in the context of the fact-finding investigation on the state of implementation of the legislative provisions on adoption and foster care. The Ombudsperson has provided its contribution to recognising the application practice of l. 4 May 1983, No. 184, on the subject of the child's right to a family, to verify its consistency and relevance.

Finally, on 27 July, the Ombudsperson was audited by the Joint Committees of the Chamber of Deputies, constitutional affairs and labour, as part of the examination of the legislative proposals laying down rules on video surveillance in nurseries and infant school, as well as at social welfare facilities for disabled elderly persons and disadvantaged minors. According to the Ombudsperson, in the case of children, a balance must be struck between the protection of their physical safety and the protection of their confidentiality from excessively invasive means. The other, also relevant, interests at stake must be interpreted in the light of the principle of the superior interest of the minor, which is of utmost priority. This balance can be achieved with a CCTV system. The images would only be viewed by law enforcement agencies, subject to authorisation by judicial authorities, upon a motivated request by interested parties or in the context of a proceeding penalty arising from criminal charges.

The Ombudsperson has taken also numerous actions in favour of some particularly vulnerable categories of minors (minors out of family and unaccompanied, children of detained parents, children belonging to ethnic minorities), as well as opportunities to meet with children and teenagers, in the implementation of the right to be listened, enshrined in the article 12 of the Convention on the Rights of the Child.

E. National Ombudsperson for the Rights of Persons in Prison or Deprived of Liberty

This Ombudsperson was established by article 7 of l.d. 23 December 2013, No. 146, converted with amendments by l. 21 February 2014, No. 10. It is collegial and consists of the Chair and two members chosen from independent people who are competent in areas relating to the protection of human rights. Members are nominated, following a decision of the Council of Ministers, by a Presidential Decree, having heard the competent parliamentary commissions, with a five-year mandate which may not be extended.

In 2017, the National Ombudsperson for the Rights of Persons in Prison or Deprived of Liberty was Mauro Palma; the other members were Daniela De Robert and Emilia Rossi.

The Ombudsperson is tasked with ensuring that custody of persons in prison and persons subject to other types of limitations on personal freedom is carried out in accordance with the rules and principles set out in the Constitution, in international conventions on human rights, and the laws of the land. To this end, it has the faculty to visit penitentiary institutions and other structures used to host persons subject to measures restricting their personal freedom without requiring authorisation.

The Ombudsperson has been identified as an independent national monitoring mechanism required under the Optional Protocol to the Convention against Torture (OPCAT), which Italy ratified in 2012.

The National Ombudsperson is also tasked with coordinating the network of local ombudspersons, promoting their solidity as an institution through the recognition of sufficient guarantees of independence and autonomy vis-à-vis the local government which appointed them.

Finally, the Ombudsperson monitors procedures relating to forced repatriations pursuant to the system provided for in article 8, para. 6, of EU Directive No. 115 of 2008. In the period January-July 2017, the National Ombudsperson conducted eight visits and monitoring activities, as shown below.

- 26 January: monitoring a joint forced repatriation operation of Nigerian citizens, carried out by air transport from Rome to Lagos.
- 9 February: visit to the *Sorella Luna* ("Sister Luna") residential therapeutic rehabilitation community. With the visit, the National Ombudsperson began monitoring the communities hosting persons deprived of personal freedom, in order to verify personal and environmental conditions, administrative regularity, as well as composition, training and rehabilitation method used by the staff.
- 23 February: monitoring a joint forced repatriation operation of 43 Nigerian citizens, carried out by air transport from Rome to Lagos.
- 23-31 March: visit to the Campania region.
- 13 April: monitoring a charter flight for the repatriation of 23 Tunisian citizens coming from Centres of Identification and Expulsion in Caltanissetta and from the hotspot of Trapani.
- 17 May: monitoring a charter flight for forced repatriation of 15 Nigerian citizens, which took place with air transport from Palermo to Lagos.
- 23 June: visit to the first reception centre for abandoned minors in difficult situations in Rome.
- 13 July: monitoring a charter flight, organised by the Ministry of the Interior and financed by FRONTEX, for the repatriation of Tunisian citizens.

In June 2017, the "CIE and Hotspot 2016-2017 Report" was also published, which collects the reports of visits to CIEs and hotspots carried out by the National Guarantor in the first year of activity. The document contains some general recommendations and a series of specific recommendations addressed to the Ministry of the Interior.

For the CIEs, the National Ombudsperson recommends:

- performing urgently all the necessary ordinary and extraordinary maintenance of the structures in order to significantly improve the living standards;

- encouraging as much as possible the separation of those who come from the criminal circuit and those who are only in a position of administrative irregularity or asylum seekers;
- setting up and equipping, with urgency, spaces suitable for the foreseen recreational activities and areas dedicated to prayers, inviting the Ministry of the Interior to perform strict monitoring activities on the actual delivery of these actions by the entity manager;
- establishing a register of critical events, to be completed daily and kept at the reference structure;
- intensifying efforts, through the managing body and the mediators present in the centres, to increase the quantity and quality of information to foreign nationals held in detention; making information forms available in a broader range of languages and providing a large number of individual and group interviews aimed at increasing the understanding and awareness of the detained citizens about the complex rights and duties that can be attributed to them.

In relation to the critical issues noted in the hotspots, the National Ombudsperson recommends:

- defining as soon as possible, with a primary regulatory source, how people stay in the hotspots, providing for judicial screening and the related remedies regarding the aspects of deprivation of personal liberty;
- adopting standardised rules in all the hotspots concerning the possibility for foreign citizens that are already identified to enter and leave the centres;
- limiting the permanence in such structures strictly to the necessary time for identification; and, in the case of vulnerable groups such as unaccompanied foreign minors or pregnant women, ensuring maximum transfer speed;
- directing actions to guarantee the essential conditions of personal dignity in the hotspots (providing clean clothes, shoes, blankets in case of adverse weather conditions) and to satisfy basic human needs, such as the possibility to wash and refreshment to recently arrived migrants. All of this precedes or, in any case, cannot be subverted by the needs of identification and photosetting;
- strengthening the coordination activities and the teamwork of the various operating teams, in order to harmonise procedures and mutual roles, especially regarding coordinating security, identification procedures and reception;
- making hotspots more accessible to the press, academics, and associations, especially those involved in protecting the rights of migrants.

VIII. Non-Governmental Organisations

In Italy, numerous non-governmental organisations are active in promoting and protecting human rights. Some that are organised in networks at national and international levels have gained consultative status with international organisations and actively participate in their programmes.

As of 31 December 2017, 118 Italian non-governmental organisations held consultative status with the United Nations Economic and Social Council, eight of which have general status; 92 have special status and 18 have roster status. There are 174 non-governmental organisations with headquarters or representative offices in Italy enjoying participatory status with the Council of Europe dealing specifically with human rights.

In addition, some of the most important international non-governmental organisations have local branches in Italy. These include Amnesty International, the International Federation on Human Rights, Save the Children, *Médecins sans Frontières* and ActionAid. The Italian associations Hands off Cain (*Nessuno tocchi Caino*) and No Peace without Justice (*Non c'è pace senza giustizia*) also have high profiles internationally.

Non-governmental organisations play an important role in monitoring the level of compliance with and protection of human rights in Italy. In 2017, the following monitoring reports, which are of particular interest, were published.

- Working group for the Convention on the Rights of the Child (CRC Group): *3rd Supplementary Report to the United Nations on the monitoring of the Convention on the Rights of the Child in Italy, 2016-2017*. The Report was published in the view of the examination that will be submitted to Italy in 2018 by the UN Committee on the Rights of the Child, reflecting the position of the 96 associations of the CRC Group and of those who, for various reasons, are involved in the promotion of the rights of children and adolescents in Italy, on issues such as: social policies and resources for children and adolescents in Italy; commitment to childhood and adolescence in international cooperation; principles of non-discrimination, higher interest, participation of minors and making sure their voice is heard; civil rights and freedom; violence against minors; family environment and alternative measures; health, disability and basic services; education, play and cultural activities; special protection measures for unaccompanied migrant minors. According to the report, although in recent years much progress has been made, especially from the legislative point of view, to make rights of children and adolescents real in Italy, the road ahead is still long; still many unresolved critical issues and increasing inequalities, starting from the evident disparity at the regional level. Therefore, the CRC Group formulates 157 recommendations to local and national institutional representatives in order to improve policies for childhood and adolescence in Italy.
- *Antigone Association – XII National Report on detention conditions – "Prison returns"*. The underlying thesis of the Report is that after some years characterised by a significant drop in the prison population, the numbers of

prisons have risen once again. In 2010, when the state of national emergency for prison overcrowding was declared, the detained population had reached unprecedented levels, since then a series of interventions have been launched on numerous fronts, which have led to a significant drop. This has increased from 68,000 inmates in 2010 to 52,000 in 2015. The decline in numbers had led to a general improvement for the Italian penitentiary system, generating an overall decrease: of the number of foreign prisoners, often detained for less serious events and longer than Italians; of the number of people in pre-trial detention, which has always been at pathological levels in Italy; the number of persons detained for short sentences; of the rate of suicides in prison. Instead, the percentage of prisoners who worked or studied had increased.

Yet, in the face of a considerable decrease in crimes, by 30 April 2017, the prison population had reached 56,436. Consequently, the rate of crowding rose from 105% in 2015 to 112.8% in April 2017. Pre-trial detainees went from 34.1% to 34.5%; the percentage of foreigners among prisoners from 33.2% to 34.1%; and prisoners for sentences of less than three years from 23.7% to 24.3%.

Another data concerns the composition of the prison population. Italy is one of the countries with the most employees in prison, even when compared to other European countries that have a greater number of prisoners, such as Spain, France, Germany, or the United Kingdom. However, 90.1% of these personnel is made up of custodians (the European average is 68.6%); criminologists and psychologists in Italy are 0.1%, compared to a European average of 2.2%, while the medical and paramedical staff is 0.2%, against 4.3% of the European average. To counter the new surge in numbers of detainees and promote an overall improvement of the Italian penitentiary system, the Report hopes that the reforms proposed by the States General of the Execution of Criminal Sentences and wanted by the Minister of Justice Orlando, are adopted (see *Yearbook 2017*, p. 102).

- *A Buon Diritto* Association: *Report on the status of rights in Italy*. The Report analyses the fulfilment of fundamental rights of the person and of the protective measures in place for minorities in Italy. The Report highlights a wide range of rights and guaranties for the full enjoyment of basic human needs: personal freedom, freedom of movement, religious freedom, freedom from discrimination of any kind, freedom of persons with disability, gender identity and sexual orientation, minority rights, rights of migrants, refugees and asylum seekers, justice and guarantees, freedom of expression and information, sensitive information, confidentiality and the right to be forgotten, protection of minors, education and social mobility, women's rights, right to health, work and wage guarantees, environmental protection.
- *Institute of International research for Disarmament Archive: Light Arms, Heavy War. 2017 Report*. The Report aims at monitoring the evolution of the framework and Italian export of arms for "civil use". According to the data in the Report, in 2016, Italy negotiated exportation contracts for small and light arms for civil use (the category including pistols and guns, ammunition and

explosives) for a total value of around €579 million. According to the latest available data, in 2015, Italy was the second largest exporter of these arms in the world. The United States (around €248 million) and EU countries (around €200 million) are the main benefactors of Italian produced arms, with non-EU countries trailing behind (€37 million). Globally in the period 2010-2015, 46% of violent deaths were caused by firearms, more often used in "peaceful" situations rather than situations of conflict.

- *Sbilanciamoci!* Campaign ("Let's flip it!")*: 2018 Report – How to use public expenditure for human rights, peace and the environment.* The Report contains 111 detailed proposals by the 47 countries signed up to the *Sblianciamoci!* campaign, starting from a detailed analysis of the quality of public spending in Italy. It aims to save and bring in more money, cut excessive or wasteful spending and allocate the money for more correct usage. It identified seven key areas: finance; work and wages; culture and knowledge; environment and sustainable development; welfare and rights; peace, cooperation and disarmament; fair trade.
- *ANCI, Caritas Italiana, Cittalia, Migrant Foundations, SPRAR Central Service (in collaboration with UNHCR): Report on Italian Protection in Italy 2017.* The participating organisations begin with an analysis of the role of the State, local authorities and third sector in the asylum and reception of immigrants with international protection. The Report aims at illustrating both the development of integrated reception in Italy over the course of the years and the increase of migration with reference to the higher numbers of vulnerable persons, such as foreign minors, stateless persons and victims of human trafficking whose conditions reflect those of refugees. The main themes of the Report are: the Italian reception system and the updates in legislation; asylum seekers requesting international protection in Italy; international protection in Europe; forced migration flows and dynamics in the world.

In November 2017, the Community of *Sant'Egidio,* the Federation of the Evangelical Church in Italia and *Tavola Valdese*, alongside the Italian Episcopal Conference, *Caritas* and *Migrants* signed a Memorandum of Understanding with the Minister of Foreign Affairs and International Cooperation and with the Minister of the Interior. The Memorandum aims to institute a transferal and integration programme, using the so-called "Humanitarian Corridors". The programme is aimed at asylum seekers in vulnerable conditions: women travelling alone with children, victims of human trafficking, old people, people with physical or mental disabilities.

This is the second deal signed after that of 2015 that allowed more than 1000 people into Italy from Libya, mostly of Syrian origin, and 500 people from Ethiopia (refugees and asylum seekers from Eritrea, Somalia and Sudan).

The collaboration mechanism foresees that the list of possible benefactors from the humanitarian corridors be evaluated by the Ministry of the

Interior, who are able to individualise and signal cases most in need of civil society protection. The Ministry of Foreign Affairs and International Cooperation will carry out any checks necessary for the release of entry visas. *Caritas Italiana,* the Community of Sant'Egidio, the Federation of the Evangelical Church and *Tavola Valdese* will organise the reception of these cases upon their arrival in Italy, guaranteeing accommodation and economic assistance for the time necessary to complete their request for international protection. The funds for humanitarian corridors come from the "8x1000" (tax donations) and from private donations to the other organisations.

At the end of 2016, pushed by *Un Ponte Per…* ("A Bridge For…") association, the *In Difesa Di – per i diritti umani e chi li difende* ("In Defense of – Human Rights and Those who Defend Them") network was created. It is made up of 30 Italian organisations and associations who deal with human rights, environment, international solidarity, peace and disarmament, workers' rights, freedom of press and the state of rights. The aim of the network is to promote campaigns and initiatives for human rights defenders, to make the public aware of this subject and to ask the Italian public institutions (Government, parliament and local entities) to develop tools and mechanisms to protect human rights defenders.

According to the latest data given by FrontLine Defenders and Amnesty International, more than 300 human rights defenders were killed in 2017, the vast majority of them being environmentalist or LGBTQI activists, mostly in Colombia, Brazil, Mexico and the Philippines. Thousands were threatened, criminalised, persecuted and arrested arbitrarily. To tackle this emerging crisis, in 2004, the European Union adopted a mechanism on human rights defenders with its programme "Protect Defenders". Some EU Member States subsequently adopted the application procedure of this EU mechanism, while the OSCE adopted a set of "guidelines" on the defence of human rights defenders, to which all Member States would have to abide by, including Italy. The protection extends not only to activists, but also to their organisations and not just in the Member State territory but in third countries. There is also a UN Special Rapporteur on the situation of human rights defenders, post currently held by Michel Frost of France, who can directly appeal to governments and non-State actors about cases of violations of human rights, about official communications and General Assembly reports on the subject of human rights defenders and the criminalisation of solidarity. It has become a global crisis, given the number of attacks and murder of human rights defenders all over the world, especially the theme "Shrinking space for civil society", which will be focussed on relative to human rights defenders.

The *In Difesa Di* network took its first steps in November 2016 with an international conference in the Chamber of Deputies. Human rights defenders from various countries participated (India, Afghanistan, Iraq, Mauritania, Syria), and in the months following the Foreign Committee of the Chamber adopted an important resolution that requires the Ministry of Foreign Affairs to reinforce their efforts to protect human rights defenders. The resolution aims to do this through diplomatic representation for the human rights defenders to actively collaborate with other EU Member States to implement the EU guidelines. In May 2017, the network organised the visit of UN Special Rapporteur on the situation of human rights defenders Michel Forst. *In Difesa Di*'s main objective is to reinforce the initiative of the Italian diplomatic corps to fulfil the EU mechanism and the OSCE guidelines, allowing activists to know about possibilities of support. Some EU Member States subsequently adopted the application procedures of the EU mechanism.

The Dutch NGO *Justice and Peace* is working on a Shelter Cities Programme sponsored by the Ministry of Foreign Affairs, thanks to an accelerated procedure to concede urgent visits to human rights defenders under threat. In Ireland, the Ministry of Foreign Affairs has made an assistance and coordination service available for support activity and for concession of humanitarian visits. Spain has also adopted some best practices with the same aim, while the Finnish, German and Irish Ministry of Foreign Affairs have their own guidelines for the application of the EU mechanism. France is also working on a network of diplomatic representation. Besides these instruments, a system for granting emergency visits for activists in risk, that would allow them entry into the country for a period of time. This would protect them from risks to their personal safety and that of their families. For the second half of 2018, the Ministry of Foreign Affairs and International Cooperation will organise an international workshop describing best practices for the protection of human rights defenders, in the context of the OSCE 2018 presidency. Cooperation can also play an important role in supporting human rights defenders' activities and the work carried out to promote them. The network will therefore work to get Italian cooperation to adopt the financial guidelines to support human rights defenders' activities. To fulfil this aim, the networks asks that specific and defined aims be placed into the framework of the "National Action Plan for Business and Human Rights" to protect human rights defenders and to prevent conflicts and attacks on environmental activists. The fourth pillar of the "toolbox" are the local entities, which present the possibility of creating a network of refuge cities where activists under threat can go if they decide to temporarily leave their home country. At the end of 2017, contact was made with the Autonomous Province of Trent and a resolution to create a shelter programme for human rights defenders was subsequently presented to the Provincial Council. This is seen as the first step to promote awareness for ANCI and other administrations involved.

IX. Teaching and Research on Human Rights in Italian Universities

The Italian a has shown growing interest in research and education in the area of human rights. This issue is now included in teaching programmes across a number of disciplines and in the curricula of various degree courses at undergraduate and post-graduate levels, as well as in interdisciplinary research programmes. The following pages offer an overview of the universities and research centres which are specifically involved with human rights issues, including the teaching of three- and five-year degree, Masters and PhD courses which were available in 2017 or which opened for registration during that year, on the subject. In the interests of precision, the list comprises only the courses and structures which include the phrase "human rights" or equivalent expressions (rights of man, rights of the person, fundamental rights) in their full title. The picture thus obtained offers reasonably reliable evidence as to how widespread and penetrating issues regarding the multifaceted aspects of the rights of the person have become in Italian academia.

University Institutions and Research Centres

University	Name	Founding year
University of Padova	University Human Rights Centre	1982
University of Salento	Inter-University Centre on Bioethics and Human Rights	1992
41 European universities in partnership	European Inter-University Centre for Human Rights and Democratisation (EIUC)	2002
University of Naples	Centre for Studies on Human Rights in the era of globalisation and conflicts	2003
University of Ca' Foscari, Venice	Human Rights Research Centre (CESTUDIR)	2003
University of Salerno	Department of Individual Rights and Comparison	2011

Source: elaboration by the 2018 Yearbook research and editorial board

Bachelor's Degree Courses

University	Name	Scientific Area
University of Padova	Political Science, International Relations, Human Rights	L-36: Political science and International Relations

Source: elaboration by the *2018 Yearbook* research and editorial board

Master's Degree Courses

University	Name	Scientific Area
University of Bergamo	Human Rights and the Ethics of International Cooperation	LM-81: Cooperation development sciences
University of Bologna	International Cooperation on Human Rights and Intercultural Heritage	LM-81: Cooperation development sciences
University of Padova	Human rights and multi-level governance	LM-52: International Relations

Source: elaboration by the *2018 Yearbook* research and editorial board

Teachings

In 2017, a total of 88 human rights teachings were run in 33 universities. Over 58% of these were delivered via degree courses in the field of political and social science (51 modules), while slightly under one-third related to the area of law (30 modules); 5 modules to the area of history, philosophy, pedagogy and psychology, and a further two to economics and statistics.

As in the years between 2010 and 2016, in 2017 the university with the greatest number of human rights teachings was Padova (16 teachings), followed by the University of Milan (10 teachings), Turin (6), Bari (5) and Bologna (5). Of the 88 teachings available, 21 are taught in English, 8 of which are at the University of Padova, 7 at the University of Milan, 2 at Bologna, as well as one at each of the following universities: Palermo, Roma Tre, Rome "La Sapienza", Salerno and Trento.

University	Area	Degree Course	Teaching	Lecturer/ Professor
Aldo Moro University of Bari	Law	5-Year Degree in Law	International Protection of Human Rights	Andrea Cannone
		MA in Designing Social Inclusion Policy	Citizenship and Human Rights	Giuseppe Campesi
	Political and social science	MA in International Relations	Theory of Human Rights	Ivan Pupolizio
			Legal Philosophy, Human Rights and Religion in the Middle and Far East	Gianfranco Longo
	History, philosophy, pedagogy and psychology	MA in Philosophy	History of the Philosophy of Human Rights	Francesca Recchia and Romana Luciani
University of Bergamo	History, philosophy, pedagogy and psychology	MA in Pedagogy	Pedagogy of Marginalisation and Human Rights	Ivo Lizzola
	Law	MA in Human Rights and the Ethics of International Cooperation	International Cooperation and Human Rights	Paolo Scevi
University of Bologna	Political and Social Science	MA in Local and Global Development	Human Rights, Constitutions and Institutions	Raffaella Gherardi
		MA in International Relations and Diplomatic Affairs	International Protection of Human Rights (Seminar)	Marco Balboni
		MA in International Cooperation, Protection of Human Rights and Intercultural Heritage	Political Power Beyond State Boundaries: Migration, Development and Human Rights	Annalisa Furia
			Public Law and Protection of Fundamental Rights	Caterina Drigo
	Law	5-Year Degree in Law	Fundamental Rights	Luca Mezzetti

University	Area	Degree Course	Teaching	Lecturer/ Professor
University of Camerino	Economics and Statistics	BA in Social Sciences for Non-profit Organisations and International Cooperation	International Protection of Human Rights	Agostina Latino
University of Ferrara	Law	5-Year Degree in Law	Human rights and humanitarian law in armed conflicts	Francesco Salerno
University of Florence	Law	BA in Science of Law Services	Legal systems and protection of rights	Beatrice Gambineri
			Welfare state and rights	Emilio Santoro, Marta Picchi, Antonio Gorgoni
		MA in International Relations and European Studies	Constitutional Courts and Multi-Level Protection of Fundamental Rights	Ginevra Cerrina Feroni
	History, philosophy, pedagogy and psychology	BA in Economic Development, International Cooperation, Social-Health and Conflict Management	Human Rights and Armed Conflict	Antonio Bultrini
University of Genova	Law	5-Year Degree in Law	Rights to Freedom and Social Rights	Astride Canepa
University of L'Aquila	Economics and Statistics	BA in Economics	Theory of Interpretation and Fundamental Rights	Francesca Caroccia
University of Macerata	Political and Social Science	BA in Political Science and International Relations	Philosophy of Human Rights	Natascia Mattucci
		MA in Theories, Cultures and Techniques for Social Work	Social and Citizenship-related Rights	Angela Cossiri
	Law	MA in International Politics	Human Rights and Differences	Ines Corti

University	Area	Degree Course	Teaching	Lecturer/ Professor
University of Messina	Politics and social science	MA in International Relations and Development Aid	International Organisations and Human Rights	Carmela Panella
Sacro Cuore (Sacred Heart) Catholic University Milan	Politics and social science	BA in Politics and International Relations	International protection of Human rights	Marinella Fumagalli Meraviglia
	Law	5-Year Degree in Law	Human Rights	Pasquale De Sena
University of Milan	Politics and Social Science	BA in International Studies and European Institutions	International Protection of Human Rights	Ilaria Viarengo
		BA in Administration and Management	Theory of Equality and Rights	Beatrice Magni
		MA in Politics and Government	Theories of Fundamental Rights	Alessandra Facchi
		MA in International Cooperation and Trans-National Social Processes	Anthropology of Human rights	Nicola Riva
	Law	5-Year Degree in Law	EU law on business and human rights	Angelica Bonfanti
			International refugee and human rights law	José Henrique Fischel De Andrade
			Legal Clinic: business and human rights in the digital era	Angelica Bonfanti
		MA in Sustainable development	Access to Justice Protecting Human Rights	Barbara Randazzo
			European Criminal Law and Human Rights	Stefano Zirulia
			Sociology of Human Rights and the Ombudsman	Marco A. Quiroz Vitale

University	Area	Degree Course	Teaching	Lecturer/ Professor
University of Milan-Bicocca	Politics and social science	MA in Sociology	Rights and European citizenship	Marina Calloni
		MA in Planning and Managing Social Policy and Social Services	Cooperation and human rights protection	Gabriella Citroni
	Law	5-Year Degree in Law	International protection of human rights	Gabriella Citroni
University of Modena and Reggio Emilia	Law	5-Year Degree in Law	Theory and practice of human rights	Thomas Casadei
University of Molise	Politics and social science	BA in Media Studies	Human rights and globalisation	Lorenzo Scillitani
Second University of Naples	Political and Social Science	BA in Politics	Protection of Rights in Multi-Cultural States: Western and Asian Models	Domenico Amirante
		MA in International Relations and Organisations	Human rights	Pasquale Femia
	Law	5-Year Degree in Law	International Protection of Human Rights	Andrea Saccucci
University of Padova	Politics and Social Science	BA in Politics, International Relations and Human Rights	Human Rights	Elena Pariotti
			Public Policy and Human Rights	Paola Degani
			General Sociology and Human Rights Sociology	Giuseppe Giordan
			Economic Development and Human Rights	Mario Pomini
			International Protection of Human Rights	Paolo De Stefani
		MA in European Studies	Fundamental Rights and European Citizenship	Costanza Margiotta Broglio Massucci

University	Area	Degree Course	Teaching	Lecturer/ Professor
		Master's Degree in Human Rights and Multi-Level Governance	European Union Law of Human Rights	Paolo Piva
			Human Rights and International Justice	Costanza Margiotta Broglio Massucci
			International Law of Human Rights	Paolo De Stefani
			Women's Human Rights	Paola Degani
			Culture, Society and Human Rights	Andrea Maria Maccarini
			Economic Globalization and Human Rights	Roberto Antonietti
			Human Rights Governance	Léonce Maria Bekemans / Pietro de Perini
			Religions and Human Rights	Giuseppe Giordan
	Law	5-Year Degree in Law	Human Rights and Public Ethics	Umberto Vincenti
	History, Philosophy, Pedagogy and Psychology	BA in Primary Education	Pedagogy of childhood, adolescence and rights of the child	Mirca Benetton
University of Palermo	Law	5-Year Degree in Law	Human rights	Ciclia Bartoli
University of Pavia	Law	5-Year Degree in Law	Constitutional Law and Fundamental Rights	Francesco Rigano
University of Perugia	Politics and Social Science	MA in International Relations	Human Rights, Crime and International Humanitarian Law	Amina Maneggia
University of Pisa	Political and Social Science	BA in Sciences for Peace: international cooperation and conflict transformation	Legal and political theories and human rights	Vittorio Benedetti
	Law	5-Year Degree in Law	Multilevel protection of human rights	Elena Malfatti

University	Area	Degree Course	Teaching	Lecturer/ Professor
Guido Carli Free International University of Social Studies – LUISS	Law	5-Year Degree in Law	International protection of human rights	Pietro Pustorino
Roma Tre University	Politics and social science	BA in Political Science for Cooperation and Development	International organisation and protection of human rights	Carlo Focarelli
		MA in International Relations	Theory of human rights	Francesco Maiolo
La Sapienza University of Rome	Politics and social science	MA in Development and International Cooperation Sciences	Human rights and bioethics	Luca Marini
			European Union Law and Human Rights	Alessandra Mignolli
		MA in International Relations	International Human Rights Law	Luigino Manca
University of Salento	Politics and social science	BA in International Relations	Human rights	Attilio Pisanò
University of Salerno	Law	5-Year Degree in Law	Human rights	Stefano Pietropaoli
			Human rights and Biolaw	Anna Malomo
University of Siena	Politics and social science	MA in International Studies	International protection of human rights	Alessandra Viviani
University of Teramo	Law	5-Year Degree in Law	Human rights	Mario Sirimarco
University of Turin	Politics and social science	MA in Sociology	Theories of human rights	Valentina Pazé
		MA in International Studies	Human rights and immigration	Alessandra Algostino
			History of human rights	Franco Motta
		MA in Social Policy and Social Services	Citizenship, social rights, justice	Franco Prina
			Vulnerable People and the Protection of Rights	Maurizio Riverditi

University	Area	Degree Course	Teaching	Lecturer/ Professor
University of Trento	Politics and social science	BA in International Studies	International Relations and Human Rights	Alessia Donà
		MA in European and International Studies	Human Rights and Natural Resources under International Law	Marco Pertile
University of Udine	Law	5-Year Degree in Law	Theory of Human Rights	Giovanni Turco
Carlo Bo University of Urbino	Law	5-Year Degree in Law	Human Rights	Maria Paola Mittica
Ca' Foscari University of Venice	History, philosophy, pedagogy and psychology	MA in Cultural Anthropology, Ethnology, Anthropological Linguistics	Human Rights and Citizenship Policies	Lauso Zagato
University of Verona	Politics and social science	MA in Social Services in challenging environments	Social and Citizenship-related Rights.	Marco Peruzzi
			Protection of Fundamental Rights	Stefano Catalano

Source: elaboration by the *2018 Yearbook* research and editorial board based on data from the prospectuses of each university

Doctoral programmes (Academic years 2015-2016 and 2016-2017)

University	Name	Area of scientific discipline
University of Camerino, School of Advanced Studies	Doctorate in Law, Politics and Social Science – Curriculum on Fundamental rights in the global society	M-STO/02; M-STO/04; M-DEA/01; M-FIL/03; M-FIL/06; IUS/04; IUS/08; IUS/09; IUS/13 – IUS/21 SECS-P/01; SECS P/02; SECS-P/04; SPS/01; SPS/02; SPS/04; SPS/06; SPS/07; SPS/11; SPS/12
University of Florence	Theory and history of law – Theory and history of human rights	IUS/18, IUS/19, IUS/20

University	Name	Area of scientific discipline
University of Padova, Western Sydney University (Australia), University of Zagrab (Croatia), Panteion University of Athens (Greece)	Joint Ph.D Degree in Human Rights, Society, and Multi-level Governance	IUS/13: IUS/20; IUS/21; SPS/04; SPS/08; SECS-P/01
University of Palermo	International Doctorate in Human rights: evolution, protection and limits	IUS/01, IUS/09, IUS/12, IUS/20, SPS/02, IUS/13, IUS/19, IUS/10, SPS/09, SECS-P/01, IUS/08
Amedeo Avogadro University of Eastern Piedmont	Local autonomies, public services and citizenship rights	IUS/05, IUS/08, IUS/09, IUS/10, IUS/21
Sant'Anna School of Advanced Studies of Pisa	Politics, human rights and sustainability	SPS/01, SPS/06, IUS/13, IUS/03, IUS/14, SPS/04, SECS-P/02, SECS-P/06, SECS-P/08
La Sapienza University of Rome	International order and human rights	IUS/13, IUS/14, IUS/08, IUS/07, IUS/01
University of Salerno	Comparison and rights of the person	IUS/01, IUS/02, IUS/07, IUS/13, IUS/14, IUS/16, IUS/17

Source: elaboration by the *2018 Yearbook* research and editorial board

Master's degree programmes – postgraduate

University	Name	Level
University of Bologna	Human rights, migration and development	I
European Inter-University Centre for Human Rights and Democratisation (EIUC, 41 European University partners)	E.MA European Master's degree in human rights and democratisation	I

University	Name	Level
Sant'Anna School of Advanced Studies of Pisa	Human rights and conflict management	I
University of Siena	European Joint Master of Human Rights and Genocide Studies	I
Aldo Moro University of Bari	Ethics of peace, human rights and inclusion	I
La Sapienza University of Rome	"Maria Rita Saulle" International protection of human rights	II
Roma Tre University	Peace studies: international cooperation, human rights and policies of the European Union	II
Italian Society for International Organisation (SIOI)	International relations and international protection of human rights	–

Source: elaboration by the *2018 Yearbook* research and editorial board

Sub-national Human Rights Structures*

I. Peace Human Rights Offices in Municipalities, Provinces and Regions

At the sub-national level, especially by virtue of the inclusion of the "peace human rights norm" in thousands of Municipal, Provincial and Regional Statutes and of the adoption of dedicated regional laws on this topic (see Part I, Italian Law, III), Italy has a number of local consultancies, offices, departments, bureaux and centres for human rights, peace, equal opportunity, development cooperation, fair trade and international solidarity.

During 2017, for example, the Municipal Advisory Board for Peace, Human Rights, Non-Violence and Disarmament took office in Palermo. It is an organism with advisory and proposing functions, which aims to assert the role of Palermo as a city of peace and to support concrete peace gestures and initiatives of peace and human rights education. Other examples of these structures have been presented in the preceding editions of the *Yearbook*.

II. Ombudspersons in the Italian Regions and Provinces

In 2017, there were 15 incumbent Ombudspersons (or Human Rights Authorities which also fulfil the duties of an Ombudsperson), of a total of 19 Regions and Autonomous Provinces (17+2) whose respective Statues or specific regional laws included provisions for such an institution: Abruzzo, Basilicata, Emilia-Romagna, Lazio, Liguria, Lombardy, Marche (Ombudsperson), Molise, Piedmont, Sardinia, Tuscany, Valle d'Aosta and Veneto (Ombudsperson for Human Rights, see this Part, Region of Veneto, VI), as well as the Autonomous Provinces of Bolzano and Trent. The post is currently vacant in Umbria (where a document for the establishment of a "Digital Ombudsperson" was presented) and in Campania, where the appointment of the new Ombudsperson, made in July 2017, was annulled by the State Council in December of the same

* Pietro de Perini

year. No Ombudsperson has ever been appointed in Calabria and Apulia. No legislative provision has been made for the role by the Regions of Sicily and Trentino-Alto Adige (where, however, the Region has delegated full responsibility in their respective territories to the Ombudspersons of the Autonomous Provinces), while in Friuli-Venezia Giulia, the laws establishing this institution was abrogated in 2008 (r.l. 14 August 2008, No. 9).

At European and international levels, in 2017, the European Ombudsman Institute (EOI) confirmed as members of its Executive Committee: Gabriele Morandell, Ombudsperson of the Autonomous Province of Bolzano, Antonia Fiordelisi, Ombudsperson of the Region of Basilicata, Daniela Longo, Ombudsperson of the Autonomous Province of Trent, and Vittorio Gasparrini, Office of the Ombudsperson of the Region of Tuscany. Furthermore, the Provincial Ombudspersons of the Autonomous Provinces of Bolzano and Trent and the Regional Ombudspersons of Lombardy, Tuscany and Valle d'Aosta are members of the International Ombudsman Institute (IOI).

III. National Coordinating Body of Ombudspersons

The National Coordinating Body of Regional and Autonomous Provinces Ombudspersons is an associative body working to harmonise and enhance the institutional role of the Ombudsperson in Italy and to guarantee every citizen, regardless of where he or she resides, protection in dealing with the public administration at all levels, whether State, regional or local.

The Coordinating Body is made up of the incumbent Ombudspersons in the Regions and the Autonomous Provinces. It operates through the office of the Ombudsperson collectively elected from time to time and its headquarters are in Rome, at the Network of the Presidents of the Legislative Assemblies of the Regions and the Autonomous Provinces, where it usually meets. The Coordinating Body also intervenes by order of the European Ombudsperson at the central offices of the State and of those Regions and Italian local authorities without a regional or local Ombudsperson. Furthermore, it represents the Italian Ombudsperson with the European Ombudsperson and it also links up with the other European Ombudspersons through a liaison officer. On 14 February 2017, the Coordinating Body elected the Ombudsperson of the Region of Abruzzo, Fabrizio di Carlo, as its new President. The Vice-Presidents are Daniela Longo, Ombudsperson of the Autonomous Province of Trent, and Enrico Formento Dojot, Ombudsperson of Valle d'Aosta.

During 2017, the Coordinating Body promoted or its representatives participated to some activities as the conference "*La dignità negata*"

("Denied Dignity"), held in Turin on 28 September 2017, which focused on the issue of confining non self-sufficient elderly people to nursing homes. On 6 October 2017, a seminar was held in Florence, entitled: "The Ombudsperson to strengthen deliberative democracy and the solution of citizens' problems", which aimed to tackle the increasingly "polycentric" aspects connected to the role of the Ombudsperson in a coordinated way, forty years after the introduction of this figure in the administrative procedure and therefore in the relationship between citizen and institutions. The event represented the first step of a significant path in the in-depth understanding of Ombudsperson issues in Italy, Italian regions and Europe.

At the time of writing this Yearbook 2018, the third periodic report of the National Coordinating Body on Ombudspersons has not been presented yet to the Italian Parliament.

IV. Network of Ombudspersons for Children and Adolescents

As of today, 17 Regions and the Autonomous Provinces of Trent and Bolzano have approved legislation introducing a local Ombudsperson for Children and Adolescents at a regional level. Ombudspersons have actually been nominated in 18 Regions (Apulia, Basilicata, Calabria, Campania, Emilia-Romagna, Friuli-Venezia Giulia, Lazio, Liguria, Lombardy, Marche, Molise, Piedmont, Sardinia, Sicily, Umbria, Veneto and the Autonomous Provinces of Trent and Bolzano). Some of these are exclusively tasked with ensuring rights for children and adolescents (Apulia, Basilicata, Calabria, Campania, Emilia-Romagna, Lazio, Lombardy, Molise, Sardinia, Sicily, Tuscany, Umbria and the Autonomous Province of Bolzano), whereas others have additional competence in areas such as those dealt with by Ombudspersons and/or ensuring rights for persons whose personal freedom is restricted (Friuli-Venezia Giulia, Liguria, Marche, Veneto and the Autonomous Province of Trent).

The approval of l. 12 July 2011, No. 112 established the figure of Ombudsperson for Children and Adolescents at the national level (see this Part, National Bodies with Jurisdiction over Human Rights, VII, D) and formally defined and established the National Network for the Protection of the Rights of Children and Adolescents, made up of the Regional Ombudspersons for Children (or equivalent). The Network is tasked with creating common lines of action to protect the rights of children and adolescents for regional and national Ombudspersons, to be promoted and supported at the international level. It is also charged with identifying ways of ensuring a constant exchange of data and information on the condition of minors living in Italy. The Network has drawn up a set of internal regulations governing its functioning.

The Network is chaired by the National Authority and meets in Rome at least twice annually to discuss common interest issues. Specially in 2017, the Network discussed the following subjects: the procedures implemented by the regional Ombudspersons and the national Ombudsperson to select and train voluntary guardians of unaccompanied foreign minors; the need to adopt a shared system for the collection of data related to the aspiring guardians, to harmonise the content of the training modules throughout the national territory and to provide a monitoring system to support the appointed guardians in carrying out their activity; the approval of the Guidelines on reporting contained in the document "Reporting Management Procedures of Regional Authorities and the Autonomous Provinces of Trent and Bolzano"; creating working groups to monitor voluntary guardians and promote family foster care.

V. National Coordinating Body of Local Authorities for Peace and Human Rights

Founded on 12 October 1986, the National Coordinating Body of Local Authorities for Peace and Human Rights is the largest Italian network of municipalities, provinces and regions involved in promoting peace and human rights: it is a unique experience in Europe and worldwide. The Coordinating Body is chaired by Andrea Ferrari and directed by Flavio Lotti.

The Coordinating Body responded to the call launched by the Secretary-General of the United Nations António Guterres and the Pope on 1 January 2017. It developed a vast campaign to renew local authorities, associations and schools commitment to peace and human rights. There are three major proposals at the centre of the initiative: (1) investing in young people and school; (2) making peace at the local level; (3) facing global challenges together.

The first part of the year was marked by the commitment to implement the National Education Programme for Democratic Citizenship *Proteggiamo la nostra casa* ("Protect Our Home"), aimed at promoting the UN 2030 Agenda for "Sustainable Development Goals" and reflect on the letter "Laudato si", written by Pope Francis.

On 5-6 May 2017, over 7,000 students and teachers, local administrators, journalists, parents and representatives of civil society across Italy met in Rome to participate in the National Meeting of Schools for peace, fraternity and dialogue "Protect Our Home".

The meeting opened with eight workshops held at the Ministry of Education, the Ministry of Foreign Affairs, the Chamber of Deputies, the Department for Equal Opportunities – Presidency of the Council of Ministers and the City of Rome. The next day, participants had the opportunity to meet Pope Francis who, for over two hours, spontaneously answered five questions posed by students and teachers.

In 2017, the Coordinating Body took care of numerous training activities for teachers from different regions (Umbria, Tuscany, Sicily, Emilia Romagna, Friuli Venezia Giulia and Marche). As part of the *La pace si insegna e si impara* programme ("Peace is Taught and Learned"), promoted in collaboration with the Autonomous Region of Friuli Venezia Giulia and the Regional School Office, the Body has worked on the elaboration of the "Guidelines for peace and glocal citizenship education". The document was distributed by MIUR in September 2017. It was written in collaboration with a group of 162 teachers from Friuli Venezia Giulia who participated in a training programme focused on the analytic observation of reality and of their own concrete experience.

Since July 2017, the Coordinating Body has been engaged in the promotion of the Human Rights Year (2018) and the Human Rights Education Programme "Rights and Responsibility". The programme was promoted for the 70th anniversary of both the Universal Declaration of Human Rights and the Italian Constitution, in collaboration with the Ministry of Education, University and Research and the University of Padova Human Rights Centre.

On 4-5 December 2017, at the "Galileo Galilei" Aula Magna of the University of Padova, the Coordinating Body and the University Human Rights Centre held the opening conference of the Human Rights Year entitled "In the spirit of brotherhood", which was dedicated to the memory of prof. Antonio Papisca, one of the foremost promoters and defenders of human rights in the world.

On 10 December, in occasion of the 69th anniversary of the Universal Declaration of Human Rights, the Body promoted the "International day of mobilisation for human rights" with numerous initiatives in many Italian cities.

During 2017, the Body collaborated in organising many projects, events, seminars, lectures, workshops, meetings, marches and public events: for example, the Regional Meeting of Schools for Peace of Friuli Venezia Giulia, "The World needs Young Peacebuilders" (Udine, 26 May 2017) and the national conference "Ernesto Balducci: Prophet and Master of Planetary Man" (Zugliano, Udine 20-24 September 2017).

On 21 September 2017, in occasion of the World Peace Day promoted by the United Nations, the Body started organising the PerugiAssisi March which will take place on Sunday 7 October 2018. The March aims to give impetus to a new extraordinary mobilisation for the implementation of human rights in the year of the 70th anniversary of the Universal Declaration of Human Rights and will be preceded by the International Meeting of Human Rights (Perugia, 5-6 October 2018).

VI. Archives and Other Regional Projects for the Promotion of a Culture of Peace and Human Rights

Besides the "Pace Diritti Umani – Peace Human Rights" Archive of the Region of Veneto, established by r.l. 18/1988 and managed by the University of Padova Human Rights Centre (see this Part, Region of Veneto, IV), there are other more recent archives and similar projects set up by Italian Regions and Autonomous Provinces to foster the promotion and dissemination of a culture of human rights and peace.

The "Peace and Human Rights" project in the Region of Emilia-Romagna was set up by the Regional Council in collaboration with the Department for Social Policies, Immigration, Youth Projects and International Cooperation and the Regional Governments Management Control and Statistics Systems Department. The project is managed by the Europe Direct Centre of the Legislative Assembly of Emilia-Romagna and follows the principles laid out in r.l. 24 June 2002, No. 12 (Regional interventions for cooperation with developing countries and countries in transition, international solidarity and the promotion of a culture of peace), aims to support activities described in the law. The commitment of the Legislative Assembly is illustrated in the page "*Pace e Diritti*" ("Peace and Rights") of the Europe Direct Centre of Emilia-Romagna, which also provides citizens with a repository of documents and videos on the topic (www.assemblea.emr.it/europedirect/pace-e-diritti).

> The commitment of the Regional Legislative Assembly of Emilia-Romagna for the promotion and protection of human rights has continued. In the two-year period 2016-2017, a number of exhibitions and conventions have been held, meetings of citizens and students and a strong commitment in the field of training for young people and teachers and initiatives on the web and on social networks. A work that continues in the current year connected by a red thread: the values of the Republican Constitution and the principles enshrined in the Universal Declaration of Human Rights and in the Charter of Fundamental Rights of the European Union.
>
> The "*Concittadini*" ("Co-citizens") project, a civic education course promoted by the Regional Assembly, has allowed more than 4,000 students a year to participate in initiatives inside and outside school on the themes of memory and legality. The activities of the Europe Direct Centre of Emilia-Romagna have involved thousands of students and hundreds of teachers in training projects on citizenship rights in Europe and in the world. There has also been

cultural activity organised by the Legislative Assembly, aimed at promoting human rights. The prizes and competitions, such as the "*René Cassin*" graduation prize, which for many years has supported three young people a year in a period of professional training for international UN projects at one of the operational offices of the KIP International School, or the "EurHope" photography competition on the feeling of European identity, aimed at students of high schools of the Emilia-Romagna Region.

The "*Forum Trentino per la pace e i diritti umani*" ("Trentino for Peace and Human Rights Forum") standing body was established in 1991 at the behest of the Provincial Council of Trent with p.l. 10 June 1991, No. 11 (Promoting and disseminating the culture of peace). Website: http://www.forumpace.it/.

The annual theme approved during the Forum Assembly on 9 March 2017 was "*Le Vie della Pace. Pratiche quotidiane per superare violenza*" ("The Paths of Peace. Daily practices to overcome violence"). It was understood as the search for new ways to find peace through daily practices of democracy and active nonviolence both by individuals and institutions. On this occasion, the Forum launched a call for participating associations to develop recommendations and actions in projects stimulating a culture of peace starting from the small daily practices of each. These projects can be either individual or in partnership.

Region of Veneto*

The Region of Veneto has been operating consistently for the promotion of human rights, the culture of peace and international cooperation, ever since 1988, the year when the first regional law on such issues was adopted in Italy (r.l. 30 March 1988, No. 18). In 1999, r.l. 18/1988 was replaced by the current r.l. 16 December 1999, No. 55, on "Regional measures for the promotion of human rights, a culture of pace, development cooperation and solidarity". With r.l. 24 December 2013, No. 37, the Region established the post of Regional Ombudsperson for the Rights of the Person which integrates the functions of the Ombudsperson, of the Ombudsperson for Children and Adolescents (both created in 1988), as well as those of promotion and protection of the rights of persons deprived of their liberty.

In the context of the Regional Government, issues concerning human rights pertain to the Councillor on Social Services, programme implementation and relations with the Regional Council, a post currently held by Manuela Lanzarin. Measures and activities concerning international relations and development cooperation are overseen directly by the Regional Governor, Luca Zaia.

In virtue of r.l. 55/1999, the Committee on Human Rights and the Culture of Peace (articles 12–13) and the Committee on Development Cooperation (articles 14–15) operate to fulfil their mandate of formulating three-year programmes and annual plans of implementation according to their respective areas of competence and intervention. In addition, the law promotes and supports the Regional Archive "Pace Diritti Umani – Peace Human Rights" (article 2), the Venice for Peace Research Foundation (article 17), the activities of the European Commission for Democracy through Law (Venice Commission) of the Council of Europe (article 19) and initiatives of decentralised cooperation promoted by the Ministry of Foreign Affairs and by the European Union (article 7). The regional infrastructure for peace and human rights is completed by the Commission for the Realisation of Equal Opportunities between Men and Women and the Regional Observatory for Immigration. Moreover, by way of r.l. 28 December 1998, No. 33, the Region promotes and supports financially the European Masters degree Programme in Human Rights and Democratisation (E.MA), located in Venice. With the adoption of

* Pietro de Perini

r.l. 22 January 2010, No. 6, the Region has recognised the social and cultural value of fair trade, proclaiming its support for the organisations which operate in this sector.

Finally, r. l. 23 April 2013, No. 5 established a Regional Coordination Table for Preventing and Combating the Violence against Women within the Regional Government.

Implementing this law, the Region has financed requests received for the year 2017 from 20 anti-violence centres, 9 shelters and 8 second-stage shelters.

I. Department for International Relations, Communications and SISTAR

Among other things, the Department is responsible for the implementation of r.l. 55/1999. In 2017, the Director managing this structure was Diego Vecchiato.

> The Regional Section oversees a series of international activities undertaken by the Region, including: the management of international relations; the signature of memoranda of understanding with national and foreign institutions; the participation in international bodies and initiatives; international solidarity; and all activities in the sectors of human rights, the culture of peace, the promotion of equal opportunities and the protection of linguistic minorities. The Section also hosts the Veneto Regional Committee for UNICEF.
>
> In the specific area human rights promotion, the Section provides technical support to the Committee for human rights and the culture of peace; it oversees the organisation of events, takes part in the activities of the Council of Europe Venice Commission and fulfils the obligations deriving from the Regions promotion and financial support of the European Masters Programme in Human Rights and Democratisation (E.MA).

During 2017, among the other activities of communication and promotion of human rights, the Department published a report on the use of educational vouchers allocated in the period 2014-2016. During this period, 236 educational courses were presented by non-profit organisations and 150 vouchers were assigned for the creation of educational paths in schools in the regional territory (97 in secondary schools and 53 in primary schools) on the following macro-themes: bullying, internet and social networks, environmental protection and children's rights. The vouchers were introduced in 2014 to create opportunities for schools and associations in the region to meet and compare ideas on human rights issues.

II. Committee for Human Rights and the Culture of Peace

Established pursuant to article 12 of r.l. 55/1999, the Committee is tasked with drawing up the three-year programmes and annual plans regarding initiatives of the Region of Veneto on human rights and a culture of peace (article 13). The Committee comprises representatives from local authorities, civil society, academia, the business world and social partners.

With Regional Council Decision No. 945 of 23 June 2017, the regional Council adopted its 2017 Annual Plan to implement regional interventions to promote human rights and the culture of peace, with a total budget of €100,000, nearly twice the value of the previous year. In addition to assuring cover for the costs associated with the "Peace Human Rights" Archive, as per the provisions of r.l. 55/1999, this financing allowed the Region to grant 100 educational vouchers to promote human rights training in schools in Veneto region (see this Part, Region of Veneto, I). Otherwise, it has not been possible to put in place direct regional human rights initiatives or calls for proposals. Among the obligations provided for by r.l. 55/1999, the 2017 Action Plan, which falls into the framework of the Region's three-year programme for the period 2016-2018 in the field of human rights (see *Yearbook 2017*, p. 127) confirms the commitment to award the Regional Prize "Veneto for Peace and Solidarity among Peoples" and the membership of the "Venice for Peace Research" Foundation. No financial allocation has been made for either of these initiatives.

III. Committee for Development Cooperation

The Committee for Development Cooperation was established pursuant to article 14 of r.l. 55/1999. The Committee is charged with contributing to the drafting of the three-year programmes and annual plans for decentralised development cooperation and international solidarity activities. The Committee comprises representatives from local administrations, civil society, academia, the business world and social partners.

In the framework of the regional three-year programme of 2016-2018 in the field of development cooperation (see *Yearbook 2017*, p. 128), with decision 23 June 2017, No. 945 the Regional Council adopted the new Annual Action Plan. €320,000 have been allocated on the regional budget for 2017 to implement this Action Plan for decentralised cooperation interventions promoted by private organisations and bodies. In the area of fair trade, regional planning provided a budget of €90,000 for initiatives in 2017.

IV. Regional Archive "Pace Diritti Umani – Peace Human Rights"

The Regional Archive was created pursuant to r.l. 18/1988 and re-confirmed by the subsequent r.l. 55/1999. The Archive is managed by the University of Padova Human Rights Centre, as laid down in article 2 of the aforementioned law, which reads: "1. The Region promotes and supports: [...] c) the Archive established by r.l. 30 March 1988, No. 18, in cooperation with the Centre of Studies and Training on the Rights of Man and of Peoples of the University of Padova, according to a special agreement [...]". It is one of the main instruments through which the Region of Veneto promotes the culture of human rights, peace, development cooperation and solidarity in Italy and abroad.

The Archive works to collect, elaborate and publish documents, thematic databases and informational resources on topics regarding regional law, particularly through the regular updating of the portal "Archivio Pace Diritti Umani" (http://unipd-centrodirittiumani.it/en/), available in Italian and English, and the distribution of knowledge on human rights through multimedia tools and social networks. In addition, it oversees publication of books, teaching aids, in-depth studies and multimedia and offers technical and scientific support to the actors most closely involved in the promotion and practice of the culture of peace, especially as concerns initiatives promoted by teachers, education staff, schools and civil society organisations. In 2017, the Archive published and distributed 16 editions of the "peace human rights" newsletter in Italian and in English to a long and qualified mailing list.

During 2017, the Archive updated the databases available on its website, notably the Italian translations of the database of international legal instruments on human rights, humanitarian, criminal and refugee law; the University of Padova Human Rights Centre publications from 1982 to present; and the associations and NGOs active in the field of human rights and development cooperation in Veneto. In addition to its usual activities of updating, providing in-depth studies and information, the Archive started the promotion of *Peace Human Rights Governance (PHRG),* the new scientific journal entirely in English of the University of Padova Human Rights Centre. The Archive also contributed to the publication and promotion of the 2017 edition of the *Italian Yearbook of Human Rights* in Italian and in English and the institutional presentation of this publication in the Aula Magna of the University of Padova, in the context of the Training, Information and Research Course on Human Rights and Global Citizenship "*In spirito di fratellanza*" ("In the Spirit of Brotherhood"), 4-5 December 2017, University of Padova (see this Part, Sub-national Human Rights Structures, V).

The Archive also helped organise a series of events at the University of Padova, in collaboration with national and international organisations and experts, namely the documentation and media side. Particularly noteworthy are the following: in addition to the aforementioned training course, the International Conference "The Role of Human Rights Research: Current Challenges and Future Opportunities (27-28 November) and the promotion activity of the General course "Human Rights and Inclusion" of the University of Padova for the academic year 2017/2018.

V. Venice for Peace Research Foundation

As was the Regional Archive, the Foundation was established by r.l. 18/1988 and reconfirmed by r.l. 55/1999. The Foundation's main goal is to carry out research, partly in collaboration with national and international institutions, on matters of security, development and peace.

In 2017, the Foundation continued to work on the *Blind Spots* project (see *Yearbook 2016*, p. 119) and supported the realisation of "Dropping Seeds", an artistic project which aimed at encouraging an exchange between words and images on permanent consequences and on offering shelter. The same year, the Foundation edited a new paperbook, entitled *Balcani. Europa. Violenza, politica, memoria* ("Balkans. Europe. Violence, Politics, Memory") (edited by R. Petri).

VI. Human Rights Authority

The Human Rights Authority of the Region of Veneto was provided for by regional law 24 December 2013, No. 37 (Regional Human Rights Authority). The first and current Authority, Mirella Gallinaro, was appointed in early 2015.

The Authority brings together the functions of the Ombudsperson and of the Ombudsperson for Children and Adolescents (both established by the Region of Veneto in 1988 and abolished following the creation of the new Authority) and the activities of promoting, protecting and facilitating the fulfilment of the rights of persons subject to restrictions to their personal freedom.

Among the various initiatives carried out in 2017 by the Authority, common to its three different functions, the following are of note:

- participating, as a member, in working and discussion meeting within the institutionalised coordinating bodies of the rights Ombudspersons equally competent in the area; i.e. the Network of Ombudspersons for Children and Adolescents (see this Part, Sub-national Human Rights Structures, IV), as well as the working meetings between the National Ombudsperson for the Rights of Persons in Prison or Deprived of Liberty and the equivalent territorial Ombudspersons created by Regions and Autonomous Provinces as provided for in the legislative provisions which established the National Ombudsperson for the Rights of Persons in Prison or Deprived of Liberty (article 7 "National Ombudsperson for the Rights of Persons in Prison or Deprived of Liberty" of l.d. 23 December 2013, No. 146 (Urgent measures concerning the protection of the fundamental rights of prisoners and the controlled reduction of the prison population), converted with l. 21 February 2014, No. 10);

– participating, as a member, in coordinating meetings of the Ombudspersons of the Regions and Autonomous Provinces of Trent and Bolzano (see this Part, Sub-national Human Rights Structures, II);

– participating, as a member, in coordinating meetings of regional Ombudspersons for the Rights of Persons in Prison or Deprived of Liberty, a free and spontaneous association between regional, provincial and municipal Ombudspersons with similar functions;

– promoting, pursuant to article 7(1)(h) of the law establishing the body, coordination, discussion and working meetings with Regional Ombudspersons for the Rights of Persons with Restricted or Limited Liberty, which are established in some municipalities in Veneto;

– participating, as a member, in observatories, inter-institutional round tables and committees established at a regional level;

– participating, as a member, to the working group "Monitoring of the institute of voluntary guardians", as established by the national Network of the regional Ombudspersons in 2017, chaired by the national Ombudsperson for Children and Adolescents and composed by the Ombudspersons of the Regions and the Autonomous Provinces;

– participating (including as a rapporteur) in meetings, seminars and round tables; these events all seek to gain an in-depth understanding of and promote debate on questions the Authority is already acting upon or on new emerging issues;

– providing information and consultancy, facilitating and mediating on public administration office procedures and activities as well as those of public service managers in the regional context, at the request of public or private entities.

In addition, the Veneto Human Rights Authority implemented a series of initiatives in 2017 that have differently affected the various areas of activities, including:

– signing a Memorandum of Understanding with the President of the Juvenile Court of Venice on 29 June, aimed at promoting and facilitating the appointment of voluntary guardians for unaccompanied foreign minors;

– joining and supporting the projects: "Care Leavers Network" (2016-2017) aimed at promoting a national network made up of young guests and former guests of educational communities, foster families and care homes and "*C.R.E.S.C.E.R.E.*" ("Building Relationships and Development Experiences Shared with Empathy, Responsibility and Enthusiasm") 2009-2021, a longitudinal study that over time monitors a sample of children and families living in the Province of Padova and in the Municipality of Rovigo during their transition from childhood to adolescence and towards adulthood;

– promoting and running training courses for people suitable and prepared to take on the protection of minors, including the possible protection of unaccompanied foreign minors and applicants for international protection;

– promoting and implementing information seminars in the various penitentiary institutions in the Veneto region, with the aim of promoting a new and different culture of penalty among prisoners and prison workers. This culture effectively respects the dignity and fundamental rights of the persons with restricted liberty and effectively oriented towards the reintegration of the condemned person into the community, bearing in mind the conclusions reached by the *États Generaux* (*Stati Generali*) on the execution of sentences.

– willingness to promote and/or share places and opportunities to create networks of information, knowledge, skills and proposals designed to create synergies and effective responses protecting human rights.

Alongside initiatives taking a proactive approach to the protection human rights, the traditional activities, seen as complementary to the former, were also performed: accepting and managing reports, applications, complaints and requests for consultancy or guidance in the field of protecting the rights of physical and legal persons against public administrations and activities promoting, protecting and facilitating the pursuit of rights for minors and the rights of persons subject to restricted personal liberty.

In 2017, the Authority published a report on the activities carried out in the period 2015-2016.

Significantly, this data reveals that there were 790 requests to the Authority for the names of people available to be appointed guardians. The Authority opened a total of 545 files of consultancy, mediation, orientation activities that, in the two years under review, concerned a total of 589 minors.

VII. Regional Commission for Equal Opportunities between Men and Women

The Commission was established by r.l. 30 December 1987, No. 62, and it is the regional consultative body on gender policies for the actual implementation of the principles of equality and equal opportunities enshrined in the Constitution and Regional Statute. The Commission was established at the Veneto Regional Council and is chaired by Elena Traverso.

> The main task of the Commission is to carry out investigations and research into the condition of women in Veneto, with particular reference to issues involving employment, labour and professional training and to disseminate information on these areas. At the same time, the Commission respects its commitment to being present on the ground and to developing new synergies with all the actors and forces involved to promote and support the realisation of equal opportunities in the social, political and economic life of the population of Veneto. It may offer opinions on the current state of implementation of laws and on bills, as well as drawing up proposals of its own. The Veneto Equal Opportunities Commission carries out its mission in contact with other Commissions at the local, regional and national level and maintains a constant exchange with all women's organisations in the region.

Among the activities and the initiatives promoted and supported by the Commission during 2017, the following are of note:

- documentary exhibition *Donne e lavoro, di ieri, oggi e domani* ("Women and Work, Yesterday, Today and Tomorrow") at the Municipality of Arcugnano (Vicenza), 1-8 April;
- conference *Imprenditrici e professioniste nei Colli Euganei* ("Business Women and Professionals in the Euganean Hills") in Arquà Petrarca (Padova), 23 June;
- free training course *Post elezione: come continua la comunicazione?* ("Post election: how does communication continue?"), in collaboration with the Interdepartmental Research Centre for Gender Studies of the University of Padova, 22 September – 20 October;
- photo exhibition: "Donne - マ", ("Women - マ) at Forte Carpenedo (Venice), 14-15 and 21-22 October;
- theatre performance *Ho ucciso l'Angelo del focolare* ("I killed the Angel in the House") – The battle of Virginia Woolf for women's access to professional work, in Verona, 24 November.

VIII. Regional Observatory on Immigration

The Observatory is a service within the Region of Veneto "Migratory Flows" organisational unit and is managed by Veneto Lavoro. Its establishment was included in the three-year plan 2007-2009 comprising measures and initiatives in the field of immigration, and was confirmed in subsequent three-year plans, pursuant to article 3 of r.l. 9/1990 (Measures in the immigration sector).

> The Observatory is a technical-scientific instrument aiming to monitor, analyse and disseminate data and information on migratory flows and integration at the regional and national level. To this end, it: collaborates with the other regional observatories which are affected in various ways by the migration phenomenon; assures the proper functioning and constant input for databases, the monitoring of immigration dynamics, further study on various thematic aspects, housing conditions, the social and educational integration of minors, schooling and training; it ensures updated reconnaissance of specialised laws, proposing training sessions to facilitate acquaintance with these laws and their correct implementation.

In March 2018, the Observatory published the fourteenth "Annual Report on foreign migration to Veneto". The Report presents a systematic analysis of data and trends in migratory flows in relation to certain aspects crucial for Veneto and for Italy as a whole, such as demographic dynamics, employment and unemployment figures and the presence of young foreigners in the regional school system, the issues of unaccompanied minors, asylum seekers and the economic integration of migrants.

In general terms, the statistical data presented in the report show that the number of foreign citizens, resident in Veneto as of 1 January 2017 was 485,477, constituting 9.6% of the total number of foreigners in Italy. This represents a fall of approximately 12,000 people compared to the figures for the previous year (497,291 constituting 9.9% of the total number of foreigners in Italy). Compared to the other Italian regions, Veneto has also this year the fourth highest number of foreign residents (after Lombardy, Lazio and Emilia-Romagna). The total percentage of foreigners within the regional population is again 10%, keeping Veneto the sixth-highest percentage after Emilia-Romagna, Lombardy, Lazio, Umbria and Tuscany. The Provinces with the highest percentage of foreigners are Verona (11.4%), Treviso (10.2%), Padova (10%). The number of foreign nationals in municipal registers who have gained Italian citizenship has continued to grow steadily compared with previous years (14,592 in 2013; 20,331 in 2014; 25,802 in 2015), reaching a total of 29,313, equivalent to 14.5% of the total citizenships granted on a national level (around 201,000). The main countries of origin of resident foreign citizens as of

1 January 2017 are Romania (24.6%), Morocco (9.4%), the Republic of Moldova (7.2%), Albania (7.2%) and China (6.9%). The largest number of residence permits in Veneto were held by foreigners from Morocco (53,764), China (40,358), Albania (35,305) and the Republic of Moldova (34,762).

Part III

Italy in Dialogue with International Human Rights Institutions

The United Nations System*

I. General Assembly

The General Assembly, which is the main deliberative body of the United Nations, comprises six Committees, each of which is made up of all 193 United Nations Member States. Human rights issues are handled mainly within the Third Committee (the Social, Humanitarian and Cultural Committee). The responsibilities of this Committee include issues such as torture and other cruel, inhuman and degrading treatment or punishment; the advancement of women; the rights of refugees and displaced persons; the promotion and protection of the rights of children; the rights of indigenous peoples; the elimination of racism, racial discrimination, xenophobia and related intolerance; the right of peoples to self-determination; and social development.

In December 2017, the 72nd General Assembly adopted 63 human rights resolutions (40 of which by consensus) which had been debated and approved by the Third Committee during October and November, on a wide range of issues; from the rights of migrants to the right to privacy in the digital age, from protection from discrimination based on sexual orientation and gender identity to country-specific situations.

In 2017, Italy's Permanent Representative to the United Nations in New York was Ambassador Sebastiano Cardi; the Deputy Permanent Representative was Ambassador Inigo Lambertini; Emilia Gatto was responsible for following the activities of the Third Committee. The chart below depicts the most significant interventions by the Italian delegation and Government representatives in General Assembly meetings in 2017.

Date	Event	Speaker
24 January 2017	High-level Dialogue on the 2030 Agenda and Sustainable Peace	Amb. Cardi
6 February 2017	GA Meeting on the Issue of Equitable Representation and the Increase in the Number of Security Council Members	Amb. Cardi

* Andrea Cofelice

Date	Event	Speaker
7 March 2017	GA Meeting on the Issue of Equitable Representation and the Increase in the Number of Security Council Members	Amb. Cardi
3 April 2017	GA Meeting on the Issue of Equitable Representation and the Increase in the Number of Security Council Members	Amb. Cardi
8 May 2017	GA Meeting on the Issue of Equitable Representation and the Increase in the Number of Security Council Members	Amb. Cardi
19 June 2017	High-level Debate on Transnational Organised Crime	Minister of Justice, Andrea Orlando, on the occasion of the commemoration of the 25th anniversary of the murder of Judge Giovanni Falcone at GA
19 July 2017	GA Meeting on the Issue of Equitable Representation and the Increase in the Number of Security Council Members	Amb. Cardi
6 September 2017	Informal Dialogue on the Report of the Secretary General on the Responsibility to Protect	Amb. Lambertini
19 September 2017	Event on the Occasion of the 72nd Session of the GA on Refugees and Migrants	Minister of Foreign Affairs and International Cooperation, Angelino Alfano, on "Italy's Path between Development Aid and Issue of Security"
20 September 2017	Opening of the General Debate at the 72nd session of the GA	President of the Council, Paolo Gentiloni
21 September 2017	Event on the Sidelines of the GA's 72nd Session Organised by Italy on "Protecting Cultural Heritage from Terrorism and Mass Atrocities: Links and Common Responsibilities"	Minister of Foreign Affairs and International Cooperation, Angelino Alfano

Date	Event	Speaker
21 September 2017	Event on the Sidelines of the GA's 72nd Session Organised by Italy on "Women Mediators Networks:. From Paper to Practice. How to Strengthen Synergies and Complementarities for Greater Efficiency and Impact"	Minister of Foreign Affairs and International Cooperation, Angelino Alfano
22 September 2017	72nd GA Ministerial Meeting of the Anti-ISIS Coalition	Minister of Foreign Affairs and International Cooperation, Angelino Alfano
28 September 2017	GA High-level Meeting on the Evaluation of the UN Global Plan to Combat Trafficking in Persons	Amb. Cardi
3 October 2017	72nd GA General Debate of the Second Committee	Amb. Lambertini
4 October 2017	72nd GA Meeting of the Third Committee	Amb. Cardi, on Crime Prevention and Criminal Justice – International Drug Control
4 October 2017	72nd GA General Debate of the First Committee	Amb. Mati
5 October 2017	72nd GA Meeting of the Third Committee	First Secretary Cupellini, on the Progress of Women
10 October 2017	72nd GA Meeting of the Third Committee	First Secretary Schettino, on the Rights of the Child
10 October 2017	72nd GA Meeting of the Third Committee	First Secretary Cupellini, on the Death Penalty
18 October 2017	72nd GA First Committee Meeting	Amb. Mati on conventional weapons
23 October 2017	72nd GA Meeting of the Sixth Committee	Director for International Legal Affairs, Min. Plen. Andrea Tiriticco, on the subject of International Law
30 October 2017	72nd GA Report of the International Criminal Court	Amb. Lambertini
1 November 2017	72nd GA Meeting of the Third Committee	First Secretary Schettino, on the Rights of Refugees and Displaced Persons
7 November 2017	GA Meeting on the Issue of Equitable Representation and the Increase in the Number of Security Council Members	Amb. Lambertini

Source: Permanent Representation of Italy at the United Nations in New York

A. Resolutions on Human Rights – Italy's Voting Behaviour

As in the past, in 2017, Italy's action in support of human rights prioritised the following thematic areas: promotion of the rule of law and strengthening of democracy; the fight against torture, xenophobia, racism and all forms of discrimination, with specific attention to religious discrimination and intolerance; the rights and protection of children; the abolition of the death penalty; combating violence against women and female genital mutilation.

More specifically, Italy presented the resolution: Strengthening the United Nations crime prevention and criminal justice programme, in particular its technical cooperation capacity (A/RES/71/209), adopted by consensus.

Italy sponsored 36 resolutions and was asked to pass an open vote on 23 resolutions (12 votes in favour, 6 against, 5 abstained), the outcome of which is shown below.

Subject	Resolution	Main sponsor of the Resolution	Information regarding Italy	Outcome of the Plenary Session
Social development	A/RES/72/140 Persons with albinism	Algeria *et al.*	Co-sponsor of the Resolution	Adopted by consensus
	A/RES/72/141 Implementation of the results of the World Summit for Social Development and of the 24th special session of the AG	Belarus, Ecuador, Kazakhstan	Co-sponsor of the Resolution Voted in favour	184 in favour, 2 against, 0 abstentions
	A/RES/72/142 Promoting social integration through social inclusion	Brazil *et al.*	Co-sponsor of the Resolution	Adopted by consensus
	A/RES/72/143 Cooperatives in social development	Australia *et al.*	Co-sponsor of the Resolution	Adopted by consensus
	A/RES/72/144 Follow-up to the Second World Assembly on Ageing	Ecuador *et al.*	Co-sponsor of the Resolution	Adopted by consensus
	A/RES/72/146 Policies and programmes involving young people	Argentina *et al.*	Co-sponsor of the Resolution	Adopted by consensus

Subject	Resolution	Main sponsor of the Resolution	Information regarding Italy	Outcome of the Plenary Session
Progress of women	A/RES/72/148 Improvement of the situation of women and girls in rural areas	Antigua and Barbuda *et al.*	Co-sponsor of the Resolution	Adopted by consensus
Refugees, displaced persons and humanitarian issues	A/RES/72/150 Office of the United Nations High Commissioner for Refugees	Albania *et al.*	Co-sponsor of the Resolution	Adopted by consensus
	A/RES/72/152 Assistance to refugees, returnees, and displaced persons in Africa	Gabon	Co-sponsor of the Resolution	Adopted by consensus
Human Rights Council Report	A/RES/72/153 Human Right Council Report	Gabon	Abstention	123 in favour, 2 against, 58 abstentions
Promotion and protection of children's rights	A/RES/72/245 Child Rights	Albania *et al.*	Co-sponsor of the Resolution Voted in favour	162 in favour, 0 against, 1 abstention
Rights of the indigenous peoples	A/RES/72/155 Rights of the indigenous peoples	Argentina *et al.*	Co-sponsor of the Resolution	Adopted by consensus
Elimination of racism, racial discrimination, xenophobia and related intolerance	A/RES/72/156 Combatting glorification of Nazism, neo-Nazism and other practices that contribute to fuelling contemporary forms of racism, racial discrimination, xenophobia and related intolerance	Russian Federation	Abstention	133 in favour, 2 against, 49 abstentions
	A/RES/72/157 A global call for the total elimination of racism, racial discrimination, xenophobia and related intolerance and the comprehensive implementation of and follow-up to the Durban Declaration and Programme of Action	Ecuador, China	Abstention	133 in favour, 109 against, 43 absentions

Subject	Resolution	Main sponsor of the Resolution	Information regarding Italy	Outcome of the Plenary Session
People's right to self-determination	A/RES/72/158 The use of mercenaries as a means of violating human rights and impeding the exercise of the right of peoples to self-determination.	Cuba	Dissenting vote	128 in favour, 51 against, 6 abstentions
	A/RES/72/160 The right of the Palestinian people to self-determination	Egypt	Co-sponsor of the Resolution Voted in favour	176 in favour, 7 against, 4 abstentions
Implementation of human rights instruments	A/RES/72/162 Implementation of the Convention on the Rights of Persons with Disabilities and its Optional Protocol: situation of women and girls with disabilities	Albania *et al.*	Co-sponsor of the Resolution Voted in favour	187 in favour, 0 against, 0 abstentions
	A/RES/72/163 Torture and other cruel, inhuman and degrading treatment and punishment	Albania *et al.*	Co-sponsor of the Resolution	Adopted by consensus
Human rights issues, including alternative approaches to improving the effective enjoyment of human rights and fundamental freedoms	A/RES/72/164 Strengthening the role of the United Nations in enhancing periodic and genuine elections and the promotion of democratisation	Argentina *et al.*	Co-sponsor of the Resolution Voted in favour	175 in favour, 0 against, 13 abstentions
	A/RES/72/165 International day of remembrance and tribute to the victims of terrorism	Afghanistan *et al.*	Co-sponsor of the Resolution	Adopted by consensus
	A/RES/72/166 UN Human Rights Training and Documentation Center, Southwest Asia and the Arab Region	Kuwait *et al.*	Voted in favour	188 in favour, 0 against, 1 abstention

Subject	Resolution	Main sponsor of the Resolution	Information regarding Italy	Outcome of the Plenary Session
	A/RES/72/167 Right to development	Cuba, China, El Salvador	Abstention	140 in favour, 10 against, 38 abstentions
	A/RES/72/168 Human rights and unilateral coercive measures	Cuba, China	Voted against	134 in favour, 53 against, 0 abstention
	A/RES/72/169 Human rights and cultural diversity	Cuba, China	Voted against	136 in favour 53 against, 0 abstentions
	A/RES/72/172 Promotion of a fair and democratic international order	Cuba	Voted against	129 in favour, 54 against, 5 abstentions
	A/RES/72/173 Right to Food	Cuba	Co-sponsor of Resolution Voted in favour	187 in favour, 2 against, 0 abstentions
	A/RES/72/174 Promotion of a fair geographical distribution in the membership of treaty bodies on human rights	China, Cuba	Voted against	134 in favour, 52 against, 0 abstentions
	A/RES/72/175 Safety of journalists and impunity	Albania *et al.*	Co-sponsor of Resolution	Adopted by consensus
	A/RES/72/177 Freedom of religion or belief	Albania *et al.*	Co-sponsor of Resolution	Adopted by consensus
	A/RES/72/178 Human right to water and sanitation	Albania *et al.*	Co-sponsor of Resolution Voted in favour	183 in favour, 1 against, 2 abstentions
	A/RES/72/179 Protection of migrants	Argentina *et al.*	Co-sponsor of Resolution	Adopted by consensus
	A/RES/72/180 Protecting human rights and fundamental freedoms while countering terrorism	Argentina *et al.*	Co-sponsor of Resolution	Adopted by consensus

Subject	Resolution	Main sponsor of the Resolution	Information regarding Italy	Outcome of the Plenary Session
	A/RES/72/181 National institutions for the promotion and protection of human rights	Afghanistan *et al.*	Co-sponsor of Resolution	Adopted by consensus
	A/RES/72/182 Protection and assistance for displaced persons	Albania *et al.*	Co-sponsor of Resolution	Adopted by consensus
	A/RES/72/183 International Convention for the Protection of All Persons from Enforced Disappearances	Argentina *et al.*	Co-sponsor of Resolution	Adopted by consensus
	A/RES/72/246 Effects of terrorism on the enjoyment of human rights	Egypt *et al.*	Abstention	95 in favour, 1 against, 58 abstentions
	A/RES/72/247 20th anniversary and promotion of the Declaration on the right and responsibility of individuals, groups and organs of society to promote and protect universally recognised human rights and fundamental freedoms	Argentina *et al.*	Co-sponsor of the resolution	Adopted by consensus
	A/RES/72/184 Effective promotion of the Declaration on the rights of persons belonging to national, ethnic, religious, and linguistic minorities	Albania *et al.*	Co-sponsor of the Resolution	Adopted by consensus
	A/RES/72/185 Globalisation and its impact on the full enjoyment of all human rights	Egypt and the People's Democratic Republic of Korea	Voted against	129 in favour, 53 against, 3 abstentions

Subject	Resolution	Main sponsor of the Resolution	Information regarding Italy	Outcome of the Plenary Session
	A/RES/72/186 Role of ombudsperson, mediator and other national human rights institutions in the promotion and protection of human rights	Argentina *et al.*	Co-sponsor of the Resolution	Adopted by consensus
	A/RES/72/187 Sub-regional Centre for Human Rights and Democracy in Central Africa	Republic of Cameroon	Co-sponsor of the Resolution	Adopted by consensus
Reports of Rapporteurs and Special Representatives on the situation of human rights	A/RES/72/188 Situation of human rights in the Democratic People's Republic of Korea	Argentina *et al.*	Co-sponsor of the Resolution	Adopted by consensus
	A/RES/72/189 Situation of human rights in Islamic Republic of Iran	Albania *et al.*	Co-sponsor of the Resolution Voted in favour	81 in favour, 30 against, 70 abstentions
	A/RES/72/190 Situation of human rights in the Autonomous Republic of Crimea and in the city of Sevastopol	Albania *et al.*	Co-sponsor of the Resolution Voted in favour	70 in favour, 26 against, 76 abstentions
	A/RES/72/191 Situation of human rights in Syria	Japan *et al.*	Co-sponsor of the Resolution Voted in favour	109 in favour, 17 against, 58 abstentions
	A/RES/72/248 Situation of human rights in Myanmar	Afghanistan *et al.*	Co-sponsor of the Resolution Voted in favour	122 in favour, 10 against, 24 abstentions

Subject	Resolution	Main sponsor of the Resolution	Information regarding Italy	Outcome of the Plenary Session
Crime prevention and criminal justice	A/RES/72/195 Improve the coordination of efforts against trafficking in human beings	Armenia *et al.*	Co-sponsor of the resolution	Adopted by consensus
International drug control	A/RES/72/198 International cooperation to tackle and combat the world drug problem	Costa Rica *et al.*	Co-sponsor of the resolution	Adopted by consensus

Source: United Nations, General Assembly

II. Human Rights Council

The Human Rights Council is the subsidiary body of the General Assembly responsible for for addressing human rights violations, promoting worldwide respect of all human rights and fundamental freedoms for all, without distinction of any kind.

Established in 2006 under General Assembly resolution 60/251, the Council is an inter-governmental body made up of 47 United Nations Member States elected by the General Assembly for an initial period of three years, extendable for not more than two consecutive terms. It meets in Geneva, in three ordinary sessions per year, for an overall period of at least ten working weeks. Furthermore, although it is a body of Government representatives, the Council is open to the contributions of nongovernmental organisations which enjoy advisory status with the ECOSOC, which may participate in the meetings and submit written documents.

The Council has established several different "mechanisms" for monitoring human rights (resolution A/HRC/RES/5/1 of June 2007), including: the Universal Periodic Review (UPR), the Special Procedures (which include mandates by Country and thematic mandates), the Advisory Committee and a Complaints Procedure.

In 2017, the Council held:

- three ordinary sessions: 34th (27 February – 24 March); 35th (6-23 June); 36th (11-29 September);
- a special session on the Rohingya Muslim minority and other minorities in the Rakhine State in Myanmar (27th session, 5 December);
- two sessions of UPR: 27th (1-12 May); 28th (6-17 November).

In 2017, Italy was represented at the Human Rights Council by H.E. Amb. Maurizio Enrico Serra, Permanent Representative of Italy to the International Organisations in Geneva, by the First Counsellors Cristina Carenza and Daniela d'Orlandi, and by the First Secretary Massimo Baldassarre. Listed below are the main interventions by the Italian mission in 2017.

Date	Event	Intervention
28 February 2017	34th Session of Human Rights Council	Benedetto della Vedova, Under-secretary of State – Ministry of Foreign Affairs, at the high-level segment
2 March 2017	34th Session of Human Rights Council	First Counsellor d'Orlandi, at the interactive dialogue with the Special Rapporteurs on Human Rights Defenders and on Torture
3 March 2017	34th Session of Human Rights Council	First Secretary Baldassarre, at the interactive dialogue with the Special Rapporteurs on the protection of human rights in the fight against terrorism and the enjoyment of cultural rights
3 March 2017	34th Session of Human Rights Council	First Secretary Baldassarre, on the occasion of the interactive dialogue with the Special Rapporteurs on the rights of persons with disabilities and the rights of persons with albinism
7 March 2017	34th Session of Human Rights Council	First Secretary Baldassarre, at the interactive dialogue with the Special Rapporteurs on violence against children and on children and armed conflict
10 March 2017	34th Session of Human Rights Council	First Counsellor Carenza, at the interactive dialogue on the human rights of migrants
14 March 2017	34th Session of Human Rights Council	First Counsellor d'Orlandi, during the discussion on human rights in Syria
14 March 2017	34th Session of Human Rights Council	H.E. Amb. Serra, at the interactive dialogue with the Commission of Inquiry on Human Rights in Syria
20 March 2017	34th Session of Human Rights Council	H.E. Amb. Serra, at the general debate on the follow-up and implementation of the Vienna Declaration and Programme of Action

Date	Event	Intervention
1-12 May 2017	27th Session of UPR	Interventions with reference to the examination of the human rights situation in the following States: Bahrain, Ecuador, Morocco, Indonesia, United Kingdom, India, Brazil, Philippines, Algeria, Poland, the Netherlands, South Africa
7 June 2017	35th Session of Human Rights Council	First Secretary Baldassarre, at the interactive dialogue with the Special Rapporteurs on the right to freedom of assembly and peaceful association and the right to education
8 June 2017	35th Session of Human Rights Council	First Counsellor Carenza, at the interactive dialogue with the Working Group on Human Rights and Transnational Corporations and with the Special Rapporteur on the human rights of migrants
9 June 2017	35th Session of Human Rights Council	First Counsellor d'Orlandi, on the occasion of the interactive dialogue with the Working Group on discrimination against women
12 June 2017	35th Session of Human Rights Council	H.E. Amb. Serra, at the interactive dialogue with the Special Rapporteur on trafficking in human beings
12 June 2017	35th Session of Human Rights Council	First Counsellor d'Orlandi, at the interactive dialogue with the Special Rapporteurs on independence of judges and lawyers and on violence against women
13 June 2017	35th Session of Human Rights Council	First Councilor d'Orlandi, on the occasion of the annual debate on the human rights of women
14 June 2017	35th Session of Human Rights Council	H.E. Amb. Serra, at the interactive dialogue with the Commission of Inquiry on Human Rights in Syria
11 September 2017	36th Session of Human Rights Council	First Counsellor d'Orlandi, at the interactive dialogue with the Special Rapporteurs on truth, justice and reparations and on forced or involuntary disappearances
12 September 2017	36th Session of Human Rights Council	H.E. Amb. Serra, at the general debate on the report of the High Commissioner on the human rights situation in the world and on the activities of the office

Date	Event	Intervention
15 September 2017	36th Session of Human Rights Council	First Secretary Baldassarre, at the discussion on the integration of the gender perspective in the work of the Human Rights Council and its mechanisms
18 September 2017	36th Session of Human Rights Council	First Secretary Baldassarre, on the occasion of the general debate on the promotion of all human rights
18 September 2017	36th Session of Human Rights Council	H.E. Amb. Serra, at the interactive dialogue with the Commission of Inquiry on Human Rights in Syria
26 September 2017	36th Session of Human Rights Council	First Secretary Baldassarre, during the discussion on the impact of multiple forms of discrimination and violence in the field of racism, racial discrimination, xenophobia, and related intolerance
26 September 2017	36th Session of Human Rights Council	First Secretary Baldassarre, at an interactive dialogue with the Group of Experts on the African descent population
27 September 2017	36th Session of Human Rights Council	First Counsellor d'Orlandi, at the interactive dialogue with the independent expert on the human rights situation in Somalia
27 September 2017	36th Session of Human Rights Council	First Counsellor d'Orlandi, at the interactive dialogue on the report of the High Commissioner on the human rights situation in Libya
6-17 November 2017	28th Session of UPR	Interventions with reference to the examination of the human rights situation in the following States: Czech Republic, Argentina, Gabon, Ghana, Peru, Guatemala, Switzerland, Republic of Korea, Benin, Pakistan, Zambia, Japan, Ukraine, Sri Lanka
5 December 2017	27th Special Session on the Muslim minority in Rohingya and Other Minorities in the State of Rakhine in Myanmar	First Counsellor Carenza

Source: webtv.un.org

A. Italy's Behaviour at the Human Rights Council in 2017

In 2017, Italy participated in the three ordinary sessions of the Human Rights Council as an Observer State (hence, without the right to vote).

Over the course of 2017, the Human Rights Council adopted 108 resolutions (eight more than 2016): 41 resolutions during the 34th session; 34 during the 35th session; and 32 during the 36th session. Of these resolutions, 73 were adopted with the consensus of all Member States, whereas a majority vote by Council members was necessary for the remaining 35 (32%), showing a slightly higher level of disagreement than in the previous year, when majority voting was required for 31% of the resolutions adopted.

The following paragraphs analyses Italy's behaviour at the Human Rights Council in 2017, with a particular focus on Italy's diplomatic efforts in the negotiation and presentation of resolutions.

On this issue, 58% of the resolutions adopted by the Council were negotiated with direct participation (sponsoring) or with diplomatic support (co-sponsoring) from Italy. Indeed, of the 108 resolutions adopted, Italy sponsored nine (compared to the eleven of 2016) and co-sponsored 54 (same as 2016).

Five of the nine resolutions sponsored by Italy are thematic and refer to the rights of children and adolescents, education and training in human rights, national human rights policies, and the contribution of parliaments to the work of the Human Rights Council.

The remaining four resolutions are on the human rights situations in Syria and Belarus.

The table below summarises the resolutions approved by the Council in 2017 and shows that, of the resolutions sponsored and cosponsored by Italy, the Council adopted 84% by consensus and 16% by a majority vote.

Human Rights Council: resolutions sponsored by Italy in 2017

Resolutions	Other sponsors of the resolution	Outcome of the Voting Process
A/HRC/RES/34/26 Situation of human rights in Syria	Saudi Arabia, United Kingdom *et al.*	27 in favour, 7 against, 13 abstentions
A/HRC/RES/35/14 Youth and human rights	El Salvador *et al.*	Adopted by consensus
A/HRC/RES/35/16 Child marriages, precocious or forced in humanitarian contexts	The Netherlands, Sierra Leone *et al.*	Adopted by consensus

Resolutions	**Other sponsors of the resolution**	**Outcome of the Voting Process**
A/HRC/RES/35/26 Situation of human rights in Syria	Saudi Arabia, United Kingdom *et al.*	27 in favour, 8 against, 12 abstentions
A/HRC/RES/35/29 Contribution of parliaments to the work of the Human Rights Council and its UPR	Ecuador *et al.*	Adopted by consensus
A/HRC/RES/35/32 National policies and human rights	Ecuador, Peru *et al.*	Adopted by consensus
A/HRC/RES/35/27 Situation of human rights in Belarus	Malta	18 in favour, 8 against, 21 abstentions
A/HRC/RES/36/12 World programme for human rights education	Brazil *et al.*	Adopted by consensus
A/HRC/RES/36/20 Situation of human rights in Syria	Qatar, United Kingdom *et al.*	27 in favour, 7 against, 13 abstentions

Source: United Nations, Human Rights Council

Human Rights Council: resolutions co-sponsored by Italy in 2017

Resolutions	**Sponsors of the Resolution**	**Outcome of the Voting Process**
34th session (27 February – 24 March)		
A/HRC/RES/34/1 Promoting reconciliation, accountability and human rights in Sri Lanka	The United States *et al.*	Adopted by consensus
A/HRC/RES/34/2 Promotion of the enjoyment of cultural rights of everyone and respect for cultural diversity	Cuba	Adopted by consensus
A/HRC/RES/34/4 Question of the realisation in all countries of economic, social and cultural rights	Portugal	Adopted by consensus
A/HRC/RES/34/5 Special Rapporteur's mandate on the situation of human rights defenders	Norway	Adopted by consensus
A/HRC/RES/34/6 Mandate of the Special Rapporteur on minority issues	Austria, Senegal, Slovenia	Adopted by consensus

Resolutions	**Sponsors of the Resolution**	**Outcome of the Voting Process**
A/HRC/RES/34/7 Right to privacy in the digital age	Brazil, Germany	Adopted by consensus
A/HRC/RES/34/9 Special Rapporteur on adequate housing as a component of the right to an adequate standard of living, and on the right to non-discrimination in this context	Namibia *et al.*	Adopted by consensus
A/HRC/RES/34/10 Freedom of religion or belief	Malta	Adopted by consensus
A/HRC/RES/34/14 Right to work	Egypt, Greece *et al.*	Adopted by consensus
A/HRC/RES/34/16 Rights of the Child: protection of rights of the child in the implementation of the 2030 Sustainable Development Agenda	Malta, Uruguay	Adopted by consensus
A/HRC/RES/34/17 Regional agreements for the promotion and protection of human rights	Belgium *et al.*	Adopted by consensus
A/HRC/RES/34/18 Freedom of opinion and expression: mandate of the Special Rapporteur on the promotion and protection of the right to freedom of opinion and expression	The United States	Adopted by consensus
A/HRC/RES/34/19 Mandate of the Special Rapporteur on Torture and Other Cruel, Inhuman or Degrading Treatment or Punishment	Denmark	Adopted by consensus
A/HRC/RES/34/20 Human rights and environment	Costa Rica, Switzerland *et al.*	Adopted by consensus
A/HRC/RES/34/22 Situation of human rights in Myanmar	Malta	Adopted by consensus
A/HRC/RES/34/23 Situation of human rights in Iran	Sweden *et al.*	22 in favour, 12 against, 13 abstentions
A/HRC/RES/34/24 Situation of human rights in the Democratic People's Republic of Korea	Japan, Malta	Adopted by consensus
A/HRC/RES/34/25 Situation of human rights in South Sudan	United States *et al.*	Adopted by consensus
A/HRC/RES/34/37 Cooperation with Georgia	Georgia	18 in favour, 5 against, 24 abstentions

Resolutions	**Sponsors of the Resolution**	**Outcome of the Voting Process**
A/HRC/RES/34/38 Technical assistance and capacity-building to improve human rights in Libya	Libya, Tunisia	Adopted by consensus
A/HRC/RES/34/39 Technical assistance and capacity-building for Mali in the field of human rights	Tunisia	Adopted by consensus
A/HRC/RES/34/40 Promoting Voluntary Technical Assistance Trust Fund to Support the Participation of Least Developed Countries (LDCs) and Small Island Developing States (SIDS) in the work of the Human Rights Council	Maldives *et al.*	Adopted by consensus
A/HRC/RES/34/41 Human rights, democracy and the rule of law	Romania *et al.*	Adopted by consensus
35th session (6-23 June)		
A/HRC/RES/35/1 70th anniversary of the Universal Declaration of Human Rights and the 25th anniversary of the Vienna Declaration and Programme of Action	Russian Federation	Adopted by consensus
A/HRC/RES/35/2 Right to education: follow-up to Resolution 8/4 of the Human Rights Council	Portugal	Adopted by consensus
A/HRC/RES/35/5 Mandate of the Special Rapporteur on trafficking in human beings, especially women and children	Germany, Philippines	Adopted by consensus
A/HRC/RES/35/6 Special Rapporteur on the Rights of Persons with Disabilities	Mexico, New Zealand	Adopted by consensus
A/HRC/RES/35/7 Mandate of the Working Group on the issue of human rights and transnational corporations and other business enterprises	Norway *et al.*	Adopted by consensus

Resolutions	Sponsors of the Resolution	Outcome of the Voting Process
A/HRC/RES/35/10 Accelerating efforts to eliminate all forms of violence against women: involving men and children in preventing and responding to violence against all women and girls	Canada	Adopted by consensus
A/HRC/RES/35/11 Special Rapporteur's mandate on the independence of judges and lawyers	Hungary *et al.*	Adopted by consensus
A/HRC/RES/35/15 Mandate of the Special Rapporteur on extrajudicial, summary or arbitrary executions	Sweden	Adopted by consensus
A/HRC/RES/35/18 Elimination of discrimination against women and children	Mexico, Colombia	Adopted by consensus
A/HRC/RES/35/19 Extreme poverty and human rights	France *et al.*	Adopted by consensus
A/HRC/RES/35/22 Achieving equal enjoyment of the right to education of every child	United Arab Emirates	Adopted by consensus
A/HRC/RES/35/23 The right of everyone to enjoy the highest attainable standards of physical and mental health in the implementation of the 2030 Sustainable Development Agenda	Brazil *et al.*	Adopted by consensus
A/HRC/RES/35/25 The negative impact of corruption on the enjoyment of human rights	Morocco *et al.*	Adopted by consensus
A/HRC/RES/35/31 Cooperation and assistance to Ukraine in the field of human rights	Ukraine	22 in favour, 6 against, 19 abstentions
A/HRC/RES/35/33 Technical assistance to the Democratic Republic of the Congo and accountability for events in the Kasai regions	Tunisia	Adopted by consensus
A/HRC/RES/35/34 Protection of human rights and fundamental freedoms in the fight against terrorism	Mexico	Adopted by consensus

Resolutions	**Sponsors of the Resolution**	**Outcome of the Voting Process**
36th session (11-29 September)		
A/HRC/RES/36/5 Unaccompanied migrant children and adolescents and human rights	El Salvador	Adopted by consensus
A/HRC/RES/36/6 Forced or involuntary disappearances	France *et al.*	Adopted by consensus
A/HRC/RES/36/7 Special Rapporteur on the promotion of truth, justice, reparation and guarantees of non-recurrence	Switzerland *et al.*	Adopted by consensus
A/HRC/RES/36/8 The full enjoyment of human rights by all women and girls and the systematic mainstreaming of a gender perspective into the implementation of the 2030 Agenda for Sustainable Development	Switzerland *et al.*	Adopted by consensus
A/HRC/RES/36/13 Mental health and human rights	Portugal, Brazil	Adopted by consensus
A/HRC/RES/36/16 Human rights in the administration of justice, including juvenile justice	Austria	Adopted by consensus
A/HRC/RES/36/17 The question of the death penalty	Benin, Mongolia *et al.*	27 in favour, 13 against, 7 abstentions
A/HRC/RES/36/18 Conscientious objection to military service	Croatia, Costa Rica, Poland	Adopted by consensus
A/HRC/RES/36/19 Renewal of the mandate of commission of inquiry on Burundi	Estonia	22 in favour, 11 against, 14 abstentions
A/HRC/RES/36/21 Cooperation with the UN, its representatives and mechanisms in the field of human rights	Hungary *et al.*	28 in favour, 0 against, 19 abstentions
A/HRC/RES/36/25 Technical assistance and capacity-building for the Central African Republic in the field of human rights	Tunisia	Adopted by consensus
A/HRC/RES/36/27 Assistance to Somalia in the field of human rights	Somalia, United Kingdom	Adopted by consensus

Resolutions	Sponsors of the Resolution	Outcome of the Voting Process
A/HRC/RES/36/28 Advancement of technical cooperation and capacity-building in the field of human rights	Thailand *et al.*	Adopted by consensus
A/HRC/RES/36/29 Promote international cooperation to support systems, processes and related human rights follow-up mechanisms, as well as their contribution to the implementation of the 2030 Agenda for Sustainable Development	Paraguay, Brazil	Adopted by consensus
A/HRC/RES/36/31 Human rights, technical assistance and capacity-building in Yemen	Egypt	Adopted by consensus

Source: United Nations, Human Rights Council

Human Rights Council: resolutions not sponsored by Italy in 2017

Resolutions	Sponsors of the Resolution	Outcome of the Voting Process
34th session (27 February - 24 March)		
A/HRC/RES/34/3 Mandate of the Independent Expert on the effects of foreign debt and other related international financial obligations of States on the full enjoyment of all human rights, particularly economic, social and cultural rights	Cuba	31 in favour, 16 against, 0 abstentions
A/HRC/RES/34/8 Effects of terrorism on the enjoyment of all human rights	Algeria, Egypt *et al.*	28 in favour, 15 against, 4 abstentions
A/HRC/RES/34/11 The negative impact of the non-repatriation of funds of illicit origin in the countries of origin on the enjoyment of human rights, and the importance of improving international cooperation	Tunisia *et al.*	30 in favour, 1 against, 16 abstentions
A/HRC/RES/34/21 Human Rights of Migrants: Special Rapporteur on Human Rights of Migrants	Mexico	Adopted by consensus

Resolutions	**Sponsors of the Resolution**	**Outcome of the Voting Process**
A/HRC/RES/34/12 The right to food	Cuba	45 in favour, 1 against, 1 abstention
A/HRC/RES/34/13 Human Rights and unilateral coercive measures	Venezuela	32 in favour, 14 against, 0 abstentions
A/HRC/RES/34/15 Birth registration and the right of every-one to recognition everywhere as a person before the law	Mexico, Turkey	Adopted by consensus
A/HRC/RES/34/27 Human Rights in the occupied Syrian Golan	Pakistan	26 in favour, 3 against, 18 abstensions
A/HRC/RES/34/28 Ensure accountability and justice for all violations of international law in the occupied Palestinian territory, including East Jerusalem	Pakistan, Palestine	30 in favour, 2 against, 15 abstentions
A/HRC/RES/34/29 The right of the Palestinian people to self-determination	Pakistan, Palestine	3 in favour, 2 against, 2 abstentions
A/HRC/RES/34/30 Situation of human rights in the occu-pied Palestinian territory, including East Jerusalem	Pakistan, Palestine	41 in favour, 2 against, 4 abstentions
A/HRC/RES/34/31 Israeli settlements in the occupied Palestinian territories, including East Jerusalem, and in the occupied Syrian Golan	Pakistan, Palestine	36 in favour, 2 against, 9 abstentions
A/HRC/RES/34/32 Combating intolerance, negative stereo-typing, stigmatization, discrimination, in-citement to violence and violence against persons based on religion or belief	Pakistan	Adopted by consensus
A/HRC/RES/34/33 Establishment of a forum on the people of African descent	Tunisia	Adopted by consensus
A/HRC/RES/34/34 Mandate of the Intergovernmental Working Group on the effective imple-mentation of the Durban Declaration and Programme of Action	Tunisia	46 in favour, 1 against, 0 abstentions

Resolutions	**Sponsors of the Resolution**	**Outcome of the Voting Process**
A/HRC/RES/34/35 Special Rapporteur's mandate on contemporary forms of racism, racial discrimination, xenophobia and related intolerance	Tunisia	Adopted by consensus
A/HRC/RES/34/36 Elaboration of complementary standards to the Convention on the Elimination of All Forms of Racial Discrimination	Tunisia	31 in favour, 4 against, 12 abstentions
35th Session (6-23 June)		
A/HRC/RES/35/3 Human rights and international solidarity	Cuba	32 in favour, 15 against, 0 abstentions
A/HRC/RES/35/4 Promotion of the right to peace	Cuba	32 in favour, 11 against, 4 abstentions
A/HRC/RES/35/8 Strengthening international cooperation in the field of human rights	Venezuela	32 in favour, 3 against, 12 abstentions
A/HRC/RES/35/9 Elimination of Discrimination Against Persons Affected by Leprosy and their Family Members	Japan *et al.*	Adopted by consensus
A/HRC/RES/35/12 The independence and impartiality of the judiciary and prosecutors, and the independence of lawyers	Hungary *et al.*	Adopted by consensus
A/HRC/RES/35/13 Protection of the family: the role of the family in supporting the protection and promotion of the human rights of older persons	Egypt *et al.*	30 in favour, 12 against, 5 abstentions
A/HRC/RES/35/17 Protecting human rights of migrants: global compact for safe, orderly and regular migration	Mexico	Adopted by consensus
A/HRC/RES/35/20 Human rights and climate change	Bangladesh, Philippines, Vietnam	Adopted by consensus
A/HRC/RES/35/21 Contribution of development to the enjoyment of all human rights	China	30 in favour, 13 against, 3 abstentions
A/HRC/RES/35/24 Human rights in cities and other human settlements	Brazil, Ecuador	Adopted by consensus

Resolutions	Sponsors of the Resolution	Outcome of the Voting Process
A/HRC/RES/35/28 Social Forum	Cuba	Adopted by consensus
A/HRC/RES/35/30 Elaboration of a draft declaration on the promotion and full respect of the human rights of the people of African descent	Azerbaijan, Brazil, Tunisia *et al.*	Adopted by consensus
A/HRC/RES/35/35 Situation of human rights in Eritrea	Djibouti, Somalia	Adopted by consensus
36th Session (11-29 September)		
A/HRC/RES/36/1 Composition of the staff of the Office of the UN High Commissioner for Human Rights	Cuba	31 in favour, 15 against, 1 abstention
A/HRC/RES/36/2 Mission by the Office of the UN High Commissioner for Human Rights to improve the situation of human rights and accountability in Burundi	Tunisia	23 in favour, 14 against, 9 abstentions
A/HRC/RES/36/3 Use of mercenaries as a means of violating human rights and impeding the exercise of the right of peoples to self-determination	Cuba	32 in favour, 15 against, 0 abstentions
A/HRC/RES/36/4 Mandate of the Independent Expert on the promotion of a democratic and equitable international order	Cuba	32 in favour, 15 against, 0 abstentions
A/HRC/RES/36/9 Right to development	Venezuela	31 in favour, 11 against, 4 abstentions
A/HRC/RES/36/10 Human rights and unilateral coercive measures	Venezuela	30 in favour, 15 against, 1 abstention
A/HRC/RES/36/11 Intergovernmental working group to consider the possibility of elaborating an international regulatory framework on the regulation, monitoring and oversight of the activities of private military and security companies	Tunisia	Adopted by consensus
A/HRC/RES/36/14 Human rights and indigenous peoples	Mexico, Guatemala	Adopted by consensus

Resolutions	**Sponsors of the Resolution**	**Outcome of the Voting Process**
A/HRC/RES/36/15 Special Rapporteur on the implications for human rights of the environmentally sound management and disposal of hazardous substances and wastes	Tunisia, Ivory Coast	Adopted by consensus
A/HRC/RES/36/22 Promotion and protection of human rights of peasants and other people working in rural areas	Bolivia *et al.*	34 in favour, 2 against, 11 abstentions
A/HRC/RES/36/23 Expert working group mandate on the people of African descent	Tunisia	Adopted by consensus
A/HRC/RES/36/24 From rhetoric to reality: a global call for concrete actions against racism, xenophobia, racial discrimination, and related intolerance	Tunisia	32 in favour, 5 against, 10 abstentions
A/HRC/RES/36/26 Technical assistance and capacity-building to improve human rights in Sudan	Tunisia	Adopted by consensus
A/HRC/RES/36/30 Technical assistance and capacity building in the field of human rights in the Democratic Republic of the Congo	Tunisia	Adopted by consensus
A/HRC/RES/36/32 Advisory services and technical assistance for Cambodia	Japan	Adopted by consensus

Source: United Nations, Human Rights Council

Italy also took part in the special session on the Muslim minority Rohingya and other minorities in the state of Rakhine in Myanmar (5 December 2017).

Italy was one of the countries which supported the request to convene the session, and also sponsored the concluding resolution (A/HRC/RES/S-27/1), adopted with 33 votes in favour, 3 against, 9 abstained.

B. Universal Periodic Review

Italy was subjected to its first Universal Periodic Review (UPR) in 2010 (7th session): on that occasion, 92 recommendations were addressed to Italy, of which it fully accepted (supported) 78, partially rejected (noted)

2 and fully rejected 12. Detailed information on the outcome of the first Universal Periodic Review for Italy is demonstrated in the 2011 edition of the *Italian Yearbook of Human Rights* (p. 169–173).

In 2014, Italy was subjected to its second cycle of the UPR (20th session), during which, 186 recommendations were addressed to Italy, of which it fully supported 176 and noted 12. Detailed information on the outcome of the second Universal Periodic Review for Italy is displayed in the 2015 edition of the *Italian Yearbook of Human Rights* (p. 161–164).

C. Special Procedures

In 2017, the Human Rights Council established a new Special Rapporteur on the Elimination of Discrimination Against Persons Affected by Leprosy and their Family Members. Consequently, all indicated, there were 44 thematic mandates and 14 Country mandates in operation at the Council.

It should be noted, in particular, that in 2017 Maria Grazia Giammarinaro held the position of Special Rapporteur on trafficking in persons, exclusively women and children.

In 2017, Italy was part of the Special Rapporteur on extrajudicial, summary and arbitrary executions' visit, Agnes Callamard (10-16 May), as part of its study on the deaths and illegal killings of migrants and asylum seekers (report A/72/335), as well as by the visit of the Special Rapporteur on trafficking in persons, in particular women and children, Maria Grazia Giammarinaro (12-13 October: report to be published in 2018).

In August, the Special Rapporteur on extrajudicial, summary and arbitrary executions issued a statement requesting explanations from the European Union, Italy and Libya in relation to the new Code of Conduct for private organisations performing search and rescue operations in the Mediterranean. The Code of Conduct, drawn up by the Italian Government and the European Commission, is structured with 13 points and includes a ban on facilitating the transfer of migrants from one vessel to another and an obligation to accept judicial police officers on board. According to the Special Rapporteur, the application of the Code may potentially hinder the activities of NGOs dedicated to saving lives in the Mediterranean, with the consequent increasing risk of lethal accidents, which, as foreseeable and preventable, could cause a violation of Italy's international human rights obligations. The Special Rapporteur calls on the European Commission to support Italy with regard to safeguarding the human rights of migrants and refugees travelling through Libya to Europe, as well as all European countries to their responsibility for reception and fair distribution of asylum seekers.

Listed below are the visits carried out, agreed (but yet to be carried out) and those requested by the Special Rapporteurs to Italy since 2002.

Visits carried out:

- Special Rapporteur on trafficking in persons, in particular women and children (12-13 October 2017): report to be published.
- Special Rapporteur on extrajudicial, summary and arbitrary executions (10-16 May 2017): report A/72/335.
- Working Group of experts on people of African descent (1-5 June 2015): report A/HRC/33/61/Add.1.
- Special Rapporteur on the human rights of migrants (2-5 December 2014): report A/HRC/29/36/Add.2.
- Working Group on arbitrary detention (7-9 July 2014): report A/HRC/30/36/Add.3.
- Special Rapporteur on freedom of opinion and expression (11-18 November 2013): report A/HRC/26/30/Add.3.
- Special Rapporteur on trafficking in persons (12-20 September 2013): report A/HRC/26/37/Add.4.
- Special Rapporteur on the rights of migrants (30 September –8 October 2012): report A/HRC/23/46/Add.3.
- Special Rapporteur on violence against women (15-26 January 2012): report A/HRC/20/16/Add.2.
- Working Group on arbitrary detention (3-14 November 2008): report A/HRC/10/21/Add.5.
- Special Rapporteur on contemporary forms of racism (9-13 October 2006): report A/HRC/4/19/Add.4.
- Special Rapporteur on the right to freedom of opinion and expression (20-29 October 2004): report E/CN.4/2005/64/Add.1.
- Special Rapporteur on the human rights of migrants (7-18 June 2004): report E/CN.4/2005/85/Add.3.
- Special Rapporteur on the independence of judges and lawyers (11-14 March 2002): report E/CN.4/2002/72/Add.3.

Agreed Visits

- UN Working Group on the use of mercenaries (to be carried out in the third quarter of 2018).

Requested Visits

- Special Rapporteur on cultural rights (visit requested in February 2016).
- Special Rapporteur on the human right to safe drinking water and sanitation (visit requested in February 2015).
- Special Rapporteur on the independence of judges and lawyers (visit requested in July 2013).

III. High Commissioner for Human Rights (OHCHR)

The Office was established by the General Assembly in December 1993 with Resolution 48/141.

The High Commissioner has a very broad mandate which includes the prevention of violations of human rights, ensuring the respect of all human rights, coordinating all United Nations activities involving human rights and strengthening national systems for protecting human rights and the rule of law. In this context, one of the crucial strategic activities for the High Commissioner's Office is supporting the establishment and development of independent human rights commissions at the national level.

In order to fulfil its mandate, the Office of the High Commissioner has consolidated its presence "on the ground", establishing 13 regional offices and 13 national offices, sending experts on integrated United Nations peace missions or dispatching independent fact-finding operations, as well as mainstreaming the human rights component in United Nations teams' activities at Country or Programme level, and in those of specialised agencies of the United Nations (such as UNDP).

The High Commissioner for Human Rights in 2017 was Zeid Ra'ad Al Hussein (Jordan), in post since 2014.

The Office of the High Commissioner is funded one-third by the ordinary budget of the United Nations, approved by the General Assembly every two years; the remaining two-thirds of the budget are voluntary contributions, mostly from States and additionally from international organisations, foundations, commercial enterprises, and private citizens.

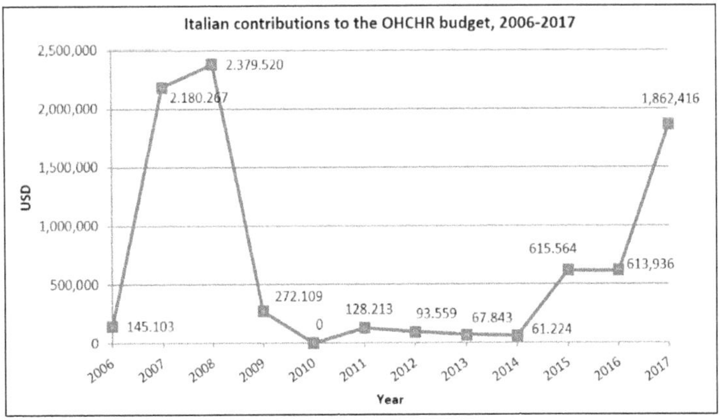

In 2017, Italy contributed to the budget of the High Commissioner's Office with funds of about $1,860,000 (ranking 21st among donors), tripling contributions compared to the previous years.

IV. High Commissioner for Refugees (UNHCR)

This Office was established by the United Nations General Assembly on 14 December 1950, with resolution A/RES/428(V).

The mandate of the Agency is to coordinate international action for the protection of refugees and the resolution of their problems all over the world. Its primary mission is to protect the rights and welfare of refugees and to ensure that all of them can exercise their right to request asylum and seek safe shelter in another State, with the option to return voluntarily to their home Country, integrate locally or to resettle into a third Country. The remit of the UNHCR also includes assistance to stateless persons.

On 1 January 2016, the General Assembly of the United Nations appointed Filippo Grandi (Italy) High Commissioner for Refugees, for a five-year mandate.

The UNHCR has had its own office in Rome since 1953. The Italian office participates in the procedures to determine refugee status in Italy and performs other duties regarding international protection, training, dissemination of information on refugees and asylum-seekers in Italy and in the various crisis areas all over the world, raising public awareness and fund-raising with Governments, companies and individual donors. Since 2006, the Italian UNHCR Office has performed as the *Regional Representative* for Albania, Cyprus, Greece, Malta, Portugal, San Marino, and the Holy See, besides Italy. In 2017, the UNHCR Spokesperson in Italy was Carlotta Sami.

According to the data provided by the UNHCR, 119,369 migrants arrived in Italy by sea in 2017 with a decrease of 34% compared to 2016 (181,436). 15% came from Nigeria, followed by Guinea, Côte d'Ivoire, Bangladesh (8% each) Mali and Eritrea (6% each), Sudan, Tunisia, Morocco and Senegal (5% each). The majority of people arriving in Italy by sea were men, followed by children (15%) and women (11%).

Around nine out of 10 children arriving by sea were either unaccompanied or separated.

Libya reportedly remained the main country of departure for people arriving in Italy by sea (in 2017: 108,409 people, equal to 91% of arrivals). Most of the new arrivals disembarked following SAR operations conducted in the high seas. Nevertheless, independent arrivals also took place, including people reaching southern Italy from Algeria, Tunisia, Turkey and Greece.

In 2017, 100,963 people arriving in Italy by sea applied for asylum; a decrease in comparison to 2016 during which 123,842 applications were submitted. The most common countries of origin for asylum seekers are: Nigeria, Pakistan, Gambia, Ivory Coast, Senegal, Eritrea, Mali, Bangladesh.

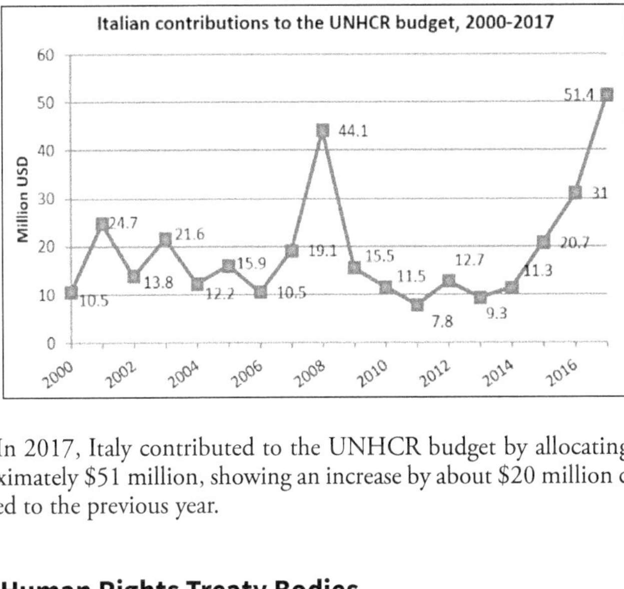

In 2017, Italy contributed to the UNHCR budget by allocating approximately $51 million, showing an increase by about $20 million compared to the previous year.

V. Human Rights Treaty Bodies

Over the years, the United Nations has established a comprehensive Human Rights Code (*International Bill of Human Rights*), whose backbone are the following nine conventions: International Convention for the Elimination of All Forms of Racial Discrimination (ICERD, 1965); International Covenant on Civil and Political Rights (ICCPR, 1966); International Covenant on Economic, Social and Cultural Rights (ICESCR, 1966); Convention against all Forms of Discrimination against Women (CEDAW, 1979); International Convention against Torture (CAT, 1984); Convention on the Rights of the Child (CRC, 1989); International Convention on the Protection of the Rights of All Migrant Workers and Members of Their Families (ICRMW, 1990); Convention on the Rights of Persons with Disabilities (CRPD, 2006); International Convention for the Protection of All Persons from Enforced Disappearance (CPED, 2006).

Italy has ratified eight conventions and relevant optional protocols (as indicated in the following table). However, it has not yet signed the ICRMW.

Convention	Ratification law	Declarations/ Reservations	Recognition of competence of the specific Committees
ICERD	l. 13 October 1975, No. 654	Yes (art. 4)	Individual communications (art. 14): Yes
ICESCR	l. 25 October 1977, No. 881	No	–
OP	l. 3 October 2014, No. 52	No	–
ICCPR	l. 25 October 1977, No. 881	Yes (art. 15.1 and 19.3)	Inter-state communications (art. 41): Yes
OP – 1	l. 25 October 1977, No. 881	Yes (art. 5.2)	–
OP – 2	l. 9 December 1994, No. 734	No	–
CEDAW	l. 14 March 1985, No. 132	Yes (general)	–
OP	Deposit date of ratification: 22/09/2000	No	Inquiry procedure (art. 8 and 9): Yes
CAT	l. 3 November 1988, No. 498	No	Individual communications (art. 22): Yes Inter-state communications (art. 21): Yes Inquiry procedure (art. 20): Yes
OP	l. 9 November 2012, No. 195	No	Visits by the Sub-Committee on the Prevention of Torture (art. 11): Yes
CRC	l. 27 May 1991, No. 176	No	–
OP – AC	l. 11 March 2002, No. 46	Binding declaration pursuant to art. 3: 17 years	–
OP – SC	l. 11 March 2002, No. 46	No	–
OP – IC	l. 16 November 2015, No. 199	No	Individual communications: Yes Inquiry procedure (art. 13): Yes

Convention	**Ratification law**	**Declarations/ Reservations**	**Recognition of competence of the specific Committees**
CRPD	l. 3 March 2009, No. 18	No	–
OP	l. 3 March 2009, No. 18	No	Inquiry procedure (art. 6 and 7): Yes
CPED	l. 29 July 2015, No. 131	No	Inquiry procedure (art. 33): Yes

Legend:

OP = Optional Protocol

OP – AC =Optional Protocol to the Convention on the Rights of the Child on the Involvement of Children in Armed Conflict

OP – SC = Optional Protocol on the Sale of Children, Child Prostitution and Child Pornography

OP – IC = Optional Protocol to the Convention on the Rights of the Child on a communications procedure

In addition to recognising human rights in legally binding treaties, the UN has created monitoring mechanisms for each treaty. These committees or conventional bodies (Treaty Bodies) are composed of 10 to 23 independent experts selected on the basis of their probity and experience recognised in the field of human rights.

In 2017, Mauro Politi was a member of the Human Rights Committee (civil and political) while Alessio Bruni was a member of the Committee against Torture.

The main function of the Committees is to examine the periodic reports on the implementation of the internationally established standards in the Contracting Country. States are obliged to present these reports periodically (usually every 4 or 5 years). The Committees can carry out monitoring functions through three other mechanisms: field surveys; examination of inter-State communications; examination of individual communications. The Committees provide their interpretation of the content of the provisions on human rights by publishing General comments (for a more in-depth analysis of these functions, see *Yearbook 2011*, p. 181-182).

Italy is monitored by eight Committees, as indicated in the following table. In 2017, Italy presented the joint report no. V and VI on the Convention on the Rights of the Child; received the concluding remarks of the Human Rights Committee, of the Committee on the Elimination of Discrimination against Women, and of the Committee against Torture.

Italy's Cooperation with United Nations Treaty Bodies

Committee	Total No. of reports presented	Latest report presented	Latest concluding observations	Reporting status
CERD	20	February 2015	December 2016	XXI report: to be submitted in February 2019
CESCR	5	August 2012	October 2015	VI report: to be submitted in October 2020
CCPR	6	October 2015	March 2017	VII report: to be submitted in 2022
CEDAW	7	October 2015	July 2017	VIII report: to be submitted in 2021
CAT	6	October 2015	November 2017	VII report: to be submitted in 2021
CRC	6	July 2017	–	Combined V and VI reports submitted and awaiting discussion
CRPD	1	November 2012	September 2016	Combined II, III and IV report to be submitted in May 2023
CED	–	–	–	I report: to be submitted in 2018

A. Committee on Economic, Social and Cultural Rights

In 2017, the Committee held three sessions: 60th (20-24 February), 61st (29 May – 23 June) and 62nd (18 September – 6 October). The Committee did not analyse reports during the 60th session while in the 61st session, the reports of Australia, Liechtenstein, the Netherlands, Pakistan, Sri Lanka, Uruguay were analysed. In the 62nd session, those of Colombia, Mexico, Republic of Korea, Republic of Moldova and Russian Federation were reviewed. During the year, the General Comment No. 24 on the obligations of States under the International Covenant on Economic, Social and Cultural Rights in the context of business activities was adopted.

The last periodic report of Italy was discussed by the Committee in September 2015, during its 56th session (see *Yearbook 2016*, p. 159-162). Italy is required to present its sixth report in 2020.

B. Human Rights Committee (Civil and Political Rights)

In 2017, the Committee held three sessions: 119th (6-29 March), 120th (3-28 July) and 121th (16 October-10 November). During the 119th session, the reports of Bangladesh, Bosnia Herzegovina, Italy, Serbia, Thailand, Turkmenistan were analysed; in the 120th, the reports of Honduras, Liechtenstein, Madagascar, Mongolia, Pakistan, Switzerland; in the 121st, the reports of Australia, Cameroon, Democratic Republic of Congo, Dominican Republic, Jordan, Mauritius, Romania. During the year, no General comments were adopted.

Latest Report Submitted by Italy

Reporting round	Report No. VI
Scheduled date for the submission of the Report	31/10/2009
Actual date of submission of the Report	08/10/2015
Report	CCPR/C/ITA/6
List of themes	CCPT/C/ITA/Q/6
Summary of the debate	CCPR/C/SR.3345, CCPR/C/ SR.3346
Concluding observations	CCPR/C/ITA/CO/6
Date of discussion of the Report	9-10 March, during 119th Session of the Committee (6-29 July 2017)

The Committee examined the 6th report of Italy during its 119th session (6-29 March 2017). The discussion on the previous report took place in November 2005. The following civil society organisations lodged their documentation: A Buon Diritto, Amnesty International, *Associazione 21 luglio* ("21 July Association"), Antigone, Article 3, Italian Coalition for Civil Rights and Freedom, European Association of Jehovah's Witnesses, Radicals Certain Rights Association, Family and Human Rights Centre, Rosario Livatino Study Centre, Fiacat, Free Association of Gynacologists for the Application of Law 194, , Centre for Reproductive Rights, Doctors for Human Rights, Non-violent, Transnational and Across-Party Radical Party, North-South XXI, Italian Forum for Disability, European Roma Rights Centre. The Agency for Fundamental Rights of the European Union (FRA) also presented its own communication.

Its concluding remarks were made available to the public on 1 May 2017. In these remarks, the Committee underlined the positive actions taken by Italy, in particular: the approval of l. 76/2016 on civil unions; the adoption of the National Action Plan 2016-2018 against trafficking and severe exploitation of human beings; the approval of the l. 119/2013 against gender violence; the adoption of the Interministerial National Strategy 2012-2020 for the inclusion of Roma, Sinti, and Travellers; the ratification of significant international instruments, such as the Optional Protocol to the UN Convention against Torture, the Optional Protocol to the Covenant on Economic, Social and Cultural Rights, the Convention on the Reduction of Statelessness, the Third Optional Protocol to the Convention on the Rights of the Child on communication procedures, the International Convention for the Protection of All Persons from Enforced Disappearance, the Optional Protocol to the Convention on the Rights of Persons with Disabilities; the withdrawal of reservations to articles 15 (1) and 19 (3) of the International Covenant on Civil and Political Rights.

The main recommendations concern the following aspects:

- *National institutions for human rights.* The Committee recommends that Italy create, without further delay, a national human rights institution, in accordance with the Paris Principles.
- *Legislation on non-discrimination.* Italy should take all necessary measures, including the adoption of comprehensive anti-discrimination legislation, to ensure that its legal framework offers complete and effective protection against all forms of direct and indirect discrimination in all sectors, including in the private sphere; deal comprehensively with all grounds for discrimination, including national origin, citizenship, birth, disability, age, sexual orientation, gender identity, and any other status; and provide effective remedies in case of violations, even in the case of multiple and intersectoral discrimination.
- *Discrimination based on sexual orientation and gender identity.* Italy is invited to reconsider the relevant legislation, to assess the possibility of allowing same-sex couples to adopt children, including the biological children of one of the couple's partners, and to ensure the same legal protection for children living in same sex families compared to those living in heterosexual families. The government should also step up efforts to combat discrimination, hate speech and hate crimes against LGBTI people.
- *Hate speech and racial discrimination.* Italy should increase its efforts to eradicate all forms of stigmatisation, stereotypes, and racist discourse against non-citizens and Roma, Sinti, and Traveller communities by conducting awareness campaigns to promote tolerance and respect for diversity; review the l. 205/1993, in order to implement aggravating circumstances for all the crimes of hate; ensure that all cases of racially motivated violence are systematically investigated, that perpetrators are prosecuted and punished and that adequate compensation is provided to victims.
- *Discrimination against Roma, Sinti and Traveller communities.* Italy is invited to: fully implement the National Strategy for the Inclusion of Roma, Sinti, and Travellers; provide effective remedies and compensation to those who have suffered human rights violations as a result of the implementation of the nomad emergency decree, taking into account the decision of the Council of

State No. 6050 of 16 November 2011; to take all possible measures to avoid the forced eviction of members of these communities and, in the event of evictions, ensure that the communities concerned enjoy legal protection and have adequate alternative housing; to take the necessary measures to repeal all security measures imposed on Roma-only settlements, including Executive Decision 19 December 2015, No. 4377 of the Municipality of Rome, which strongly limits the rights to privacy and the movement of residents and their visitors; suspend any plan that could lead to the creation of new segregated fields or segregated housing areas; accelerate the examination of current legislation to try to recognise the Roma, Sinti and Traveller communities as a national minority.

- *Voluntary interruption of pregnancy*: Italy should take the necessary measures to ensure unhindered and timely access to legal abortion services in its territory, including by setting up an effective reference system for women wishing to turn to such services.
- *Excessive use of force and mistreatment:* Italy has taken all measures to prevent the police forces and security forces resorting to excessive use of force by introducing a code of conduct for such titles and requiring them to wear identification labels. It should also reexamine the article 582 of the Penal Code and ensure that the accusation of mistreatment and excessive use of force are subjected to thorough investigations, even if the victim has not lodged a complaint. Finally, the government should ensure that perpetrators are prosecuted and, if convicted, punished with sanctions commensurate with the gravity of the crime, and that the victims are properly compensated.
- *Statelessness and citizenship*: Italy should take the necessary measures to simplify the procedures for determining statelessness, reform the law on citizenship and speed up the adoption of appropriate legislation aimed at reducing statelessness cases.
- *Migrants, asylum seekers and refugees:* The Committee recommends that Italy implement l. 67/2014, in order to repeal the crime of illegal entry and stay; refrain from making collective expulsions of migrants, ensuring that all expulsion orders are based on an individual assessment of the situation of each migrant, taking into account the special needs of personal protection; to ensure that bilateral and multilateral agreements are applied in such a way as to guarantee full respect for the rights of the Covenant and strict compliance with the principle of non-refoulement, suspending any agreement that does not include effective protection of human rights; ensure that the detention of migrants is applied for the shortest possible time and as a last resort measure; increase the number of available places in reception centres and take all necessary measures to improve living conditions in these centres; ensure information and legal assistance, where necessary, in relation to pre-identification, identification, and asylum application procedures.
- *Unaccompanied minors:* Italy should ensure that the age assessment procedure is based on safe and scientifically valid methods, taking into account children's mental well-being; review the guardian assignment procedure to ensure that each unaccompanied child is promptly supported by a legal guardian; ensure

adequate living conditions for unaccompanied minors in reception facilities; take all necessary measures to prevent the disappearance of children and track down those who have left.

- *Trafficking in human beings and exploitation of work:* Italy should fully implement the National Action Plan against trafficking and the serious exploitation of human beings (2016-2021); establish clear procedures to identify victims of trafficking and continue to provide the necessary training for police officers and immigration police personnel working in reception facilities; conduct individual risk assessments before victims of trafficking return to their country of origin; strengthen labour inspections in those sectors where most migrants are employed, with particular reference to the agricultural sector; establish effective complaints procedures to allow migrant workers to file complaints against employers, without fear of reprisals, strengthening lgs.d. 109/2012 (so-called Rosarno law) for this purpose.
- *Conditions of detention:* The Committee recommends that Italy continue its efforts to reduce overcrowding in prisons; deal with the over-representation of foreigners in prisons, including by conducting a study on discrimination against foreigners in criminal proceedings and by developing appropriate and realistic alternative measures to detention; take measures to improve the conditions of detention, including access to health services, provision of adequate and adequate food, taking into account the health conditions and food needs of prisoners; ensure that the special detention regime, pursuant to article 41 *bis* of l. 26 July 1975, No. 354 (penitentiary order), both in line with the Agreement Covenant.
- *Right to a fair trial*: Italy should continue its efforts to reduce the duration of criminal and civil proceedings; take the necessary measures to improve access to legal aid, including by extending the legal assistance criteria and providing information on these services available to the public.
- *Right to online and digital privacy:* Italy is called upon to review the regime that regulates the interception of personal communications, the hacking of digital devices and the conservation of communication data, in order to guarantee that these activities comply with the obligations under article 17 of the Agreement Covenant, with particular reference to the principles of legality, proportionality, and necessity; that there are independent surveillance and interception systems; that the judicial authority is involved in the authorisation of such measures, offering effective remedies to those affected in case of abuse and including, where possible, an ex post notification of the fact that they have been placed under surveillance or that their data have been violated; that measures be taken to ensure that all companies under the jurisdiction of the State, in particular technology companies, comply with human rights standards when carrying out operations abroad.
- *Offense of defamation:* The Committee recommends that Italy decriminalise blasphemy; consider the complete decriminalisation of defamation and, in any case, limit the application of criminal law to the most serious cases; reviewing its legislation, including article 13 of Press Law and article 595 of the Penal Code, in order to make it compliant with the obligations established by the

Agreement Covenant, taking into account the General Comment No. 34 (2011) of the Committee on Freedom of Opinion and Expression; ensure that legal actions are not used as a tool to reduce freedom of expression beyond the restrictions permitted by article 19 of the Covenant.

– *Freedom of information*: Italy should monitor closely the implementation of the Freedom of Information Act 2016; ensure that the authorities present the reasons behind any refusal to provide access to information; establish effective legal redress measures involving a review of any refusal to provide access to information and any failure to respond to a request for such access.

In November 2017, the Committee published its decision regarding the Communication 2378/2014, A.S.M. and *R.A.H v. Denmark*. The applicants are a couple of citizens who, as regards the persecutions by the Al-Shabaab group for having cooperated with the government, decided to leave their country in November 2008. In April 2009, the applicants entered Italy and applied for asylum. In October 2009, they were granted refugee status under the 1951 Convention and subsidiary protection for humanitarian reasons, and residence permits were issued.

After benefiting from the first six months of the protection system for asylum seekers and refugees, the applicants have managed to receive financial support and social housing from the Italian authorities and, unable to find a regular job, start a shift around various Italian cities (including Bologna, Rome and Perugia), living in conditions of poverty of homeless persons, or occasionally hosted by compatriots or voluntary companies (including Caritas).

In December 2012, the applicants decided to move to Denmark and apply for asylum. In December 2013, the Danish Immigration Service established that, as the applicants had already had a residence permit for Italy, they were not able to obtain asylum in Denmark and had to be transferred back to Italy.

After having exhausted all the available domestic remedies, the applicants decided to submit a communication to the Committee, stating that the transfer to Italy, on the basis of the "first country of asylum" principle, as foreseen by the Dublin regulation, would apply to them and their three minor children (two of whom were born, in the meantime, in Italy and one in Denmark) to a contrary treatment, in particular, in article 7 of the International Covenant on Civil and Political Rights (prohibition of torture and cruel, inhuman or degrading punishment or treatment). The applicants base their arguments, inter alia, on the socio-economic situation they would have to face and on the lack of access to adequate forms of social assistance in Italy, as evidenced by their experience, as well as by the general reception conditions for asylum seekers and refugees in Italy. They also argued that, having already benefited from the reception system on their arrival in Italy, they would neither have had access to social housing or temporary shelters, nor would they have been able to find adequate housing or work, and would therefore have been forced to live again in conditions of poverty as homeless persons with their minor children.

According to the opinion of the Committee, the information received, as well as that of public domain, indicates that there is a genuine lack of available places in the reception facilities for asylum seekers and returnees in Italy, under the Dublin regulation. Returnees, as in the case of the applicants, who have already obtained a form of protection and have benefited the reception facilities when they were in Italy, do not have the right to accommodation through the government reception centres for asylum seekers; although in Italy the beneficiaries of international protection have the right to work and social rights, the social system of the country is, in general, insufficient to assist all people in need, particularly in the current socio-economic situation.

Despite the mentioned difficulties, the Committee believed, however, that the mere fact that the applicants could meet such situations does not in itself mean that they would have necessarily found themselves in a special situation of vulnerability, or in a situation significantly different from many other families. In conclusion, their return to Italy would have been a violation of Denmark's obligations under article 7 of the Covenant. In this case, the Committee noted that during their stay in Italy, following the recognition of refugee status, the applicants received health insurance cards and had access to medical care, including for the birth of their first two children. Moreover, one of the applicants was able to get a job in Italy in the past and did not explain convincingly why he would have not been able to work again or asked for the protection of the Italian authorities in case of abuse by an employer.

In the light of these considerations, the Committee considered that, although the applicants did not agree with the decision of the Danish authorities to transfer them to Italy, they failed to explain why such a decision was manifestly unreasonable or arbitrary. Consequently, with a dissenting opinion, the Committee could not conclude that Denmark's transfer of applicants and their children to Italy constituted a violation of article 7 of the Covenant.

C. Committee against Torture

In 2017, the Committee held three sessions: (18 April – 12 May), 61st (24 July – 11 August) and 62nd (6 November – 6 December). During the 60th session, the reports of Afghanistan, Argentina, Bahrain, Lebanon, Pakistan, Republic of Korea were analysed; in the 61st the relations of

Ireland, Panama, Paraguay; in the 62nd, those of Bosnia and Herzegovina, Bulgaria, Cameroon, Italy, Mauritius, Republic of Moldova, Rwanda, Democratic Republic of Timor-Leste. During the year, no General Comment was adopted.

Latest Report Submitted by Italy

Reporting round	Report No. VI
Scheduled date for the submission of the Report	15/07/2015
Actual date of submission of the Report	21/10/2015
Report	CAT/C/ITA/5-6
List of themes	CAT/C/ITA/Q/6
Summary of the debate	CAT/C/SR.1582, CCPR/C/SR.1585
Concluding observations	CAT/C/ITA/CO/5-6
Date of discussion of the Report	14-15 November, during 62nd Session of the Committee (6 November – 6 December 2017)

The Committee examined the sixth report of Italy during its 62nd session (6 November – 6 December 2017). The previous report was examined in 2007. The following civil society organisations released written reports: Amnesty International, the Radical Association of Rights, Antigone Association, Luca Coscioni Association, Italian Radicals, Fiacat. The Ombudsperson for the Rights of Persons detained or deprived of personal freedom filed its own report.

The Committee welcomes Italy's adoption of the following legislative and political measures: l. 10/2014, which paves the way for establishing the National Authority (Ombudsperson) for the Rights of Persons detained or deprived of personal freedom, which constitutes the national prevention mechanism for torture together with the prevention mechanisms existing at regional and urban level; l. 119/2013 on urgent security provisions and on combating gender-based violence; National Action Plan against trafficking and severe exploitation of human beings (2016-2018); National Action Plan to combat violence against women (2017-2020); the establishment of the Directorate-General for Training at the Department of Prison Administration of the Ministry of Justice (2015). The Committee also appreciates the significant efforts made by Italy to respond to the great flow of asylum seekers, people in need of international protection and irregular migrants arriving on its territory.

At the end of the discussion, the following concluding observations and recommendations were adopted:

- *Definition and criminalisation of torture:* The Committee recommends Italy to standardise the content of article 613 *bis* of the Penal Code (introduced with l. 14 July 2017, No. 110) to article 1 of the Convention, eliminating all the superfluous elements and inserting the reference to the status of public official of the offender and to the reasons for or rationale behind the use of torture (i.e. obtaining information or confession, punishing the victim, intimidating the victim or a third person, or any other reason based on discrimination of any kind). In this regard, the Committee draws Italy's attention to General Comment No. 2 (2007) on the implementation of article 2, which states that serious discrepancies between the definition of the Convention and that incorporated into national law create real or potential pretexts for impunity. Lastly, the Committee recommends that Italy ensure that the torture offense is not subject to limitation, in order to exclude any risk of impunity.
- *National and regional mechanisms for the prevention of torture:* Italy should guarantee the functional, structural, and financial independence of the existing regional and municipal prevention mechanisms for the prevention of torture; ensure implementation of the recommendations made, following the monitoring activities by the National Authority for the rights of persons detained or deprived of personal freedom, in accordance with the Guidelines on National Prevention Mechanisms of the Subcommittee on Prevention of Torture and other Cruel, Inhuman or Degrading Treatment or Punishment (CAT/OP/12/5, para. 13 and 38).
- *National institutions for human rights:* Remembering its previous recommendations, the Committee calls on Italy to create, without further delay, a national institution for human rights, in accordance with the Paris Principles.
- *Fundamental legal safeguards:* Italy should take effective measures to guarantee to all prisoners the fundamental safeguards from the beginning of their deprivation of freedom, in accordance with international standards, including the right of access to a lawyer, particularly during investigations and questioning stages, the right to have an interpreter's assistance, if necessary, and the right to promptly inform a relative or any other person of their arrest; widen the criteria for access to legal assistance, particularly in the case of foreigners; reduce the maximum period within which a person can be kept in custody after being arrested for a criminal charge to less than five days before being brought before the judicial authority, even in exceptional circumstances.
- *Non-refoulement:* Reminding the previous recommendations (CAT/C/ITA/CO/4, para. 10-12), the Committee calls on Italy to ensure that no person can be deported or extradited to a State where there are substantial grounds for a foreseeable risk of being subjected to torture; to ensure that all asylum seekers have the opportunity for an individual examination and are protected against refoulement and collective expulsions; to amend its legislation in order to provide rejected asylum seekers with an effective judicial remedy with automatic suspensory effect against expulsion decisions; ensure that the accelerated procedures foreseen by the readmission agreements and by l. 46/2017 are subject to an in-depth assessment on a case-by-case basis in relation to the risks of violation of the principle of non-refoulement. Furthermore, Italy should

take all necessary legal, political, and diplomatic measures to ensure that any bilateral or regional migration management agreement is consistent with the aims of the Convention and with the obligations under international law on human rights and rights of refugees. In this context, the government is invited to provide the Committee with information on the implementation of the Italy-Libya agreement. In order to ensure the proper use of EU funds, Italy should also consider urgently the establishment of an effective mechanism to monitor the conditions on the ground in Libya for the implementation of cooperation projects.

– *Monitoring of reception and detention centres for migrants:* Italy is invited to: clarify the legal basis for deprivation of freedom and use of force to obtain the fingerprints of asylum seekers and migrants who do not cooperate in the identification process; ensure that all allegations of excessive use of force are subjected to timely, complete and impartial investigations, and that perpetrators are prosecuted and punished; ensure that law enforcement officers receive adequate professional training, including on how to avoid excessive use of force and on how to handle situations in which asylum seekers and migrants do not cooperate in the identification process; take the necessary measures to ensure adequate reception conditions for asylum seekers and irregular migrants; formulate guidelines and adequate training on the identification, between asylum seekers and migrants, of persons in need of international protection, including victims of torture and trafficking; ensure that the National Authority for the rights of persons detained or deprived of personal liberty and its regional counterparts can visit the places of deprivation of liberty, as set forth in articles 4 and 29 of the Optional Protocol; authorise non-governmental human rights organisations and other civil society actors to undertake monitoring activities in reception centres for asylum seekers and migrants, including "crisis centres" and centres for unaccompanied minors.
– *Training:* The Committee recommends Italy to develop mandatory in-service training programmes to ensure that all civil servants, in particular police officers, prison staff and medical personnel employed in prisons, are well acquainted with the provisions of the Convention; ensure that all personnel involved, including medical personnel, are specifically trained to identify cases of torture and ill-treatment, in accordance with the Handbook for effective investigation and documentation of torture or other cruel, inhuman or degrading treatment or punishment (known as the Istanbul Protocol); develop and apply a methodology to evaluate the effectiveness of training programs related to the Convention and the Istanbul Protocol.
– *Conditions of detention:* The Committee, drawing attention to the United Nations Minimum Standards for the Treatment of Prisoners (a.k.a. Mandela Rules) and United Nations Rules for the Treatment of Women Prisoners and Non-custodial Measures for Women Offenders (a.k.a. Bangkok Rules), calls on Italy to continue its efforts to improve conditions of detention and reduce overcrowding of prisons and other detention facilities, including through the application of non-custodial measures; to guarantee, legally and practice-wise, that preventive detention is not prolonged excessively; review the special de-

tention regime provided for by article 41 *bis* of the l. 26 July 1975, No. 354 (penitentiary order), to align it with international human rights standards, ensuring, in particular, that video surveillance in the custody facilities does not interfere with the privacy of prisoners or with their right to confidential communication with their lawyer or doctor.

- *Excessive use of force:* Italy should ensure that timely, impartial and effective investigations are carried out on all allegations concerning excessive use of force by police and other law enforcement officials, ensuring that abusers are prosecuted and that victims are properly compensated; increase efforts to systematically provide training in law enforcement on the use of force, especially in the context of public demonstrations, taking into account the basic principles of the use of force and the use of weapons by police officers; ensure that members of the police and other law enforcement officers can be effectively identified at all times during the performance of their duties; provide the Committee with detailed information on the number of complaints, investigations, prosecutions, convictions and judgments issued in cases of excessive use of force.
- *Compensation and rehabilitation of victims:* The Committee, drawing attention to its General Comment No. 3 (2012) on the implementation of article 14, calls on Italy to ensure that all victims of torture and ill-treatment obtain reparation, including fair and adequate compensation for the most complete rehabilitation possible. The government should also provide the Committee with information on compensation measures for victims of torture or ill-treatment ordered by the courts or other bodies of the State.
- *Gender violence:* The Committee encourages Italy to: redouble its efforts to combat all forms of gender-based violence, ensuring that complaints are subjected to thorough investigation; that the accused are prosecuted by the judicial authority and, if found guilty, punished appropriately; ensure that victims receive full compensation for the damage suffered; provide mandatory training on judicial proceedings for gender-based violence to all law enforcement and judiciary officials; to promote awareness on all forms of violence against women through campaigns.
- *Trafficking in human beings:* Italy should: step up efforts to prevent and combat trafficking in human beings, including by effectively implementing the 2016 National Anti-Trafficking Action Plan and providing protection for victims, including safe havens and psychosocial assistance; ensure that cases of trafficking in human beings are thoroughly investigated, and that suspected perpetrators are prosecuted and, if found guilty, punished appropriately; ensure that victims receive full compensation for the damage suffered.

D. Committee on the Elimination of Racial Discrimination

In 2017, the Committee held three sessions: 92nd (24 April – 12 May), 93rd (31 July – 25 August) and 94th (20 November – 8 December). During the 92nd session, the reports of Armenia, Bulgaria, Cyprus, Finland, Kenya,

Republic of Moldova were analysed; in the 93rd, the reports of Canada, Djibouti, Ecuador, Kuwait, New Zealand, Russian Federation, Tajikistan, United Arab Emirates; in the 94th, those of Algeria, Australia, Belarus, Jordan, Serbia, Slovakia. During the year, no General Recommendations were adopted.

The last periodic report of Italy was discussed by the Committee in December 2016, during its 91st session (see Yearbook 2017, p. 174-177). Italy is expected to present its twenty-first report in 2019.

E. Committee on the Elimination of Discrimination against Women

In 2017, the Committee held three sessions: 66th (13 February – 3 March), 67th (3-21 July) and 68th (23 October – 17 November). During the 66th session, the reports of El Salvador, Germany, Ireland, Jordan, Micronesia, Rwanda, Sri Lanka, Ukraine were analysed; in the 67th, those of Barbados, Costa Rica, Italy, Montenegro, Niger, Nigeria, Romania, Thailand; in the 68th, those of Burkina Faso, Democratic People's Republic of Korea, Guatemala, Israel, Kenya, Kuwait, Monaco, Nauru, Norway, Oman, Paraguay, Singapore. Two General Recommendations were also adopted: No. 35 on gender-based violence against women; No. 36 on women's and girls' right to education.

Latest Report Submitted by Italy

Reporting round	Report No. VII
Scheduled date for the submission of the Report	01/07/2015
Actual date of submission of the Report	27/10/2015
Report	CEDAW/C/ITA/7
List of themes	CEDAW/C/ITA/Q/7
Summary of the debate	CEDAW/C/SR.1502, CEDAW/C/SR.1503
Concluding observations	CEDAW/C/ITA/CO/7
Date of discussion of the Report	4 July 2017, during 67th Session the Committee (3-21 July 2017)

The Committee examined the report VII of Italy during its 67th session (3-21 July 2017). The following civil society organisations submitted their reports to the Committee: 21 July Association, Global Initiative to the End of the Corporal Punishment of Children, Human Rights Watch,

Italian Disability Forum, Italian Network for Women's Rights, CEDAW Work in Progress Platform, StopIGM Italy. At the end of the discussion, the following concluding observations and recommendations were adopted:

- *Refugee women and asylum seekers:* The Committee, recalling General Recommendation No. 32 (2014) on gender-related dimensions of refugee status, asylum, nationality and statelessness of women, calls on Italy to adopt individual screening and evaluation procedures that are attentive to gender, cultural origin and age, in order to guarantee a systematic and timely identification of refugees and asylum seekers, in particular women and girls who have been or are at risk of gender-based violence; increase the number of places in reception centres and ensure adequate reception standards for refugees and asylum seekers, with particular attention to the needs of women and girls; provide adequate services to refugees and asylum seekers placed in administrative detention, in particular women with specific needs and vulnerabilities; ensure that migration-related detention is only applied as a last resort measure, determined on a case-by-case basis and imposed for the shortest possible period; scrupulously observe the principle of non-refoulement for all women and girls in need of international protection, by modifying the procedures to ensure that no individual is expelled without an individualised risk assessment; increase collaboration and financial support for civil society organisations working with refugee women and asylum seekers; continue to allow NGOs' emergency ships to dock at Italian ports and the people rescued to disembark; pursue and strengthen cooperation with the countries of the region, in particular the EU Member States, with sharing economic burdens and provide for the needs of refugees, including resettlement and opportunities for humanitarian admission.
- *Legislative framework and access to justice:* The Committee, recalling General Recommendation No. 33 (2015) on women's access to justice, urges Italy to strengthen the legislative framework on gender equality and eliminate any discrimination based on gender; amend article 3 of the Constitution and l. 205/1993 to protect LBTI women from intersectoral forms of discrimination or hate crime; speed up judicial proceedings and improve the treatment of women who are victims of violence by eliminating gender stereotypes in the judicial system; to ensure that complex forms of discrimination are adequately dealt with by the courts, including through the training of judges and lawyers.
- *Women, peace and security:* The Committee recommends harmonising the legislation governing the control of arms exports with article 7 (4) of the International Arms Trade Treaty and the common position of the Council of the European Union 2008/944/CFSP, common rules for the control of exports of technology and military equipment. The Committee calls on Italy to integrate a gender dimension in its strategic dialogues with countries that purchase weapons produced in Italy, and to conduct, before granting export licenses, complete and transparent assessments on the impact on women of the abuse of small arms and light weapons.

- *National Machinery for the advancement of women*: Italy is invited to: increase the resources allocated to the Department for Equal Opportunities and consider the possibility of re-establishing the Ministry for Equal Opportunities as the highest government application suitable to initiate, coordinate and implement gender equality policies; accelerate the adoption and effective implementation of a national gender policy, ensuring that the gender dimension is applied consistently in the formulation and implementation of all laws, regulations, and programmes of ministries and decentralised government structures; strengthen coordination between national institutions, clearly defining the mandate and responsibility of each institution in relation to women's rights, and regular monitoring of such coordination; guarantee the full compliance of the Department for family policies with the principles established by the Convention.
- *National institutions for human rights:* Recalling its previous recommendations, the Committee calls on Italy to create a national human rights institution without further delay, in accordance with the Paris Principles.
- *Stereotypes:* Italy is called to adopt a proactive and adequately supported global strategy to eliminate or modify patriarchal attitudes and gender stereotypes, with particular attention to women of minorities who are often the subject of acts that incite hatred and racist violence, through reviewing school textbooks and curriculum and producing awareness campaigns for women and men in general, media and advertising agencies in particular.
- *Gender-based violence against women:* Recalling its General Recommendations No. 19 (1992) on violence against women and No. 35 (2017) on gender-based violence against women, the Committee recommends that Italy rapidly adopt organic legislation to prevent, combat, and punish all forms of violence against women and approve the new national Action Plan against gender-based violence, ensuring that adequate human, technical and financial resources are allocated for the implementation, monitoring and systematic evaluation of these instruments; monitor the adequacy of the police and judiciary reactions to complaints about sexual offenses; introduce mandatory training for judges, prosecutors, police officers and other law enforcement officers on the application of criminal law provisions on gender-based violence against women and on the use of gender-sensitive questioning procedures for women victims of violence; encourage women to report incidents of domestic and sexual violence to law enforcement agencies, avoiding any stigmatisation of victims and ensuring that women have effective access to the courts to obtain restraining orders against those convicted of such crimes; ensure that alternative dispute resolution mechanisms, such as mediation, conciliation and restorative justice, are not used by the courts in cases of gender-based violence, as they may be an obstacle to women's access to justice through harmonising the relevant national legislation with the Istanbul Convention; ensure that racist, xenophobic and sexist acts against women are thoroughly investigated, that those offenders are prosecuted and that sentences are commensurate with the gravity of the crime; improve the protection and assistance provided to women victims of violence, promoting a network of safe shelters throughout

the country and strengthening the cooperation of the state with NGOs that offer shelter and rehabilitation to victims; collect statistical data on domestic and sexual violence disaggregated by gender, age, nationality and relationship between the victim and the offender.

- *Trafficking and exploitation of prostitution:* Gender-sensitivity; investigate, prosecute and punish all cases of trafficking in human beings, especially women and girls, ensuring that the sentences imposed on the perpetrators are commensurate with the gravity of the crime; adopt appropriate mechanisms for the immediate identification of victims of trafficking, so that they can receive protection and assistance in a coordinated manner after arrival by sea and throughout the asylum procedure; allocate adequate resources for the effective and sustainable implementation of the existing protection system for victims of trafficking, in particular migrant women, refugees and asylum seekers; preventing and combating all forms of exploitation related to trafficking, in particular sexual exploitation and forced labour, servitude and modern forms of slavery; provide victims of trafficking with adequate access to health and psychological care, providing technical, financial and human resources to these services; to ensure that victims of trafficking, regardless of their ethnic, national or social origin and legal status, obtain adequate protection, compensation and rehabilitation; strengthen the assistance provided to women and girls wishing to abandon prostitution, providing them with opportunities to generate alternative income and step up efforts to reduce the demand for prostitution, sensitising clients on the desperate situation of those providing these services; strengthen measures to address the root causes of trafficking, such as poverty and high unemployment among women and girls; continue the efforts of international, regional and bilateral cooperation with countries of origin, transit and destination, including through information exchange and the harmonisation of procedures, to prevent trafficking and to bring those responsible to justice.
- *Participation in public and political life:* Italy should strengthen the representation of women in top positions in political life, in the judicial system, in boards of directors and in public administration; introduce gender equality into both parliamentary chambers in the reform of the electoral law; intensify awareness campaigns for politicians, journalists, teachers and the general public on the importance of full, equitable, free and democratic participation of women on the basis of equality with men in political and public life as a prerequisite for the full implementation of the women's human rights; consider adopting specific legislation to combat political harassment and sexist attacks.
- *Statelessness:* The Committee recommends that Italy adopt the Senate bill 2148 aimed at introducing an organic law on the exercise of the rights of stateless persons; remove obstacles and procedural difficulties and improve procedures for the identification and protection of stateless persons, especially women and children; facilitate access to nationality for stateless persons, with particular attention to women and girls; allow children of stateless persons not formally recognised, including single mothers, to obtain Italian nationality; guarantee

the retroactive application of the law on nationality so that children whose parents have been officially recognised stateless after their birth can obtain Italian nationality.

- *Education:* Italy is invited to break down the discriminatory stereotypes and structural barriers that keep girls away from fields traditionally dominated by men, including mathematics, computer science and natural sciences; ensure that all gender stereotypes are removed from textbooks and that school curriculum, university programmes and vocational training for teachers deal with women's rights and gender equality; complete and implement national education guidelines for affection, sexuality and reproductive health, in line with the European Sexual Education Standards developed by the Regional Office of the World Health Organization for Europe; take effective measures to promote school attendance of girls of Roma origin, including through temporary special measures, such as grants and free supply of textbooks, by conducting a gender impact assessment of the implementation of the National Strategy for Inclusion of Roma, Sinti and Travellers.
- *Work:* The Committee recommends that Italy take all measures, including temporary special measures (positive discrimination: article 4 of the Convention and General Recommendation No. 25 of the Committee) in order to achieve substantial equality between women and men in the labour market; take effective measures, including professional training and incentives, to encourage women to work in non-traditional sectors and eliminate occupational segregation, both horizontal and vertical, in the public and private sectors; take steps to narrow down and close the wage gap between men and women; increasing women's access to full-time employment, including by promoting the fair distribution of domestic and family tasks between men and women, providing more and better childcare facilities and increasing incentives for men taking parental leave; adopt temporary special measures to promote equal participation of women in the labour market, particularly of migrant women, refugees and asylum seekers, Roma, Sinti, Travellers, elderly women, single mothers and women with disabilities, and undertake efforts on employment and on the working conditions of these women.
- *Women migrant workers:* Italy is invited to guarantee an effective implementation of the law to combat undeclared work and exploitation of labour in the agricultural sector; strengthen the capacity of the State Labour Inspectorate to implement legislation to combat the exploitation of labour, monitoring the working conditions of women on farms and preventing cases of sexual exploitation and ensuring that employers who abuse migrant women's rights are punished; establish effective procedures to allow migrant women to file complaints against their employers without fear of reprisals, arrest, detention or deportation, modifying for this purpose lgs.d. 22 June 2007, No. 109 (a.k.a. Rosarno law); provide access to fundamental services to all women migrant workers, regardless of their immigration status.
- *Health:* Recalling its General Recommendation No. 24 (1999) on women and health, the Committee urges Italy to increase the budget for the health sector, in order to ensure the full realisation of the right to health, including

sexual and reproductive rights, for all women and girls; ensure that the essential levels of assistance are respected uniformly throughout the national territory; increase the budget for the prevention of sexually transmitted infections, especially HIV, and improve access to new generations of contraceptives, including by ensuring coverage by the national health service; guarantee the full application of the l. 194/78 throughout the national territory, making sure that the exercise of conscientious objection by health personnel does not represent an obstacle for women wishing to terminate a pregnancy; develop and implement a health care protocol based on rights for intersex children, ensuring that children and their parents are adequately informed of all options; that children are involved, as far as possible, in the decision-making process on medical interventions to be undertaken; that their choices are respected and that no child is subjected to unnecessary interventions or treatments.

- *Women with disabilities:* Italy should adopt specific measures to promote the access of women with disabilities to inclusive education, the open labour market, health care, public and social life and decision-making processes; to increase and effectively apply the quotas reserved for persons with disabilities in public and private companies to promote inclusion, especially for women with disabilities, in the open labour market; increase financial support for women with disabilities, to enable them to live independently throughout the country; implement awareness-raising campaigns and promote appropriate training for public officials on the special rights and needs of women and girls with disabilities.
- *Women in custody:* Recalling the United Nations Rules on the treatment of women prisoners and non-custodial measures for women who commit crimes (a.k.a. Bangkok Rules), the Committee recommends Italy to collect disaggregated data on the number of women detained, even in preventive and administrative detention, and provide information on their conditions of detention, in particular on access to basic health and social services; develop mandatory training programmes for prison staff on gender equality, dignity and women's rights; assigning human, technical and financial resources to expand the opportunities for education, employment and access to health services for women in detention; provide alternative measures to detention, especially for pregnant women and mothers with young children, taking into account the best interests of the child.
- *Marriage and family relationships:* The Committee urges Italy to discourage the use of "parental alienation syndrome" theory by experts and courts in custody cases and custody of children (it is a controversial psychological theory that recognises a behavioural disorder in the child involved in the conflict between parents and that, prompted by one of the two, refuses the figure of the other); to adequately address the specific needs of women and children in determining child custody in cases of gender-based violence in the domestic sphere; to ensure that women are fully aware and informed about the consequences of premarital agreements regarding the distribution of property upon divorce or separation; establish a mechanism that takes into account the disparity in earning capacity and personal potential between separated spouses, a conse-

quence of the greater investment of women in childcare and domestic work at the expense of their careers.

F. Committee on the Rights of the Child

In 2017, the Committee held three sessions: 74th (16 January – 3 February), 75th (15 May – 2 June) and 76th (12-29 September). During the 74th session the reports of Barbados, Central African Republic, Democratic Republic of Congo, Estonia, Georgia, Malawi, Saint Vincent and Grenadines, Serbia were analysed; in the 75th the reports of Antigua and Barbuda, Bhutan, Cameroon, Lebanon, Mongolia, Qatar, Romania; in the 76th the reports of the People's Democratic Republic of Korea, Denmark, Ecuador, Republic of Moldova, Tajikistan, Vanuatu. Three General comments were also adopted: No. 21 on children in street conditions; No. 22 in the context of international migration – general principles; No. 23 in the context of international migration – obligations of States Parties with particular reference to countries of transit and destination.

Italy presented (yet to be discussed) its latest report in July 2017.

Latest Report Submitted by Italy

Reporting round	Joint Reports No. V and VI
Scheduled date for the submission of the Report	04/04/2017
Actual date for the submission of the Report	05/07/2017
Report	CRC/C/ITA/5-6

The report outlines the policies and programmes for children and adolescents carried out by the Italian government in the period 2008-2016 and is divided into 11 sections: general application measures; definition of a child; general principles; civil rights and freedom; violence against children; family environment and alternative assistance; disability, health and basic services; educational, cultural and leisure activities; special protection measures; implementation of the Optional Protocol concerning the sale of children, child prostitution and pornography; implementation of the Optional Protocol concerning the involvement of children in armed conflicts.

The drafting of the report has benefited from the survey work on the condition of children and adolescents in Italy, carried out by the National Centre for documentation and analysis for children and adolescents for the preparation of the Regular Report to Parliament, as well as the outcomes of the comparison exercises and thematic analysis carried out by the working groups of the National Observatory on Childhood and Adolescence on the occasion of the drafting of the IV National Action Plan for Children and Adolescents.

G. Committee on the Rights of Persons with Disabilities

In 2017, the Committee held two sessions, the 17th (20 March – 12 April) and the 18th (14 August – 1 September). During the 17th session, the reports of Armenia, Bosnia Herzegovina, Canada, Cyprus, Honduras, Iran, Jordan, Republic of Moldova were analysed; in the 18th, the relations of Latvia, Luxembourg, Montenegro, Morocco, Panama, United Kingdom. During the year, General Comment No. 5 on the right to independent life (article 19 of the Convention) was adopted.

The last periodic report of Italy was discussed by the Committee in August 2016, during its 16th session (see *Yearbook 2017*, p. 178-182). Italy is bound to present the second, third and fourth periodic reports jointly in May 2023.

H. Committee on Enforced Disappearances

In 2017, the Committee held two sessions, the 12th (6-17 March) and the 13th (4-15 September), during which the closing remarks were made regarding Cuba, Ecuador and Senegal (12th session), Gabon and Lithuania (11th session).

Italy is required to present its first periodic report in 2018.

VI. Specialised United Nations Agencies, Programmes and Funds

A. International Labor Organization (ILO)

Established by the Treaty of Versailles in 1919, the ILO became the first specialised agency of the United Nations in 1946.

> The ILO is devoted to promoting decent and productive work for men and women in conditions of freedom, equality, safety and dignity. Its chief objectives are: to promote rights at work, to encourage decent employment opportunities, to enhance social protection and to strengthen dialogue on work-related issues. The ILO is the only United Nations agency which has a tripartite structure: representatives of Governments, employers and workers

jointly elaborate the policies and programmes of the Organisation. 185 States are members of the ILO.

Since its foundation, the ILO has adopted 189 conventions. Of these, the ILO has identified 8 which it defines as "fundamental" or "core" (No. 29 on Forced Labour, 1930; No. 87 on Freedom of Association and Protection of the Right to Organise, 1948; No. 98 on the Right to Organise and Collective Bargaining, 1949; No. 100 on Equal Remuneration for Men and Women Workers for Work of Equal Value, 1951; No. 105 on the Abolition of Forced Labour, 1957; No. 111 on the Elimination of All Forms of Discrimination in Employment, Occupation, Vocational Training and Terms and Conditions of Employment, 1958; No. 138 on the Minimum Age for Admission to Employment or Work, 1973; and No. 182 on the Elimination of the Worst Forms of Child Labour, 1999) and 4 defined as "priority" (or "governance": No. 81 on Labour Inspection, 1947; No. 122 on Employment Policy, 1964; No. 129 on Labour Inspection [Agriculture], 1969; and No. 144 on Tripartite Consultation [International Labour Standards], 1976).

Italy has been a member of the ILO since 1919 (amongst the founding members); it withdrew from the Organisation in 1937 but joined again permanently in 1945. The ILO is present in Italy with its offices in Rome, which have been operating since 1920, and the International Training Centre, established in Turin in 1965.

Italy has ratified 113 conventions adopted by the ILO (of which 82 in force and 31 denounced), including the 8 fundamental ones, the 4 priority ones and 101 of the 177 technical conventions.

In order to monitor the application of conventions ratified by States, in 1926, the ILO established the Committee of Experts on the Application of Conventions and Recommendations, a body made up of twenty eminent jurists and social professionals, who are independent of Governments and appointed on individual merits. The monitoring mechanism requires each Member State to submit periodic reports on the steps they have taken, in law and in practice, to apply each of the conventions it has ratified. At the same time, Governments are required to submit copies of their reports to employers' and workers' organisations, which are entitled to make comments and supply further information. Government reports are initially examined by the Committee of Experts, which can make two different kinds of comments: observations and direct requests. The observations contain comments on fundamental questions raised by the application of a particular convention by a State, and are published in the Committee's annual report. On the other hand, direct requests relate to more technical requests or requests for further information; they are not published in the report but are communicated directly to the Governments concerned.

Upon conclusion of its considerations, the Committee presents an annual report to the International Labour Conference, the most representative body of the ILO, comprising representatives from all the ILO Member States and including all its observations and recommendations, which are carefully examined by the Conference Committee on the Application of Standards, a tripartite standing committee made up of Government, employer and worker delegates. This Committee selects a number of observations from the report for more in-depth discussion. The Governments referred to in these comments are invited to respond before the Conference Committee to provide information on the situation in question. In many cases, the Conference Committee adopts conclusions recommending that Governments take specific steps to remedy a problem or to invite the ILO to come on a mission to their Country or to request technical assistance.

In 2017, Italy received six direct requests and three observations by the Committee of Experts on the application of the Conventions and Recommendations.

With direct requests, the Committee can obtain further information on the legislative, administrative and political instruments related to the implementation of the following conventions: No. 94 – Labour clauses (public contracts); No. 97 – Migrant workers (revised); No. 100 – Equal remuneration; No. 111 – Discrimination (employment and profession); No. 122 – Employment policy; No. 143 – Migrant workers (additional provisions).

The observation was relative to Convention No. 181 – Private Employment Agencies.

Convention No. 111 on discrimination (employment and profession).

- *Article 1: discrimination based on sex.* The Committee requests the Italian Government to provide information on the specific measures adopted pursuant to lgs.d 80/2015 and of r.l. No. 81/2017 and their impact on reducing the incidence of resignation among working women. Noting that, in light of the disproportionate impact of the practice of "blank dismissal" on women with children under 3, the reasons provided by women to validate their resignation may conceal a structural form of discrimination against women based on pregnancy and maternity, the Committee calls on the government to step up its efforts to prevent and eliminate all forms of discrimination against women based on such basis and to supply information on specific measures taken to this point.
- *Article 2: equality of opportunity and treatment regardless of race, colour, or nationality.* While appreciating the information provided by the government on the number of initiatives taken over time to combat discrimination and promote equal opportunities and treatment, the Committee notes an ongoing absence of specific information on the practical application of these rules and the results they produce, which prevents the Committee from assessing progress made in pursuing the objectives of the Convention. The Committee encourages the government to collect data to this effect and to provide information on exercises of UNAR.

Convention No. 135 on workers' representatives.

The Committee calls on the Italian Government to continue providing updated information on the number of port workers, broken down by gender, age and type of contract, and on the results achieved in implementing the national strategic port work and logistics plan and on the measures taken to promote cooperation between the social partners in order to improve the efficiency of work in ports (article 5).

Convention No. 413 on migrant workers (additional provisions).

- *Migrants in irregular conditions.* While recognising the broad scale of this phenomenon and the efforts of the Italian government to find appropriate solutions, the Committee asks the government to continue taking all necessary measures to promote national cooperation (with workers and employers' organisations), bilateral, multilateral and regional to address the issue of irregular immigration in full respect of the human rights of migrant workers, and to prosecute and punish those who organise irregular flow of migrants.
- *Minimum standards of protection: access to justice.* The Committee asks the government to indicate the specific meaning of the concept of "particularly exploitative working conditions", as per article 1(1)(b) of lgs.d. 109/2012, and to provide information on how migrant workers who find themselves in an irregular situation can seek compensation from the courts regarding the violation of their rights deriving from previous employment, including non-payment or underpayment of wages, social security and other benefits. The Committee also calls on the government to provide information on how to ensure adequate legal defense for irregular migrant workers, as well as on inspections in the construction, agriculture and other sectors to detect irregular employment of migrants.
- *National policies on equal opportunities and treatment of regular migrant workers.* The Committee asks the government to continue to provide information on developments related to national policies on equal opportunities and the treatment of migrant workers, including all forms of cooperation with employers' and workers' organisations. The Committee also calls on the government to indicate the impact of the actions taken to implement these policies, starting from the 2007-2013 multi-annual programme, any obstacles encountered and the measures taken to close the pay gap between national and migrant workers, in particular in sectors where the gap is higher.

In 2017, Italy contributed 3.75% to the ILO's regular budget, with a sum of around 17 million Swiss francs. For the two-year period 2016-2017, Italy allocated a further voluntary contribution to the ordinary budget of $451,000, appearing among the eight donor countries, together with Belgium, Denmark, Germany, Luxembourg, the Netherlands, Norway and Sweden.

B. United Nations Educational, Scientific and Cultural Organisation (UNESCO)

The human rights which fall under the responsibility of UNESCO are the right to education, the right to benefit from scientific progress, the right to participate freely in cultural life and the right to information, including freedom of opinion and expression. In connection with these, the right to freedom of thought, conscience and religion, the right to seek, receive and impart information and ideas through any instrument and across borders, the right to protection of the moral and material interests resulting from any scientific, literary or artistic production are pertinent, as are the right to freedom of assembly and association.

Italy has been a member of UNESCO since 1948. In 2017, Amb. Vincenza Lomonaco was Italy's Permanent Representative to UNESCO. Since its establishment, UNESCO has adopted 28 conventions, 20 of which have been ratified by Italy.

In the field of education, it should be noted that in 1991, the 26th General Conference of UNESCO established the International Programme for University Cooperation (IUC – International University Cooperation). The Programme works to foster the creation of a network of centres of excellence (UNESCO Chairs) able to implement advanced teaching and research programmes in disciplines related to UNESCO policies, with particular reference to the issues of peace and human rights, democracy and intercultural dialogue. There are over 700 UNESCO Chairs created all over the world; in 2017 in Italy there are 25 Chairs (as in 2016), 3 of which deal specifically with human rights, reporting the wording in the denomination: Chair "Human Rights, Democracy and Peace", established in 1999 at the University of Padova; Chair "Human Rights and Ethics of International Cooperation", established in 2003 at the University of Bergamo; Chair "Bioethics and Human Rights", established in 2009 at the Pontifical Athenaeum "Regina Apostolorum", European University of Rome.

In the field of bioethics, two committees operate at UNESCO: the International Bioethics Committee (IBC) and the Intergovernmental Bioethics Committee (IGBC).

The IBC was established in 1993, particularly thanks to the efforts of Director-General of UNESCO at that time. It is a body made up of 36 independent experts coming from different geographical and disciplinary backgrounds. Its mission is to follow progress in life science and its applications in order to ensure respect for human dignity and human rights and to promote reflection on the ethical and legal issues raised by research in the life sciences and their applications. To this end, over the years the IBC has published a number of recommendations and other documents, the most significant of which is the Universal Declaration on Bioethics and Human Rights, adopted by the UNESCO General Conference in 2005.

The IGBC was created in 1998 pursuant to article 11 of the IBC Statute. It is comprised of 36 Member States who are elected by the UNESCO General Conference and meets at least once every two years to examine the proposals and recommendations of the IBC and to forward these proposals, accompanied by its own opinions, to the other UNESCO Member States.

As in previous years, in 2017, Italy contributed about 4.5% of the regular budget of UNESCO (which covers the regular expenses for the maintenance of the staff and for the main activities of the Organisation), with an equal amount of approximately $14.4 million, ranking in seventh place among the main contributors of the Organisation. In 2017, Italy is not among the countries that have made voluntary extra-budget donations (with which the multiannual cooperation programmes managed by UNESCO are financed).

UNESCO Machinery

Italy was not involved with any of the organisation's monitoring mechanisms in 2017.

C. The Food and Agriculture Organisation of the United Nations (FAO)

The FAO was established in 1945 in Ville de Quebec, Canada, and has its headquarters in Rome. José Graziano da Silva (Brazil) has been the Director-general of the Organisation since 1 January 2012. The Organisation budget for the biennium 2018-2019 has amounted to $2.6 billion.

As of 30 November 2017, Italy was the seventh largest contributor to the FAO with over $12 million in contributions. Italy collaborates with the FAO through the FAO/Italy Cooperation Programme, whose main components, financed by Italian voluntary contributions, are the traditional programme; the Italian Trust Fund for food security and the decentralised cooperation programme.

D. World Health Organization (WHO)

The primary objective of the Organisation, established in 1948, is the attainment by all peoples of the highest possible level of health, understood not as the absence of disease but as a state of complete physical, mental and social well-being.

In Italy, there is a WHO office (Venice), while 22 collaborating centres are currently accredited. The latter, specialised institutions to which the WHO does not grant any funding, are identified by the WHO Director General and are part of a worldwide network of organisational support in the various medical-scientific fields. In Italy, their activity is coordinated by the Ministry of Health.

On 13 September 2017, Italy and the WHO signed the first national cooperation strategy. This document, which covers the period 2017-2022, defines a medium-term strategic framework for bilateral cooperation in the context of the 2030 Agenda for Sustainable Development. The document includes 4 strategic priorities:

- implement the Health 2020 agenda, with particular reference to: governance and leadership; support Italian health policies; tackle inequalities to address the social determinants of health, refugee and migrant health, climate change, the environment and health;
- promote well-being throughout life, addressing and mitigating the impact of major risk factors for non-transmittable diseases, and governing innovation of the national health system on the basis of results in the field of genomics;
- address transmittable diseases through the approach of *One Health*, including the implementation of the national vaccination plan and support for strengthening global responses to international health emergencies;
- strengthen the role of Italy as a donor country in the global health field, through the WHO global programs and through greater collaboration between the WHO and Italy in the countries considered as priorities by the Italian Development Cooperation Agency.

The first "Summer School on Refugee and Migrant Health" of the WHO Regional Office for Europe took place in Syracuse from 10-14 July 2017. The Summer School was the starting point to learn about and improve the way the WHO Regional Office protects and promotes the health of refugees and migrants.

E. United Nations Development Program (UNDP)

The United Nations Development Programme (UNDP) was established by the General Assembly in 1965 and has the role of central agency for the coordination and funding of development cooperation of the United Nations system.

UNDP action pursues the general objective of "human development", understood as not only economic growth but also as social development, based on gender equality and respect for human rights. UNDP conducts research and analysis, preparing studies and reports. Of the most significant, worth noting are the Annual Report on Human Development and the report on the state of achievement of the Sustainable Development Goals.

In 2017, Italy contributed about $5.9 million to the UNDP's regular budget, keeping it in 16th place among the major contributing countries.

F. United Nations Environment Program (UN-Environment)

UN-Environment is the leading global environmental authority that defines the global environmental agenda, promotes the coherent implementation of the environmental dimension of sustainable development within the system of nations. Its mission is to coordinate and promote the creation of a global partnership for the development of projects and activities to protect the environment so that nations and peoples can improve their quality of life without compromising that of future generations.

Erik Solheim has been the Director General since 13 May 2016. The Representative at the UN-Environment and also the Head of Mission of the Italian Embassy in Nairobi is Amb. Mauro Massoni.

On 6 February 2017, the "Financing the future" report, the final product of the "National Dialogue for Sustainable Finance" launched by the Ministry of the Environment and the Protection of the Territory and the Sea, was presented in Rome, thanks to the collaboration with UN-Environment. It aimed at taking stock of the best financial systems and mechanisms available for measures to combat climate change and reduce greenhouse gas emissions, as well as to contribute to the development of renewable energy.

G. United Nations Program for Human Settlements (UN-HABITAT)

United Nations Program for Human Settlements, UN-HABITAT is invested with the mission to foster sustainable urbanisation from the social and environmental point of view with the ultimate aim of guaranteeing everyone the right to decent housing. The current General Director is Maimunah Mohd Sharif (Malaysia), succeeding Joan Clos (Spain) in December 2017; the representative at the UN-HABITAT and also the head mission of the Italian Embassy in Nairobi is Amb. Mauro Massoni.

UN-HABITAT works in close collaboration with local authorities, including Municipalities, Provinces and Regions, thanks above all to the special report established with UNACLA, the UN Advisory Committee on Local Authorities. The latter is made up of mayors and representatives of umbrella organisations of local authorities chosen by the UN-HABITAT Director-General on the basis of their competence and commitment in implementing the UN agenda on human settlements.

H. United Nations Children's Fund (UNICEF)

UNICEF is the permanent fund of the United Nations which is assigned the mandate to protect and promote the rights of children, girls and adolescents with the aim of improving their living conditions. Since 1 January 2018, the Executive Director is the American Henrietta H. Fore.

In Italy, the UNICEF Research Centre is located at the *Istituto degli Innocenti* in Florence. Since 1974, the Italian Committee for UNICEF has been working in Italy; it is a non-governmental organisation whose activities are overseen by a cooperation agreement signed with UNICEF International. Giacomo Guerrera has been President since November 2011.

In 2017, UNICEF employed a total of over $13 million received from Italy in programmes located in 24 different countries. In 2017, UNICEF spent $1.3 million received from the Italian Committee for UNICEF.

UNICEF has launched an extensive programme in Italy for migrant and refugee minors, in particular those not accompanied by adult family members, with the aim of providing assistance measures ranging from the very first reception to the transfer to smaller and more stable facilities, from monitoring human rights standards to school and cultural inclusion in local communities. In 2017, the action to improve reception standards and the technical and organisational support to local institutions was mainly concentrated in Calabria and Sicily.

Since the beginning of 2017, UNICEF has also been present on Italian Coast Guard ships, together with the NGO Intersos, to carry out activities in favor of migrant and refugee minors. The presence of UNICEF on board is foreseen by a Memorandum of Understanding signed in December 2016, which in turn is part of an agreement signed on 27 May 2016 with the Ministry of the Interior. As part of the rescue operations, UNICEF intervenes with teams composed of cultural mediators and other specialised operators, tasked with welcoming children, teenagers and mothers who have just been rescued by the Coast Guard crews on board.

On 30 May 2017, UNICEF and the Research Institute on Population and Social Policies of the National Research Council (CNR-IRPPS) launched the report "The Lost. Stories of minors arrived alone in Italy ". The report, whose goal is to unearth the migratory experience of minors and to reshape their journey to Italy, reveals that half of the migrant children in the world live in only 15 countries and that Italy, hosting 400 thousand minors, is in 20th place. According to the report, 12,360 unaccompanied minors were identified in Italy in 2015, equal to 75% of all minors disembarked, whereas in 2016, there were 25,846 identified, equal to 92% of minors disembarked. The latter arrived mainly from Syria, Eritrea, Egypt, and Somalia. A particularly significant figure in the report is that, over the last few years, the number of migrant minors who have gone missing after arriving in Italy is growing: they have gone from 1,754 in 2012 to 6,558 at the end of November 2016.

I. International Organization for Migration (IOM)

Established in 1951, the IOM is the major inter-governmental organisation which deals with migrant issues. Its mission is to promote orderly migration based on respect for human dignity; to this end, it collaborates with Governments and civil society.

> The IOM Coordination Office for the Mediterranean countries is based in Rome and the main activities of the IOM offices in Italy concern: providing assistance to vulnerable groups and minors, migration and employment; migration and health; migration, climate and development, reuniting families; supporting voluntary return; relocation and resettlement.

Dedicated to the economic contribution of the migrant population in Italy, the second Briefing of the IOM published in 2017. The Briefing, which collects and analyses the most up-to-date data from institutional and academic sources on the migratory presence in the Italian labour market, reveals that migrants are 10.5% of the workforce in Italy and produced about 9% of Italian GDP in 2016.

On 20 July 2017, the report prepared by the IOM Coordination Office for the "Trafficking in Human Beings through the Central Mediterranean Route" was published. According to the Report, the number of potential victims of trafficking for sexual exploitation arrived by sea in Italy has increased by 600% in the last three years. It is a rise that involves increasingly younger girls – often underage – who have already been subjected to violence and abuse on their way to Europe. According to the report, the phenomenon affects nearly 80% of girls arriving from Nigeria, whose number has increased from 1,500 in 2014 to over 11,000 in 2016.

Council of Europe*

Established on 5 May 1949, the Council of Europe (CoE, 47 Member States) is the first and most advanced regional system for the promotion and protection of human rights. The Permanent Representative of Italy to the Council of Europe is Amb. Marco Marsilli. The Italian official Gabriella Battaini-Dragoni holds the position of Deputy Secretary-General of the Organisation. Since 2011, Italy has been home to an external office of the CoE in Venice, whose international legal status was recognised in June 2017 following the signing of a Memorandum of Understanding between Italy and the Council of Europe. The activities of this office focus on the integration of minorities, gender equality, participation of citizens in democratic processes, the role of women in the Euro-Mediterranean context, the integration of the Roma and the Day of Remembrance.

In 2017, Italy made a contribution worth €34,984,652 to the activities of the CoE, €27,486,110 of which was allocated for the ordinary budget (In 2016, the total contribution was €34,721,576, €27,332,430 of which was allocated for the ordinary budget). In 2017, the voluntary contributions provided by Italy amounted to €590,318 (€587,328 in 2016).

The following pages will illustrate the activities of the Parliamentary Assembly and the Committee of Ministers with reference to Italy; those of six bodies established by a treaty: the European Court of Human Rights, the Committee for the Prevention of Torture, the European Committee of Social Rights, the Advisory Committee on the Framework Convention for the Protection of National Minorities, the Group of Experts on Action against Trafficking in Human Beings and Group of Experts on Action against Violence against Women and Domestic Violence; and of four bodies established by the Committee of Ministers: Commissioner for Human Rights, the European Commission against Racism and Intolerance, the European Commission for Democracy through Law and the Group of States against Corruption.

I. Parliamentary Assembly

In the Parliamentary Assembly of the Council of Europe (PACE), made up of delegations from the national parliaments of the Member

* Pietro de Perini

States of the CoE, 18 members of the Senate and the Chamber of Deputies sit for Italy; there are an equal number of alternate members.

PACE is a forum for discussing the main issues underlying the Organisation's mandate and it has advisory functions in relation to all international conventions drawn up in this context. It elects the judges of the European Court of Human Rights, the Commissioner for Human Rights, the Secretary General of the CoE and their deputy.

The following are the members and alternate members (a) of Italian PACE in 2017: Ferdinando Aiello (a), Francesco Maria Amoruso (a), Anna Ascani (a), Deborah Bergamini, Anna Maria Bernini, Maria Teresa Bertuzzi, Tamara Blazina (a), Nunzia Catalfo, Elena Centemero, Massimo Cervellini (a), Khalid Chaouki (a), Vannino Chiti, Eleonora Cimbro (a), Paolo Corsini, Luca D'Alessandro (a), Cristina De Pietro (a), Manlio Di Stefano, Sergio Divina, Claudio Fazzone (a), Giuseppe Galati (a), Adriana Galgano (a), Adele Gambaro, Florian Kronbichler, Francesco Maria Giro, Carlo Lucherini (a), Emanuela Munerato (a), Michele Nicoletti, Luis Alberto Orellana (a), Laura Puppato (a), Lia Quartapelle Procopio, Andrea Rigoni, Vincenzo Santangelo, Milena Santerini, Maria Edera Spadoni (a), Francesco Verducci (a), Sandra Zampa (a).

The President of the Italian delegation was Michele Nicoletti who in January 2018 was appointed as the President of the Parliamentary Assembly. With reference to the role of Italian MPs in the various committees of PACE, in 2017, Manlio Di Stefano was President of the Subcommittee on Children and Youth Refugees and Migrants and Andrea Rigoni was President of the Subcommittee on Diasporas (both are part of the Committee on Migration, Refugees and and Displaced Persons).

As concerns the actions of the Italian members of the Parliamentary Assembly in 2017, six reports were submitted to the relevant membership committees on the basis of which PACE subsequently adopted a series of resolutions and/or recommendations: the report by Adele Gambaro on *online media and journalism: challenges and responsibilities* (presented on 9 January 2017, Resolution 2143 adopted on 25 January 2017); Andrea Rigoni's reports on *Migration as an opportunity for European development* (presented on 7 June 2017, Recommendations 2108 and 2109 and Resolutions 2173 and 2175 adopted on 28 June 2017) and on the *Situation in Belarus* (presented on 6 June 2017, Recommendation 2107 and Resolution 2172 adopted on 27 June 2017); Eleonora Cimbro's report on *Youth Against Corruption* (presented on 15 September 2017, Resolution 2192 adopted on 13 October 2017); Michele Nicoletti's reports on the *Request for a summit of the Council of Europe to reaffirm European unity and to defend and promote democratic security in Europe* (presented on 15 September, Recommendations 2113 and 2114 and Resolution 2168 adopted on 11 October 2017) and on *Promoting integrity in governance to counter political corruption* (presented on 16 June 2017, Recommendation 2105 and Resolution 2170 adopted on 27 June 2017).

Among the resolutions adopted by PACE in 2017, Resolution 2174 on the *Implications for Human Rights of the European Response to Transit Migration through the Mediterranean* (adopted on 28 June 2017, rapporteur: Miltiadis Varvitsiotis) makes a specific reference to Italy. After underlining the benefits of the implementation of the 2016 EU-Turkey agreement for Greece, the Resolution notes that this agreement and the closure of the borders on the Western Balkans route had no impact on the central Mediterranean route between Northern Africa and Italy. In fact, the number of arrivals to Italy increased by 30% in the first months of 2017 while the reception conditions and the protection procedures for asylum seekers in the country, although improving, still require urgent action. In particular, while the level of search and rescue operations ought be maintained, the European Union should increase its efforts in order to effectively combat the networks of traffickers operating in the Mediterranean and to increase cooperation with the Libyan Coast Guard on guaranteeing an effective respect, on both sides, of the essential provisions of international human rights law (right to leave a country, the right to seek asylum and the prohibition of refoulement). PACE stresses that the lack of safe routes causes enormous risks for refugees and migrant seeking to cross the sea; for this reason, use of the existing legal arrangements for entering Europe (such as family reunification or resettlement) would contribute substantially to reducing irregular migrations across the Mediterranean.

In addition to addressing suggestions and requests to the European Union and Greece, the PACE resolution includes a series of specific recommendations for the Italian authorities. Concerning the reception conditions, Italy is requested to: increase the number of suitable facilities to accommodate unaccompanied minors and other vulnerable asylum seekers and to process their requests for protection; ensure that asylum seekers are not held in hotspots for periods longer than permitted by the law; increase the number of places in permanent shelters and to avoid the use of temporary facilities for long-term accommodation; establish national standards for refugee centres and camps by enhancing transparency and monitoring processes; and make a commitment to the prevention and combating of sexual violence, gender-based violence and all types of exploitation occuring in refugee centres. The report of the procedures of the request for international protection, PACE requires the Italian authorities to review the asylum requirements in order to enhance their effectiveness in light of the significantly increased number of requests and to ensure that the appeal systems are compliant to the procedural requirements of an effective remedy; to urgently address the problem related to the examination of the requests for protection presented by unaccompanied children and, in particular, to clarify the procedures that allow their relocation and guarantee a rapid implementation of the "Zampa law" on unaccompanied children (l. of 2017).

II. Committee of Ministers

On the subject of human rights, the Committee of Ministers (CM) relies on the work of the Steering Committee for Human Rights, an intergovernmental body composed of representatives of the 47 Member States which performs, among other things, standard-setting and follow-up.

> The CM adopts recommendations regarding the Member States and on matters for which a common policy is agreed upon – in accordance with its role in the implementation of the European Social Charter (article 29) – with the aim of asking some States to adapt their laws and public policies with the provisions contained in the Charter. In addition, it is ultimately responsible for monitoring the Framework Convention on National Minorities (article 26). In this context, it adopts specific resolutions by Country based on the opinions of the Advisory Committee of the Framework Convention.
>
> With regard to its role in relation to the European Court of Human Rights, the CM has the function of supervising the execution of judgments of the Court, ensuring that Member States act in accordance with the rulings issued by the same. The Committee terminates each case by adopting a final resolution. Finally, the CM may apply to the Court for a ruling on issues related to difficulties of interpretation of the judgments of the Court itself which would impede their implementation and if it finds that a Member State fails to comply with a final judgment, it may refer the issue to the Court.

In 2017, the CM adopted 18 final resolutions on the execution of the ECtHR judgments by Italy: CM/ResDH(2017)6 on the case *Ganci and other 12 cases*, CM/ResDH(2017)80 on the case *Di Belmonte and 1 other case*, CM/ResDH(2017)104 on the case *Centro Europa 7 SRL and Di Stefano*, CM/ResDH(2017)103 on the case *Maiorano and others*, CM/ResDH(2017)121 on the case *Anghel*, CM/ResDH(2017)138 on the case *Belvedere Alberghiera SRL and 106 others cases*, CM/ResDH(2017)182 on the case *Oliari et al*, CM/ResDH(2017)157 on the case *Ceni*, CM/ResDH(2017)156 on the case *Pilla*, CM/ResDH(2017)207 on the case *Baratta*, CM/ResDH(2017)206 on the case *Gallardo Sanchez*, CM/ResDH(2017)205 on the case *Antonio Messina*, CM/ResDH(2017)289 on the case *Abate and 118 other cases*, CM/ResDH(2017)308 on the case *Zeciri and 2 other cases*, CM/ResDH(2017)307 on the case *Craxi*

(No. 2), CM/ResDH(2017)424, on the case *Luordo and 23 other cases*, CM/ResDH(2017)423 on the case *Ceteroni and other 1723 cases*, CM/ResDH(2017)423 on the case *Bagnato and other 14 cases*.

Concerning the ongoing monitoring of the implementation of ECtHR judgments against Italy, the Committee of Ministers adopted five decisions in 2017.

On 10 March 2017, during its 1280th session, the CM adopted a decision on the case *Cestaro and others* (CM/Del/Dec(2017)1280/H46-16), related to the violence during G8 Summit held in Genoa in 2001 and the ineffectiveness of investigations and judicial proceedings related to the occurrences (see *Yearbook 2015*, p. 20, *Yearbook 2016*, p. 255). In the decision, the CM was saddened that it is no longer possible to initiate a new investigation of the actions of torture inflicted by the police, due to the limitation. The CM therefore pointed out the fact that individual measures are no longer possible in this case. With reference to the general measures, the CM noted with concern that, despite the clear indications provided by the ECtHR on this subject, the Italian legal system does not yet have provisions of criminal law capable of imposing appropriate penalties for persons responsible for torture or other forms of mistreatment prohibited by article 3 of ECHR. The Court insisted, in particular, on the urgent adoption of the bill aimed at establishing the crime of torture (still under discussion at the Italian Parliament at the time of adoption of this decision by the CM, see *Yearbook 2017*, p. 21-22).

Lastly, the CM invited the authorities to provide new information on the measures that regulate the disciplinary responsibility of law enforcement agencies and on the provisions concerning the final identification of the agents taking part in operations similar to those carried out in the case in question.

On 7 June 2017, during its 1288th session, the CM adopted a decision on the *Sharifi* case and others v. Italy and Greece (CM/Del/Dec(2017)1288/H46-17), concerning the automatic return from Italy to Greece of irregular migrants intercepted as clandestine passengers on ferries arriving at the Italian port of Ancona and the consequent impossibility for applicants to have an access to asylum procedures in Italy (see *Yearbook 2015*, p. 311). With reference to the individual measures, the CM invited the Italian authorities to provide further information on the actions taken to clarify the situation of the three applicants who have not been granted international protection in Italy. In relation to the general measures, the CM took note of the information provided by the Italian authorities about the measures taken to ensure an appropriate management of the massive migration flows that the country faces, but noted that this information does not display that the shortcomings identified by the judgement concerning the treatment of migrants in the Adriatic ports have been corrected. In this regard, the CM required the Italian authorities to provide the missing information by September 2017, with particular reference to the current organisation and functioning of the system of reception of migrants in these places and to the procedures followed upon their arrival, as well as to confirm that the country has stopped transferring to Greece people who wish to apply for international protection in Italy.

On 21 September 2017, during its 1294th session, the CM adopted a decision on the case group *Mostacciuolo Giuseppe No.1, Gaglione and others, and Olivieri and others* (CM/Del/Dec(2017)1294/H46-15), related to insufficient quantity and delays compared to the payment of the so-called "Pinto" remedy. The CM decided to conclude the monitoring of the 119 cases connected to these issues also in the light of the important developments that took place following the measures adopted by the Italian authorities. With reference to the 2012 reform of the "Pinto" law, the CM urges the Italian authorities to provide information on the issues previously raised with relation to the access to the "Pinto" remedy and the exclusion of compensation for procedures lasting six years or less. Finally, on the question of the ineffectiveness of the "Pinto" remedy with regard to the excessive length of administrative procedures (a question raised by Olivieri and others), the CM called on the authorities to promptly provide information on the measures taken and/or planned to remedy this situation.

On 7 December 2017, during its 1302nd session, the CM adopted a decision on the *Ceteroni* case group (CM/Del/Dec(2017)1302/H46-16) concerning the issue of the excessive length of civil proceedings. The CM notes that the individual measures have been established for all cases in the group and therefore decided to conclude the supervision of 1723 cases (CM/ResDH(2017)423). With reference to the general measures, the CM noted that encouraging results have been achieved related to the average duration of civil proceedings before the courts of first instance and the specialised corporate courts; it therefore encouraged the authorities to continue to monitor closely the impact of the measures taken in order to consolidate these results and further reduce the average length of disputes in similar type of proceedings. Moreover, the CM noted with satisfaction that the positive trend of reduction of the arrears observed since 2011 has been further consolidated in recent years and therefore encourages the Italian authorities to continue with this effort until the total elimination of the multi-year backlog is achieved. However, the CM noted with concern the presence of a negative trend regarding the increase in pending cases and the average length of criminal trials at the Court of Cassation. It therefore invited the Italian authorities to provide an updated analysis of the situation, in particular in relation to the appeal courts and the Court of Cassation, so as to enable the Committee to fully assess the impact of the measures adopted and the state of implementation of this set of cases. It decided that the problems related to the general measures of these cases will be followed in the cases of *Trapani* and *Muso*.

During the same session, the CM also adopted a decision on the *Luordo* case group (Cm/Del/Dec(2017)1302/H46-17), concerning the limitation of the applicants' rights following bankruptcy procedures and, in some cases, to its excessive duration. Within the same decision, the CM noted that the individual measures and the payment of equal satisfaction have been resolved in all cases of this group and decided therefore to conclude the supervision (CM/ResDH(2017)424). With reference to the general measures, the CM indicated with interest the lgs.d. 38/2017 which entrusts the Government with the mandate to carry out a profound reform of the bankruptcy procedures and encourages the authorities to quickly take the necessary steps to implement the measures recommended in this act legislative framework, keeping the Committee updated about the progress. The general measures related to these cases will be followed by the CM in the case *Collarile and others*.

On 5 April 2017, the CM adopted the resolutions CM/ResChS(2017)3 and CM/ResChS(2017)4 on the decisions of the European Committee of Social Rights concerning the collective complaints against Italy presented, respectively, on 2 August 2013 by the National Association of Judges of Peace (102/2013) (see *Yearbook 2017*, p. 208) and, on 22 April 2014, by the "La Voce dei Giusti" trade union (105/2014) (see this Part, Council of Europe, V). In these resolutions, the CM took note of the decisions of the European Social Rights Committee which identify, in both cases, a violation of the (revised) European Social Charter, and of the information communicated by the Italian delegation following these decisions, and remained in waiting for information on any progress related to the implementation of the aforementioned Charter, which Italy will be required to present in the next annual report to the Committee which will cover the provisions in question.

On 5 July 2017, the CM adopted a resolution on the implementation by Italy of the Framework Convention on the Protection of National Minorities (CM/ResCMN(2017)4). In the same resolution, the CM called on the Italian authorities to take into consideration the recommendations included in the fourth opinion of the Advisory Committee of the Framework Convention (see *Yearbook 2017*, p. 218-221). The CM draws attention to a series of these recommendations to be implemented immediately: the adoption of a legislative framework at national level for the protection of Roma and Sinti; the revision of the status and mandate of the UNAR; promoting access to the media for people belonging to minorities and providing adequate resources for the teaching of and in minority languages. Other recommendations highlighted in the resolution concern the need for the Italian authorities to: promote tolerance and respectful behavior towards minorities among the population, consult representatives of Roma, Sinti and Travellers in their projects and activities, increase financial resources for projects aimed at maintaining and developing the cultural heritage of minorities; put forward significant efforts to promote the use of minority languages by persons belonging to minorities in dealing with administrative authorities (including provision of properly funded help desks); review the procedures for appointing representatives of national minorities in the work of the Technical Committee set up to implement l. 482/1999 in order to ensure that the legitimate interests of all recognised linguistic and historical minorities are represented.

Finally, on 5 July, the CM adopted Resolution CM/ResCSS(2017)10 on the application of the European Social Security Code (with reference to the period from 1 July 2015 – 30 June 2016). Based on the report prepared by the Italian Government, and after presenting the new reporting methodology adopted by the CM on the basis of the new ILO approval in order to ensure consistency between the information on social security issues provided in the national reports to the mechanisms of monitoring of the ILO and the CoE, the CM formulates a series of observations and requests for information to be implemented by Italy. In particular, with reference to Part XI of the Code (Standard to be respected through the provision of periodic payments), the CM requires the Italian authorities to explain in the next report the substantial differences in the calculation of the amount of remuneration of skilled and unskilled workers, especially in cases where the rate of replacement of benefits recalculated on the basis of the reference remuneration of the structure of Earnings Survey (SES) would not reach the percentage prescribed in the Code. With reference to Part XIII (various provisions), referring to the new methodology adopted on the basis of ILO indications, the CM identifies a series of gaps and inaccuracies in the previous reporting activity of Italy on the implementation of the Code and therefore, requires to provide the missing information supported by updated statistical data and the necessary technical clarifications, especially with reference to the legislative provisions recalled by Italy in the previous periodic reports. In the case of emergence of divergent or controversial data, the CM invites the Italian authorities to check the consistency of the data, align them on the same temporal basis to ensure a comparison and specify the official sources of the statistical data that from now on will be used continuously by the Government when drawing up their periodic reports.

III. European Court of Human Rights

The European Court of Human Rights (ECtHR), the first international court specifically designed for the protection of human rights in a particular region of the world, guarantees the respect of the commitments laid down in the ECHR and its protocols by Member States of the CoE.

The Italian judge who now sits at the Court is Guido Raimondi, appointed President of the ECtHR in September 2015. Of the 668 members of the Registry, which provides legal and administrative support to the Court in exercising its functions, 24 are Italian.

The statistical data provided by the Court and updated in December 2017 shows that the total number of complaints pending against Italy amounted to 4,650, corresponding to about 8.3% of the total. In a worse situation are Romania with 9,900 appeals pending, equal to 17.6% of the total, the Russian Federation (7,750, 13.8%), Turkey (7,500, 13.3%) and Ukraine (7,100, 12.6%). During 2017, the Court received 1,374 valid individual appeals complaining of a violation of the rights contained in the ECHR by Italy (there were 1,409 in 2016 and 1,885 in 2015). In the same period, 1,973 complaints were declared inadmissible or struck from the register; 31 led to a judgment on the main action (relating to 133 individual appeals), 28 of which identified at least one violation of the Convention; 1,441 appeals were communicated to the relevant Country in view of a hearing on their merits. The Court also received 47 requests for urgent measures pursuant to article 39 of the Court's regulations, mostly regarding the suspension of deportation proceedings for as many applicants, only 7 of which were granted by the ECtHR.

An analysis on the Court's judgments concerning Italy in 2017 is presented in Part IV, Italy in the Case-law of the European Court of Human Rights.

IV. Committee for the Prevention of Torture

The European Committee for the Prevention of Torture and Inhuman or Degrading Treatment or Punishment (CPT) was established by the 1987 Convention of the same name, conceived as complementary to the regulations under article 3 of ECHR which sets forth an absolute ban on torture. The CPT is a body composed of independent experts and has one member for each State Party to the Convention for the Prevention of Torture (all the CoE countries are party to it). The members of the Committee are elected by the Committee of Ministers. Elisabetta Zamparutti was elected as Italian member from 7 October 2015 until 19 December 2019.

The Committee's main function is to verify, by means of inspections, the treatment of persons deprived of their liberty in order to strengthen, if necessary, their protection from torture and inhuman or degrading treatment or punishment (article 1). CPT is not an investigative body, but a preventive body. At the end of each visit, the Committee draws up a detailed report and sends it to the State involved, to which it requests an answer in relation to any critical issues raised in it. The action of the CPT is based on the principles of cooperation with national authorities and confidentiality. Therefore, its reports and the responses of the Governments are initially reserved and only subsequently, at the request of the country concerned, may they be made public together with the replies and observations provided by the national authorities.

In 2017, the committee carried out 18 visits to 17 countries: Albania, Azerbaijan, Belgium, Bulgaria, Cyprus, Croatia, Estonia, Hungary, Italy, Montenegro, Poland, Russian Federation (with reference to the Chechen Republic), Serbia, Slovenia, Turkey, United Kingdom (2, 1 with reference to Northern Ireland, 1 in relation to British military bases on the island of Cyprus) and Ukraine. In the year under review, the CPT published 15 reports on visits previously carried out in the following CoE Member States: Azerbaijan (2 reports), Former Yugoslav Republic of Macedonia, Germany, Greece, Italy, Latvia, Liechtenstein, the Netherlands, Slovenia, Spain, Turkey, United Kingdom (2, 1 on the visit to the military bases in Cyprus) and Ukraine.

In total, the CPT conducted 13 visits to Italy (7 periodic visits and 6 ad hoc visits). The last one took place between 7-13 June 2017 to examine the situation of people detained in migrant centres. The report on this visit has not yet been published publicly.

On 8 September 2017, the CPT published, together with the observations of the Italian authorities and at their request, the report on the visit to the country from 8-21 April 2016 (see *Yearbook 2017*, p. 200). During this periodic visit, the Committee examined the measures taken by Italy as part of the wider reform of detention facilities aimed at reducing prison overcrowding, and the ongoing reform process of forensic psychiatry. To this end, the CPT has visited numerous detention facilities and psychiatric institutions and met the Justice Minister Orlando, the sub-secretaries of the Ministry of Justice and the Ministry of the Interior and officials and representatives of the Ministry of Health, *Carabinieri*, Fiscal Police, and of the State Police. The CPT also met with the newly appointed National Ombudsperson for the rights of prisoners and persons deprived of their personal freedom.

Concerning the *crime of torture*, not included in the criminal code at the time of adoption of the report in question, the CPT recommended its introduction, and highlights the need for the crime of torture to be defined in accordance with the provisions from the 1984 UN Convention against

Torture. In relation to the National Prevention Mechanism foreseen by the Optional Protocol to that Convention, the function entrusted to the National Ombudsperson, the Committee anticipates that the office of the new Authority will be provided as soon as possible with the resources necessary to conduct its main activities and that the assigned personnel are selected following the criterion of autonomy, in line with the OPCAT regulation.

The first part of the report set its focus on the *locations of deprivation of freedom other than prisons* (police stations, *Carabinieri* barracks, *Carabinieri* stations, etc.). To begin with the various reports received in relation to the ill-treatment suffered by the detainees, especially by officials of the State Police and *Carabinieri*, the CPT recommends that the Italian authorities, at the highest political level, issue a formal declaration to be addressed as an order to remind them that the rights of the persons subject to their custody must be respected, and that any mistreatment of these persons will be prosecuted and sanctioned accordingly. In particular, with reference to the observed use of handcuffs during interrogations, the CPT requires that the necessary measures must be taken to ensure that the use of this instrument takes place in cases where it is essential and only for the strictly necessary period of time; moreover, a person should never be handcuffed to a fixed object. In the case of agitated or violent behaviour, the person involved should be subject to forms of supervision in an appropriate environment rather than being handcuffed. If the state of agitation derives from the health conditions, the instructions given by healthcare professionals ought to be followed.

In relation to the *mistreatment investigations*, the CPT requires detailed information on the number of law enforcement officers who have been taken to the court in the years 2013-2016 following the implementation of the articles 608, 582 and 572 of the penal code and on any convictions imposed. Among the measures to ensure protection against matration, the CPT focuses on the necessity to guarantee to all persons deprived of their freedom an effective possibility of informing a relative or any other person regarding the condition of detention from the moment of deprivation of their freedom and to ensure that lawyers are able to provide their assistance effectively during the period of custody in police stations, whether the latter are chosen by the detained person, or whether they are appointed by the office. Furthermore, the Italian authorities are called on to guarantee all persons detained by law enforcement to enjoy the right to speak privately with a lawyer from the moment of deprivation of freedom, including by amending, where necessary, the Code of Criminal Procedure. Furthermore, the CPT requires the Italian authorities to take urgent measures to ensure that all medical examinations on the persons detained in these areas are conducted outside the interrogation, and, unless the doctor involved asks for it, away from sight of law enforcement officials. According to the CPT, Italy should also take the necessary legislative measures to ensure that those detained by the police have access to a doctor of their choice and at their own expense from the moment of deprivation of their freedom. Other aspects on which Italy should focus without further delay concern the need to ensure that anyone who is detained by the police is fully and clearly informed in verbal and written form about all the fundamental rights entitled from the moment of initial privation of freedom. In addition, the detainees should be required to sign a statement indicating that they have been informed about their rights and reporting if they have decided to use or waive their rights. Regardless of the reason why a person is deprived of his personal freedom by law enforcement, including issues related to the identification process, this must be noted in a separate registry. These records must be meticulously and punctually maintained and should provide a counter-signature space for the suspect.

With reference to the *detention conditions*, while acknowledging that the status of the security chambers visited at the Police Headquarters and the Police Stations is generally acceptable, the CPT notes that some of these chambers have a series of problems related, in particular, to ventilation and hygiene. Thus, the committee asks the Italian authorities to remedy it. For example, some security chambers of the Florence Police Headquarters, already considered inadequate in a previous CPT recommendation in 2012 (see *Yearbook 2014*, p. 232), were in use at the time of the visit despite the assurances received from the authorities regarding their disposal. The Committee therefore calls for urgent action to be taken to restructure and improve these security chambers and to be careful about the progress of the work. Since none of the security chambers visited is considered suitable for prolonged detention (which in Italy may last up to four days according to current legislation), the CPT reiterates a series of recommendations made in the previous report, including that of providing adequate hygienic services and guaranteeing access to natural light and the possibility for detainees to do outdoor exercise on a daily basis.

The second part of the report focuses on the situation in the penitentiary institutions. On this issue, the CPT makes a general recommendation that the Italian authorities continue their efforts to eradicate the overcrowding and it requests information on the measures that they intend to take to address the new increase in the registered prison population since 2016. Furthermore, it recommends to the Italian authorities to work to ensure that the minimum standards established by the CPT ($6m^2$ of space for single cells, excluding health services, and $4m^2$ for inmates in multiple cells, excluding compartmentalised health facilities) are applied systematically in all prisons in Italy and that the necessary measures are taken to implement the most favourable provisions on the living space for prisoners under national legislation.

With regard to the issue of *ill-treatment in prisons*, the CPT recommends that custodial personnel must be informed that physical abuse, excessive use of force and verbal abuse of prisoners are not acceptable and will be treated accordingly. The administration of each prison should show greater vigilance on this aspect, ensuring the regular presence of prison administrators in places of detention, their direct contact with prisoners, the analysis of complaints presented by them and staff training.

In particular, the CPT calls for the adoption of appropriate measures to increase the ability to manage high-risk situations on the part of prison staff without involving force, including by providing training opportunities on how to prevent crisis situations. and defuse tensions and the use of safe methods for the control and moderation of such events. Furthermore, according to the Committee, prison staff should be placed under closer scrutiny by the prison administration and receive special training on control and confinement techniques of detainees with suicidal or self-harm tendencies.

The CPT asks the Italian judicial authorities to provide information on the measures taken in response to a series of cases of physical abuse referring to the delegation by the Ivrea prison director during the visit and on the outcome of the investigations conducted in this regard. Furthermore, it underlines the need to impose disciplinary sanctions in the event that prison officials abuse alcohol, as reported by numerous prisoners who have reported abuse in the prisons of Genoa Marassi and Como. The CPT also recalls the duty of the prison administration to take care of the detainees against him. This includes the responsibility to protect them from other inmates, acting preventively against this type of violence.

To this end, personnel in charge must be able to recognise the signs of these problems and be well trained to intervene decisively when necessary. Also on these aspects should be provided for specific training methods at all levels of staff.

In relation to *conditions of detention in prisons*, the CPT recommends that all structures work to ensure compliance with the minimum space requirements available to detainees and to implement the most favorable standards developed in national legislation, providing specific recommendations for each prison institute visited. Furthermore, the CPT requires the Italian authorities to redouble their commitment to enrich the programme of activities, including job opportunities and vocational training for prisoners, in particular at the prison facilities of Ascoli Piceno, Como, Genoa Marassi, Ivrea, Sassari and Turin.

The CPT also requires a revision of the "hard" detention regime envisaged by the so-called "41-*bis*". According to the Committee, all persons subjected to 41-*bis* should be provided with a wider range of propositional activities and should be allowed to use them at least four hours a day outside their cells. In addition, an open visit of one hour per week should normally be guaranteed, assessing the length and nature of this visit on the basis of a risk assessment of each individual case. The Italian authorities should guarantee for prisoners subject to 41-*bis* the right to accumulate unused visit permits and grant them at least one phone call per month, regardless of whether they receive visits or not in the same period. It should be ensured that the decisions of the supervisory judges are promptly and completely implemented by the prison administration and that the material shortcomings encountered in the "41-*bis*" detention centres of the penitentiary establishments visited (repairs, ventilation problems, TV access).

Concerning *health care services*, the CPT identifies a series of specific problems for each structure visited and recommends the necessary improvements (for example, it is necessary to correctly file the health records of the detainees at the Como prison and appoint appropriate medical staff at the "Security rooms" of the hospital *Le Molinette* of Turin; the nursing staff at the jails of Sassari, Como and Ivrea should be further strengthened, and better specialised care should be made available to detainees in the penitentiary institutions of Como and Sassari; the presence of a physiotherapist should be guaranteed in the prison of Ascoli Piceno at least once a week). The CPT also focuses on the steps taken by the Italian authorities regarding the introduction of telemedicine for specialist consultations at national level. Moreover, to avoid situations, such as those reported by some prisoners in the Ivrea prison, where requests for medical consultation must be presented verbally and in some cases are filtered or rejected by prison staff, the CPT requires efforts to allow prisoners to contact health care in a confidential manner and to prevent officials from monitoring requests for detainees for this purpose. Other recommendations made by the CPT on health care services concern the need to: improve the hygiene and infrastructure of some cells and to ensure that closed-circuit surveillance ensures the privacy of prisoners when using the toilet (Turin prison); to ensure that the signs of injury observed at the time of access or following an incident of violence in prison are carefully recorded together with any relevant statement by the detainee and the conclusions of the doctor (Sassari prison).

In this regard, the CPT recommends that the necessary measures to be taken to ensure that all injuries observed on detainees at the time of their entry into prison are photographed and re-registered with medical certificate, especially when they are transferred to a hospital to assess their suitability for detention. A registry should be kept in every Italian prison to systematically store this information.

Furthermore, according to the CPT, the Italian authorities should adopt a series of measures, possibly also by amending the relevant legislation, to ensure that the medical examinations of the detainees are conducted outside the interrogation, unless the doctor concerned otherwise provides in a specific case and out of sight of non-medical personnel. Finally, the Committee is particularly concerned about the practice, found in some prison institutions visited, of keeping a naked person in a room of medical isolation. This practice is listed as equivalent to degrading treatment.

The CPT recommends that the Italian authorities take the necessary measures, especially in the prisons of Como, Sassari and Turin, to abolish actions of this kind. In particular, under no circumstances should an inmate subject to quarantine be handcuffed to a bed.

The CPT report also focuses on *female prisoners with dependent children*. At this point, the Committee confines itself to recommending to the Italian authorities to allocate the necessary funds for the establishment of protected family houses to ensure that all mothers with children are housed in adequate environments, as required by l. 62/2011.

On the subject of *protection in disciplinary procedures*, the CPT regrets that none of the recommendations addressed to the Italian authorities has been implemented since 2008. According to the CPT, legislation and public policies must be reviewed in such a way that they are faced with disciplinary accusations being allowed to call witnesses against them to question the evidence against them in contradictory and to have a lawyer during the hearing before the disciplinary committee. Inmates who find themselves in this situation should receive a copy of their decision to inform them of their motives and how to appeal. Detainees should confirm in writing that they received this document. Furthermore, the Italian authorities should immediately abolish the practice that sees prison doctors actively participate in disciplinary commissions in the entire Italian prison system.

Finally, on the subject of *daytime isolation*, the CPT argues that imprisonment in prison is a punishment in itself and aggravating potentials of a life imprisonment as part of the punishment are not acceptable. The prolonged and punitive measure of the daytime isolation found by the Committee delegation in some institutions during its visit to Italy can therefore be fully considered an inhumane and degrading treatment. The principle of proportionality requires that any solitary isolation regime be imposed only on the basis of an individual risk assessment for the shortest period of time possible. The penal code should be modified on the basis of these observations.

The third and final part of the report focuses on *psychiatric institutions.* In general, the CPT welcomes the measures taken by the Italian authorities to implement the long-awaited reform of forensic psychiatry services and, in particular, the transfer of patients from judicial psychiatric hospitals to smaller regional structures, as well as the therapeutic environment and the philosophy of care put in place by the health staff in the new Residences for safety measures execution (REMS). Nonetheless, the CPT identifies a number of issues that Italian authorities could remedy to ensure full implementation of the potential of the care philosophy embodied by the REMS.

First of all, the CPT requires updated information on the closure of two judicial psychiatric hospitals (Barcellona Pozzo di Gotto and Montelupo Fiorentino) that remained operational despite the provisions of l. 9/2012 and on the discharge and transfer of patients to other psychiatric facilities. Additional information requested by the Committee concerns the strategies in place and the existing structures to ensure the transition from judicial psychiatric hospitals' stance of imprisonment to the idea of rehabilitation of patients in order to reintegrate them into the REMS community. On receiving complaints from some REMS patients located in Castiglione delle Stiviere about being subjected to imprisonment measures, the CPT recommends the administration to exercise continuous vigilance and to remind patients at regular intervals that they must be treated with respect and that any form of mistreatment against them, be it verbal or physical, is absolutely unacceptable and will be treated accordingly.

In relation to the *living conditions of patients*, the CPT recommends that these should go hand in hand with those favoured in REMS even for patients hosted in the remaining judicial psychiatric hospital of Montelupo Fiorentino. In some REMSs, the CPT recommends to remedy the lack of a room equipped to accommodate patients with physical disabilities; in others to reconsider the policy of locking patients' rooms overnight, limiting this practice to cases identified through appropriate risk assessments; for other REMSs, at the same time, the CPT's recommendation is to reconsider the practice of preventing patients in the various facilities from having access to their room for some parts of the day; more generally, the CPT recommends that measures be taken to provide all patients with a single or double room, or to ensure that the rooms do not accommodate more than four patients.

With reference to the *care provided*, the CPT requires information on the difficulties reported in the judicial psychiatric hospital of Montelupo Fiorentino to access consultations with a psychologist and the lack of activities involving exercise. Furthermore, the Committee invites the Italian authorities to further clarify on a series of critical issues identified in some of the REMSs visited regarding integration with local and regional health systems and the full development of the philosophy of care of this type of facility, the restructuring of ensure an adequate level of care, including the relationship with health personnel and access to activities and the need to ensure the presence of cultural mediators in these areas.

The relation to the *containment tools*, the CPT encourages the initiatives developed in Italy to avoid the use of mechanical restraints and asks to be informed about any development related to these tools, including the results of any monitoring process undertaken. The Committee also considers that the use of forms of isolation and restraint, although understandable in some cases, must be managed through a written procedure and all the requests must be reported in a dedicated registry. The CPT, nevertheless, emphasises that the use of these tools to punish patients is totally unacceptable and could be considered a form of ill-treatment. It is therefore necessary to put an end immediately to all practices of this kind. Other recommendations of the CPT on these aspects concern specific cases observed by the CPT during the visit, such as the need to stop using psychotropic medicine to manage the risks of a patient's escape. In general, the CPT recommends that the Italian authorities take the necessary measures to ensure that the isolation and other modalities of restraint are implemented in accordance with a set of principles and standards indicated by the Committee itself (to be used only as a last resort and if expressly ordered by a doctor or brought to the attention of a doctor for his approval, the restraint must always be of the shortest possible duration and there must always be a continuous form of monitoring by the administrative staff, etc.), that these principles are subject to a comprehensive protocol covering all the psychiatric institutions in which restraint is practiced and that these principles and standards are implemented. If necessary, the relevant legislation should also be adapted. This process of reviewing the policies and rules relating to restraint should be accompanied by periodic training and refresher courses for all the personnel involved (doctors, nurses, orderlies, etc.).

With regard to *forms of protection*, the CPT emphasises that decisions and reviews of aspects regarding patient accommodation must be made on the basis of evaluations put forward by independent psychiatrists who are not involved in patient care. Furthermore, the Committee recommends that the Italian authorities establish a clear legislative framework for the involuntary treatment of forensic psychiatry patients, who should be able to appeal to a competent court against a mandatory treatment decision and be informed, in writing, of this right.

A significant development in relation to psychiatric forensic services concerns the aforementioned institution of the National Ombudsperson, which, as well as dealing with all forms of deprivation of freedom, has also delivered with reference to the REMS. Having indicated the wish to visit these facilities as soon as the necessary personnel are available, the CPT encourages the Italian authorities to provide the resources necessary to ensure the full fulfillment of the mandate of the new guarantee body.

The CPT also recommends that an informative brochure presenting the routine of the psychiatric facility, patient rights related to legal assistance, review of the destination, consent to treatment and complaint procedures be made available in an appropriate variety of foreign languages, and that this brochure is delivered to all patients and their families upon admission to the facility. Patients who are unable to understand the contents of this brochure should receive appropriate assistance. In addition, all patients should have access to a support office that is able to explain patients' rights and help them to make use of them.

With reference to measures to ensure the *safety of facilities*, the CPT recommends that no armed guards are used within the REMS, especially in positions where these may have contact with patients. Moreover, finding that in most of the places visited the security personnel does not have specific training for the management of pediatric patients, the Committee recommends reviewing the pre-procedures for the selection of security personnel employed at the REMS visited and for their training. Detailed regulations should also be adopted regarding the duties of security personnel working in the psychiatric facilities.

Finally, in relation to the *issue of general adult psychiatry* and, specifically, of *involuntary civil procedure placement procedures*, the CPT does not notice any improvements with respect to the previous visit. (see *Yearbook 2014*, p. 234-235) It therefore invites the Italian authorities to ensure that the formal decision includes a person during a psychiatric diagnosis and treatment service is always carried out on the basis of the opinion of at least one qualified doctor. Other criteria to take into account in these situations are that doctors prepare detailed medical certificates, which, as far as possible, do not require the attending psychiatrist to prepare the initial validation certificate concerning the involuntary admission of a patient in a psychiatric service and that patients are normally heard in person by the competent custodial judge, possibly in a hospital setting.

V. European Committee of Social Rights

The European Committee of Social Rights (ECSR) was established pursuant to article 25 of the European Social Charter of 1961 in order to determine whether the legislation and practice of States Parties comply with the provisions of the European Social Charter, its Protocols and the

European Social Charter (revised) (ESC-R). Currently, the Committee is composed of 15 independent experts elected by the Committee of Ministers for a six-year mandate renewable only once. The Italian expert Giuseppe Palmisano has been re-elected for the period 2016-2022 as the President of the Committee.

Italy ratified the European Social Charter in 1965 and the revised European Social Charter in 1999, accepting 97 of its 98 paragraphs. The only non-accepted provision is article 25 ESC-R, which protects the right of workers in the case of the insolvency of their employer. In 2002, the CM decided that, every five years, countries must also inform the European Committee of Social Rights on the status of rights protected under provisions that they have not accepted. Italy's most recent communication on this issue dates back to 2014 (see *Yearbook 2016*, p. 183); the Committee's next assessment of article 25 ESC-R is scheduled for 2019.

As concerns the analysis of provisions it has accepted, from 1967-2015 the Italian Government submitted 20 annual reports on the application of the 1961 Charter and 15 on that of the revised Charter. Based on these, the Committee adopted its conclusions each year on the status of protection of social rights in Italy. Their most recent *Conclusions* on Italy were published in January 2018. The document concerns the sixteenth report, submitted in 7 March 2017 that covers the provisions of the Revised Charter in the thematic group 2, "Health, social security and social provision (articles 3, 11, 12, 13, 14, 23, 30 ESC-R) with reference to the period of 1 January 2012 – 31 December 2015. Furthermore, the report from the Italian Government contains the information requested by the 2015 Committee of Conclusions on the thematic group No. 4 "Children, families and migrants" (articles 7, 8, 16, 17, 19, 27, 31 ESC-R) related to those conclusions of non-compliance due to the persistent lack of information requested in previous reports from the Italian authorities (see *Yearbook 2016*, p. 184-186).

Overall, the 2017 *Conclusions* refer to the Italian situation in relation to 19 articles and numbered paragraphs of the revised Charter. In these, the Committee recognises 7 situations of compliance, often underlining that these assessments are carried out pending additional information on the considered issues and 6 situations of non-compliance. For the 6 situations, the Committee decides to wait for further elaborated information from the Italian authorities, in the next annual report on of the same thematic group of articles.

Summary Table of 2017 Conclusions on Italy by Paragraph

ESC-R Article	Conclusions of conformity	Conclusions of non-conformity	Requests for further information
Art. 3 ESC-R (right to safe and healthy working conditions)		Para. 4 (sanitary services for workers)	Para. 1 (occupational safety and health) Para. 2 (safety and health regulations) Para. 3 (enforce safety and hygiene regulations)
Art. 11 ESC-R (right to benefit from any measures enabling him to enjoy the highest possible standard of health attainable)	Para. 1 (remove as far as possible the causes of ill-health) Para. 2 (consultancy and education services) Para. 3 (prevent diseases and accidents)		
Art. 12 ESC-R (right to social security)	Para. 2 (maintain the social security system at a satisfactory level at least equal to that necessary for the ratification of the European Code of Social Security)	Para. 3 (raise progressively the system of social security) Para. 4 (social security for people that move to different countries)	Para. 1 (establishment of social security system)
Art. 13 ESC-R (right to social and medical assistance)	Para. 3 (prevent, remove, or alleviate personal want) Para. 4 (specific emergency assistance for non-state residents)	Para. 1 (adequate care assistance for people in need)	Para. 2 (non-discrimination on the exercise of socio-political rights)

ESC-R Article	**Conclusions of conformity**	**Conclusions of non-conformity**	**Requests for further information**
Art. 14 ESC-R (right to benefit from social welfare services)	Para. 2 (participation of individuals in the establishment and maintenance of social services).		Para. 1 (incentivise or organise services)
Art. 23 ESC-R (right of elderly persons to social protection)		The whole of the one-paragraph article.	
Art. 30 ESC-R (right to be protected against poverty and social exclusion)		The whole of the one-paragraph article.	

Specifically, with reference to article 3 ESC-R (right to safe and healthy working conditions), the Committee postpones its conclusions pending additional information on three of the four numbered paragraphs of which it is composed. The Committee requests further information in relation to para. 1 (health and safety and work environment), on the implementation of the National Prevention Plan (2014-2018). It also requires to provide a formal risk assessment document that includes occupational health and safety hazards according to various risk factors, indicate the criteria used by the Italian authorities to assess the risks and present a declaration by the employer working on prevention and protection measures implemented to eliminate identified risks or reduce them to an acceptable level. Furthermore, the Committee requests confirmation that all employers must undertake a risk assessment regardless of the size of their business activity and request information on the permanent advisory committee on health and safety at work (article 6 of lgs.d. 81/2008) and on its role in relation to risk assessment. In relation to para. 2 (safety and hygiene regulations), the Committee asks whether existing regulations include work-related stress, aggression and violence at work, especially for atypical workers.

Other information requested by the Committee concerns measures for the elimination of asbestos and the minimum protection of workers from radiation, measures to ensure safety and hygiene in relation to domestic workers and the procedures for consulting their respective safety organisations and the hygiene of temporary, temporary workers and those with a fixed-term contract. In relation to para. 3 (implementation of safety and hygiene regulations), the required information concerns the way in which the occupational disease is conceived in Italy, the mechanisms for the recognition, examination and review of these diseases, the most frequent diseases recorded during the period under review and the preventive measures taken or planned. The Committee also requests to provide further information on the work of the labour inspectorate and the measures taken to guarantee the health and hygiene of domestic workers. With reference to para. 4 (health services for workers), the Committee concludes that the situation in Italy does not comply with the provision in question because there is no evidence that there is a strategy to gradually provide access to these services by all workers in all sectors.

In relation to article 11 ESC-R (right to protection of health), the Committee concludes that, pending a series of additional information, it considers the Italian situation to conform to all three numbered paragraphs that constitute this article. In relation to para. 1 (elimination of the causes of a health deficit), the additional information requested concerns, among other aspects, the main causes of death and the measures taken to prevent them, the maternal mortality rate in all regions of Italy, the availability of services and care for mental illnesses and their prevention; the availability of dental care and services.

With reference to para. 2 (consultants and education services), the Committee asks Italy to notify whether health education and reproductive health are included in the school curricula. In relation to para. 3 (prevention of diseases and injuries) the information requested by the Committee concerns the implementation of the measures adopted by Italy in the field of environmental pollution, the presentation of updated data on pollution levels and the related trends, the cases of contamination of the drinking water and food poisoning during the reporting period and waste management. It also asked for further information on the impact and results of the measures taken to combat smoking, alcoholism (in particular the phenomenon of binge drinking) and drug addiction together with updated consumption data. Other information requested relating to this provision concern measures for the prevention of accidents, especially at home.

Regarding the article 12 ESC-R (right to social security), the Committee decides to postpone its assessment in relation to para. 1 (existence of a social security scheme). The information requested by the Committee in relation to this paragraph concerns the insurance coverage rate, also by private way, in order to allow an overall assessment of the total personal coverage and the number of insured persons in relation to the active population for each sector of the social Security.

Furthermore, it asks whether the retirement pension continues to cover the branches of invalidity and veterans and, if not, the reasons regarding. With regard to sickness allowance, the Committee asks the authorities to specify whether this compensation is calculated on the basis of the days worked by the employee or on each day of the week following the initial three days of non-eligibility. It also asked to disclose the proportion of staff that is suitable only for the minimum daily salary rates and which categories of employees could potentially be paid according to these rates.

Finally, the Committee asks the Italian authorities to explain whether sickness allowance can be combined with other additional allowances. Furthermore, noting that among the circumstances of suspension of unemployment benefit there is a refusal to accept a relevant job offer, the Committee requests clarification as to the actual meaning of this expression.

On this subject, the Committee also calls for clear and comprehensive information on the various allowances that can be applied to unemployed persons during the reference period. In relation to the issue of disability allowances, the Committee requests information on the estimate of the amount to be paid to individuals with, respectively, 66% and 100% disability and the minimum contributions recorded.

Finally, the Committee requests information on compensation deriving from accidents and occupational diseases, of which Italy's report does not mention. In relation to para. 2 (maintaining the social security system at a level satisfactory or at least equal to that required for the ratification of the European Social Security Code), the Committee considers the Italian situation to be in conformity with the disposition of the Charter. With reference to para. 3 (development of the social security system) the Committee concludes that Italy presents a situation of non-compliance as it has not been demonstrated that measures have been taken to raise the social security system to a higher level. A negative conclusion is also adopted in relation to para. 4 of this article (social security for people moving between different countries). In this case, the situation of non-compliance is due to the fact that equal treatment is not guaranteed in relation to access to family benefits for citizens of all States Parties and that the duration of the period of residence required to be holders of social allowances for foreign citizens who are not protected by EU regulations or agreements in force with Italy (10 years) is excessive.

In relation to article 13 ESC-R (right to social and medical assistance), the Committee confirms the previous conclusion of non-compliance in relation to para. 1 (adequate assistance for every person in need) because the level of social assistance is not adequate (see *Yearbook 2014*, p. 239). With reference to para. 2 (non-discrimination in the exercise of social and political rights), the Committee refers to its conclusions by asking the Italian authorities whether the provisions which establish the principle of equality and prohibit discrimination in the exercise of political and social rights are interpreted in practice in order to prevent discrimination based on receipt of social or medical assistance.

The Committee adds that if this information is not provided in the next report, there will be no basis for concluding that the situation in Italy is in conformity with the provision of the Charter. In relation to para. 3 (preventing, eliminating or alleviating the state of need), pending more detailed information on how the requirements of this provision are satisfied in the legislation and in practice, the Committee believes that the situation in Italy is in line with the Charter. A conformity situation is also identified in relation to para. 4 of this article (specific emergency assistance for non-residents).

In relation to article 14 ESC-R (right to use social services) the Committee refers to its conclusions with reference to para. 1 (incentivising or organising services) waiting to receive more information, already requested in the previous conclusions on this article (see *Yearbook 2014*, p. 239-240).

This information concerns, first of all, the measures adopted or planned by the Italian authorities to ensure that users of social services in the various Italian regions are not at risk of being subjected to unequal treatment. In the absence of such information in the next report, there will be no basis for arguing that the situation in Italy is in line with the provision in question. Other information necessary for the Committee to make this assessment concerns the total number of people employed in social services and their qualifications, both in the public sector and in the private sector.

In relation to para. 2 (public participation in the establishment and maintenance of social services), the Committee identifies a situation of compliance, but requires information about the impact of the introduction of the Information System on non-profit organisations on the quality of social services provided.

With reference to article 23 ESC-R (right of elderly people to social protection), the Committee concludes that the Italian situation does not comply with the provisions of the Charters since the level of contributory and non-contributory seniority pensions is explicitly inadequate.

Also in relation to article 30 ESC-R (right to protection against poverty and social exclusion), the situation examined by the Committee is considered non-compliant on the grounds that in Italy there is no adequate coordinated and comprehensive approach to tackling poverty and social exclusion. The seventeenth report of Italy, expected by 31 October 2017, focuses on the follow-up of decisions on the merits of collective complaints in which the Committee has found a violation by the country.

With regard to the collective complaints procedure established by the 1995 Protocol, the Committee's conclusions were published on 15 March 2017 in case No. 104/2014. The collective appeal, presented by the trade union "La Voce dei Giusti", claimed that the Italian law prevented third-rate substitute teachers from having free access to specialised training courses to become support teachers for students with disabilities, in violation of article 10 ESC-R (right to professional training), read alone or in conjunction with the general non-discrimination clause set out in article E. The Committee unanimously concludes that there has been a violation of the provisions invoked, recognising a situation of indirect discrimination to the detriment of third-level substitute teachers who, although in a situation comparable to qualified teachers, can not access the same conditions as vocational training courses to obtain the qualification of support teachers.

During 2017, the Committee adopted some decisions on the admissibility of collective complaints filed against Italy in previous years. In particular, the complaint (No. 140/2016), presented by the Italian General Confederation of Labour (CGIL), concerning the alleged violation of article 5 (trade union rights) and 6 (right to bargain collectively) ESC-R with reference to members of the *Guardia di Finanza* (decision of 10 May 2017) and complaint No. 133/2016, presented by University Women of Europe (UWE) on effective equality and fair payment between men and women (decision of 4 July 2017). The complaint n. 122/2016 was declared inadmissible since the proponent, in this case, the Movement for the freedom of psychoanalysis-Italian cultural association, was not one of the three categories of subjects authorised to submit collective complaints pursuant to the 1995 Protocol.

Furthermore, in 2017, seven new collective complaints against Italy were presented. The first (complaint No. 143/2017), presented by the General Workers' Union – National Federation of Forestry Corps of the State and Autonomous Forest Environmental Police Syndicate, concerns the alleged violation of articles 1 (right to work), 5 (right to trade union), 6 (right to bargain collectively), as well as the letters E (non-discrimination) and G (restrictions) of the ESC-R. According to the trade unions, the application of d.lgs. 177/2016, to the extent that it provides for the absorption of the State Forestry Corps in the *Carabinieri* Armament and therefore the assumption of a military status, would deprive members of the latter of all trade union protection in violation of the aforementioned provisions of the Charter. On 13 September 2017, the complaint was declared admissible.

Complaints 144/2017 and 146/2017, presented respectively by the General Confederation of Trade Unions and the Professional and Trade Union Association, concern the alleged violation of articles 1 (right to work), 4 (right to fair remuneration), 6 (right to bargain collectively), 24 (right to protection in the event of dismissal) and E (non-discrimination) ESC-R. According to the claims of the applicant organisations, the Italian legislation on fixed-term contracts in the public sector, especially in the school sector, improperly authorises the renewal of these contracts, compromising the possibility for workers in the sector to enjoy the above-mentioned safeguards. Complaint No. 147/2017, presented by the National Union of State Executives, raises the same questions as the previous ones, albeit with reference to the workers in the finance sector. On 12 September 2017, all three appeals were declared admissible.

On 12 July 2017, complaint No. 152/2017 presented by the union base – public sector employment was registered. It concerns the alleged violation by Italy of articles 1 (right to work), 4 (right to fair remuneration), 6 (4) (right to take collective action), 10 (right to professional training) and E (non-discrimination) ESC-R due to the situation of temporary workers employed by the Ministry of Justice and, in particular, with respect to their career rights. On 28 January 2018, the complaint was declared admissible.

The same trade union organisation, on 13 July 2017, also filed a complaint No. 153/2017. This concerns the alleged violation of articles 1 (right to work), 4 (right to fair remuneration), 5 (right to trade union), 6 (4) (right to take collective action), 24 (right to protection in the event of dismissal) and E (non-discrimination) ESC-R with reference to the situation of precarious workers in the public sector of Sicily, employed by forward contracts to cover vacant positions. Also in this case, the complaint was declared admissible with a decision of the Committee adopted on 28 January 2018.

The seventh and last complaint (No. 158/2017) was presented by the Italian General Confederation of Labour (CGIL). It concerns the alleged violation of article 24 ESC-R (right to protection in the event of redundancy) in relation to the provisions of lgs.d. 23/2015 on the protection of workers in the private sector in the event of an unlawful dismissal.

VI. Commissioner for Human Rights

The Commissioner for Human Rights is an independent non-judicial institution established by the Committee of Ministers' Resolution (99)50 of 7 May 1999. Nils Muižnieks (Latvia) is the current Commissioner for Human Rights of the Council of Europe (in office since 1 April 2012).

The Commissioner's duties are to promote effective respect for human rights, to support the 47 Member States in implementing the relevant CoE standards and to promote education and awareness of human rights. Its main activity is to conduct a permanent dialogue with Governments of the Member States, including visits to their respective territories. At the end of the mission, the Commissioner draws up a report that includes both an analysis on human rights and the improvement thereof; this report is published and spread widely. In addition, the Commissioner conducts follow-up visits to evaluate the progress made regarding the implementation of the previous recommendations and relevant reports are also rendered public.

In 2017, the Commissioner conducted visits and missions in: Bosnia-Herzegovina, Croatia, Czech Republic, Cyprus, Finland, Kosovo, Latvia, Liechtenstein, Luxembourg, Malta, Monaco, Poland, Portugal, Republic of Moldova, Slovenia, Sweden, Switzerland and Ukraine. He drew up public reports on visits conducted (in 2016 and 2017) in the following countries: Bosnia and Herzegovina, Ireland, Lithuania, Slovenia, Switzerland.

The Commissioner conducted five visits to Italy. The last one was held on 3-6 July 2012 with the aim to review a series of critical issues with particular reference to the excessive duration of judicial processes and the protection of the rights of migrants, asylum seekers, Roma, and Sinti people. The concluding report was published on 18 September 2012 (CommDH(2012)26) (see *Yearbook 2013*, p. 255-260). Although the last visit and the last report date back to five years ago, the Commissioner maintained his dialogue on human rights with the Italian authorities by sending letters (see, for instance, *Yearbook 2017*, p. 209-210). Three letters were prepared during 2017.

In the first, addressed to the President of the Senate Pietro Grasso on 16 May, the Commissioner expressed his concern about the draft law on the efficiency of civil judicial proceedings (Senate bill 2284), which envisages transferring the competences of juvenile justice from courts and judicial services specialised in ordinary ones. The Commissioner reiterates that children's rights are better protected in a system where justice is issued by specialised professionals with exclusive skills, as currently practised in Italy. The President of the Senate therefore warns that the planned transfer of powers would be a step in the wrong direction since it might lead to the weakening of the capacity of judges and prosecutors in paying adequate and specific attention to the needs of minors and, therefore, to reduce the protection of the rights of children who come into contact with the judicial authority.

The second letter was sent on 21 June to the Presidents of the Chamber of Deputies and the Senate, to the Presidents of the Justice Commissions of both branches of Parliament and to the President of the Extraordinary Senate Commission for the protection and promotion of human rights. In it, the Commissioner asks the Italian Parliament to improve the draft law to incorporate the crime of torture into the Italian criminal code (Chamber of Deputies bill 2168-B, 14 July 2017, No. 110, see *Yearbook 2017*, p. 21-22). While the Commissioner welcomes the establishment of legislation on torture in the Italian legal system, he is, on the other hand, concerned about the compatibility of certain aspects of the bill in accordance with international human rights standards. In particular, it refers to the case of the crime of torture contained in the bill, which may lead to not dealing with cases of torture or inhuman or degrading treatment or punishment. In the letter, the Commissioner stresses in particular the need to ensure that the authorities who commit acts of this kind are held responsible. He additionally stresses that the possibility for victims to be compensated are not undermined by the prescription or other measures.

Lastly, on 11 October, the Commissioner published the third letter, addressed this time to the Minister of the Interior, Marco Minniti. The letter concerns Italy's maritime operations in the territorial waters of Libya aimed at managing the migration flow. The Commissioner expressed appreciation for the country's efforts to save lives in the open sea and to manage migrant arrivals on the Italian shores. However, it underlines the duty of States to protect and safeguard the human rights of migrants even when migratory flows pose additional difficulties. In particular, after noting that delivering migrants to the Libyan authorities may subject them to a real risk of torture, inhuman or degrading treatment or punishment, the Commissioner calls on the Italian Government to clarify the type of aid he expects to provide to the Libyan authorities in the waters of Libya, and the forms of protection that have been put in place to avoid such risks for people intercepted or rescued by Italian ships in Libyan waters. The Commissioner also requires information concerning measures to ensure that search and rescue operations in the Mediterranean, including those conducted by non-governmental actors, continue to be carried out effectively and safely.

Among other activities carried out by the Commissioner for Human Rights in 2017 include the online publication of several *Human Rights Comments*, short posts in which the Commissioner concisely analyses and comments on relevant and current aspects related to the human rights situation in Europe. In the year under review, 10 comments were published (9 in 2015, 11 in 2016). Three of these contain explicit references to the human rights situation in Italy.

High time for investing in alternatives to migrant detention (31 January 2017); the Commissioner emphasises that the use of forms of detention for migrants throughout Europe, aimed at preventing asylum seekers and other migrants from entering or leaving the country, has always been a serious concern for respect for human rights. Indeed, detention constitutes a large interference with the right to freedom of migrants. The experts also confirmed the harmful effects of this practice on the mental health of migrants, especially minors. It is therefore imperative that States work for the abolition of detention for migrants, although in several European countries the trend is going exactly in the opposite direction: Italy, for example, is mentioned for the planned opening of 16 new detention centres for migrants. In support of his comment, the Commissioner directly refers to the sentence of the ECtHR on the *Khlaifia case and others v. Italy*, in which the Court emphasises that such a serious measure as detention is justified only where other less severe measures have been taken into account and considered insufficient. The case in question refers also when the Commissioner reiterates the need to provide alternatives to any form of detention, even taking into consideration the fact that what defines such a detention status is the deprivation of freedoms of persons regardless of the name of the structure in which this happens.

Afrophobia: Europe should confront this legacy of colonialism and the slave trade (25 July 2017). In this comment, the Commissioner starts from the observation of numerous manifestations of consolidated or emerging forms of racism to minority members observed during, especially those with African descendancy who are subjected to racism and intolerance in many aspects of their daily life. Among the cases of incitement to hatred against black people related to Italy, the comments made reference to the insults addressed by some politicians against the then Minister for integration Cécile Kyenge in 2013 and, the case of the player Sulley Muntari, the victim of racist insults by fans of the opposing team who, instead of being protected, was expelled by the referee after reporting these behaviours. Another aspect that worries the Commissioner is the discriminatory practice of racial profiling by the police forces that, with reference to Italy, was identified and reported during the 2015 visit to the country by the United Nations Expert Group on the population of African descent (see *Yearbook 2016*, p. 152).

The long march against homophobia and transphobia (31 August 2017): The Commissioner notes that in parallel with the increased visibility and victories for the equality of lesbian, gay, bisexual, transsexual, and intersex people (LGBTI), there has been a negative backlash in recent years, manifested through forms of discrimination, indifference, and persecution of persons belonging to these groups. In reviewing examples of these behaviours in many European countries, the Commissioner notes that transgender people continue to pay a particularly high price. According to the "Transgender Europe Murder Monitoring" project, more than 110 transgender people have been murdered in Europe since 2009, with 30 of these cases occurring in Italy.

According to the Commissioner, in the light of these incidents and many other events of intimidation and discrimination, urgent action is needed, starting from the consideration that LGBTI people do not ask for special or additional rights, but simply enjoy the same human rights as any other human-being.

Finally, two issue papers were published by the Office of the Commissioner, aimed at informing the public, authorities and NGOs working in the field of human rights, on these issues: *Realising the right to family reunification of refugees in Europe* (June 2017) and *Women's Sexual Reproductive and Health Rights* (December 2017).

VII. European Commission against Racism and Intolerance

The European Commission against Racism and Intolerance (ECRI), established in 1993, is a monitoring body of the Council of Europe specialised in combating any form of racism, xenophobia, anti-semitism and intolerance in a human rights perspective. The members of ECRI remain in office for five years. They are selected for their moral authority and their recognised experience in the field of combating racism, xenophobia, anti-semitism and intolerance; they act on an individual basis and independently. The Commission is composed by a member and, if a Government so wishes, a deputy member for each State of the Council of Europe. In 2017, the Italian expert was Vitaliano Esposito. Constance Hermanin was appointed in 2017 as an alternate member. An Italian official, Stefano Valenti, was responsible for the External Relations of the Commission Secretariat, part of the Directorate-general Human Rights and the Rule of Law of the Council of Europe.

The mandate of the ECRI covers all measures to combat violence, discrimination and prejudice against people (or groups of people) on the basis of racial, linguistic, religious, national, or ethnic preconditions. The Commission carries out an in-depth analysis of the situation regarding racism and intolerance in each of the Member States of the CoE and write suggestions and proposals by drawing up reports. The report is on the basis of an analysis of documentary sources, site visits and a confidential dialogue with national authorities and civil society organisations. ECRI also directs general policy recommendations to all Member States and promotes cooperation with relevant actors, in particular NGOs, mass media and youth associations.

In 2017, the Commission published reports of the fifth monitoring cycle for Andorra, Denmark, Luxembourg, San Marino, Spain, Sweden and Ukraine; the report of the second monitoring cycle relating to Montenegro; those of the third cycle relating to Bosnia-Herzegovina and Serbia. In addition, ECRI presented the conclusions on the priority recommendations to the following countries in the context of the fifth cycle reports already published: Belgium, Bulgaria, Germany, Greece, Norway, Romania, Slovakia and Switzerland. In 2017, ECRI also conducted visits, within their respective monitoring cycles, in Croatia, Latvia, Liechtenstein, Malta, Portugal, Republic of Moldova, Slovenia.

The last report on Italy prepared by ECRI was the one relating to the fifth monitoring cycle. The report, adopted on 18 March 2016 and made public on 7 June (CRI(2016)19), was followed by a visit by an ECRI delegation in Italy between 13 and 18 September 2015 and was discussed in *Yearbook 2017*, p. 162-166. The next report will concern the implementation of the priority recommendations addressed to Italy within this cycle: providing all students and students with the information, protection and support they need to live in harmony with their sexual orientation and their gender identity; and guarantee full independence and autonomy to UNAR and extend its competences to all possible fields where discrimination can occur.

VIII. Advisory Committee on the Framework Convention for the Protection of National Minorities

The Committee is a monitoring body instituted pursuant to article 26 of the Council of Europe Framework Convention for the Protection of National Minorities. It is composed of 18 independent experts with recognised expertise in the field of the protection of national minorities. It is composed of 18 independent experts with recognised expertise in the field of protection of national minorities who sit on the Committee in their individual capacity for a period of four years. In 2017, there were no Italian experts on the Advisory Committee.

The Advisory Committee serves to assist the CM in evaluating the implementation of the Framework-Convention in States Parties, through the examination of periodic State Reports. The results of this evaluation are expressed in a detailed opinion which serves as a basis for the preparation of the CM's conclusive resolutions on the Country in question. Follow-up meetings are generally organised by the Advisory Committee with a view to bringing together all actors – governmental and non-governmental – interested in the implementation of the Convention and to examine ways of implementing the results of the monitoring procedure.

During 2017, within the framework of the respective monitoring cycles, the Consultative Committee of the Framework Convention conducted visits to the following countries: Azerbaijan, Bosnia and Herzegovina, Latvia,

Romania, Russian Federation, Slovenia, Sweden; has adopted, but not yet published by virtue of the confidentiality principle, opinions on Azerbaijan, Bosnia-Herzegovina, Kosovo, Romania, Slovenia and Ukraine and has published opinions on the situation of national minorities in Armenia, Austria, the former Yugoslav Republic of Macedonia, Malta, Norway, Republic of Moldova, Sweden and the United Kingdom.

The opinion of the Advisory Committee on Italy concerning the fourth monitoring cycle of the Framework Convention, based also on the visit conducted by the latter in Italy between 29 June and 3 July 2015, was adopted on 19 November 2015 (ACFC/OP/IV(2015)006) and published on 12 July 2016 together with the comments provided by the Italian Government on the observations made by the Advisory Committee (see *Yearbook 2017*, p. 218-221). The resolution of the Committee of Ministers concluding this monitoring cycle was adopted on 5 July 2017 (CM/ResCMN(2017)4, see this Part, Council of Europe, II).

IX. European Commission for Democracy through Law

The Commission, also known as the Venice Commission, is the Council of Europe's advisory body on constitutional issues; it was established in 1990 and receives financial support by a law of the Region of Veneto.

The Commission is composed of independent experts with extensive experience in the area of democratic institutions or excellence in the legal and political domains. Members are designated for four years by the participating countries which, as well as the 47 Member States of the CoE, include Algeria, Brazil, Chile, Israel, Kazakhstan, Kyrgyzstan, Mexico, Morocco, Peru, South Korea, Tunisia and United States. Belarus is an associate member, while Argentina, Canada, the Holy See, Japan and Uruguay participate in the work of the Commission as observer countries. The European Commission, Palestinian National Authority, South Africa and the *Association of Constitutional Courts using the French Language* have a special co-operation status.

Since 2009, Gianni Buquicchio has been President of the *Venice Commission*. Two Italian experts participate in the Commission's activities as alternate members: Marta Cartabia e Cesare Pinelli.

Among its activities, the Commission put forwards studies and opinions on subjects covered by its competence, also at the request of other bodies such as the Parliamentary Assembly of the CoE and promotes in-depth seminars. In 2017, the Venice Commission adopted 27 opinions with regard to the adoption of laws or bills of law on matters of constitutional importance in the following countries: Armenia (3 opinions), the former Yugoslav Republic of Macedonia, Georgia, Hungary (3), Kazakhstan (2), Poland (2), Republic of Moldova (7), Romania, Slovakia, Turkey (2), Ukraine (3), Venezuela.

In 2017, the Venice Commission was invited by the ECtHR to present an *amicus curiae* intervention in the case of *Berlusconi v. Italy* (No. 58428/13), on the question of the minimum procedural guarantees that a State should provide in the context of an interdiction measure from public offices. The intervention, which refers to the previous reflection of the Court and the same Commission on the matter, was adopted by the Venice Commission on 7 October 2017 (CDL-AD (2017) 025).

According to the Commission's findings, the ECtHR previously stated that States may decide to leave to the courts the determination of proportionality of a measure that limits the voting rights of convicted prisoners, or to incorporate provisions in their laws that define the circumstances in which such a measure should be applied. In the latter case, it will be up to the legislator to balance competing interests in order to avoid any general, automatic and indiscriminate restrictions. This possibility applies to a fortiori of disqualification by invalidating an elective mandate, since stricter requirements on the admissibility to apply for election to the Parliament can be clearly set (and, in the opinion of the Commission, even more in the event of an interdiction that annuls the mandate election), distinct from eligibility to vote. According to the Commission, legal disqualification must take into account factors such as the severity and nature of the crime committed and the behavior of the perpetrator. The interdiction should therefore be provided only in relation to certain types of crimes or with particularly long sentences. It is also appropriate for the law to adapt the duration of the measure to the imposed sentence and therefore, for the same reason, to the gravity of the crime. According to a comparative study of the legislation on procedural guarantees provided in relation to the issue of interdiction from public offices that the *Venice Commission* conducted on 62 States in order to provide this *amicus curie* intervention and made available to the Court (CDL-REF(2017)041), in States where the ban does not operate automatically, but requires an executive decision by the Parliament, its decision does not represent an autonomous interference with the right of the representative to be elected. For this reason, only limited procedural requirements apply, in particular the right of the Member to assert his arguments, to appear before the Parliament in person and to be assisted by a lawyer, the holding of a public hearing, the public nature of the decision. An appeal to the Constitutional Court against Parliament's decision seems to be an additional logical guarantee in countries where direct access to the Constitutional Court is already foreseen, but should not be considered necessary.

X. Group of Experts on Action against Trafficking in Human Beings

The Group of Experts (GRETA) was established pursuant to article 36 of the Council of Europe Convention on Action against Trafficking in Human Beings and is charged, together with a Committee made up of the representatives in the CM of the States Parties to the Convention (Committee of the Parties), with monitoring the implementation of the obligations contained in the Convention.

> The Group is made up of 15 independent experts known for their recognised competence in the fields of human rights, assistance and protection of victims of trafficking in human beings or having professional experience in the areas covered by the Convention. The monitoring procedure is divided into 4-year rounds. The Group of Experts starts the dialogue with the Party under evaluation by sending out a questionnaire, which may be followed by requests for further information. If the Group of Experts deems it necessary, additional information may be requested from civil society organisations or gathered by organising a visit to the Country concerned. The draft report is sent to the relevant Government for comments. On receiving them, GRETA prepares its final report and conclusions and transmits it to the Country concerned and to the Committee of the Parties, which can adopt recommendations on the basis of the contents of the document. Each Party to the Convention appoints a contact person to cooperate with the Group of Experts.
>
> In 2017, the Expert Group published the evaluation reports on the implementation status of the Convention in: Armenia, Belarus, Belgium, Bosnia-Herzegovina, France, Greece, Ireland, Latvia, Malta, the Netherlands, Norway, Poland and Portugal. They conducted in-depth visits to the following countries: Azerbaijan, Estonia, Hungary, Luxembourg, the Netherlands, Spain, Sweden and Ukraine.

The first evaluation cycle on the implementation of the Warsaw Convention by Italy concluded with the recommendation of the Committee of the Parties (CP(2014)16), adopted on 5 December 2014, which confirmed the recommendations previously made by the Group of experts (GRETA(2014)18, see *Yearbook 2015*, p. 226-229). Furthermore, on 30 January 2017, GRETA published the report on an urgent visit by a delegation in Italy from 21-23 September 2016 to address the issue of Italy's removal of possible victims of trafficking through forced repatriation flights to Nigeria, as part of joint removal operations organised and coordinated by the FRONTEX European Agency (see *Yearbook 2017*, p. 222-225).

The second round of monitoring of the implementation of the Warsaw Convention in the country began with the response to the questionnaire of the Expert Group presented by the Italian authorities on 30 October and published by GRETA on 27 November 2017 (GRETA/2017/33). The subsequent visit to the country is scheduled between January and June 2018.

XI. Group of States against Corruption

The Group of States against Corruption (GRECO) was established in 1999 in order to monitor the compliance of CoE Member States with the anti-corruption standards and rules of the Organisation. These benchmarks are contained in the legal instruments adopted by the Council of Europe on actions against corruption – the Criminal Law Convention on Corruption with its Additional Protocol and the Civil Law Convention on Corruption – as well as the recommendations and resolutions adopted by the Committee of Ministers (in particular resolution (97)24 on the 20 Guiding Principles for the Fight against Corruption).

The Group comprises 49 States (47 Member States of the CoE plus Belarus and the United States). GRECO's main objective is to improve the capacity of its members to fight corruption by monitoring their compliance with Council of Europe anti-corruption standards through a dynamic process of mutual evaluation and peer pressure. It helps to identify shortcomings in national anti-corruption policies, prompting the necessary legislative, institutional and practical reforms. GRECO also provides a platform for sharing best practices. The GRECO monitoring system takes place in periodic cycles and includes: a "horizontal" evaluation procedure involving all the members and ending with the elaboration of recommendations on the necessary reforms in the legislative and institutional field; and a "compliance" procedure whose purpose is to assess the measures taken by Member States to implement these recommendations.

Italy has been a member of GRECO since 30 June 2007 and has undergone three evaluation rounds to date. The first two rounds were dealt with jointly and concluded in 2013 with the adoption by the Group of States of an *addendum* to the compliance report (see *2014 Yearbook*, p. 252-253). On 23 June 2014, on the basis of information previously provided by the Italian Government, GRECO adopted the compliance report (Greco RC-III(2014)9E) on the measures adopted by the Italian authorities to implement the 16 recommendations received in the course of the third monitoring round regarding two themes: I) incrimination for corruption and II) transparency of party funding (see *Yearbook 2015*, p. 229-232). In 2016, GRECO adopted two reports on Italy: the second compliance report, relative to the third monitoring cycle, adopted and published on 2 December 2016, and the evaluation report on Italy after the fourth evaluation round (GrecoEval4Rep(2016)2), adopted on 28 October 2016 and published in January 2017 (see *Yearbook 2017*, p. 225-228)

The fifth monitoring cycle was launched by GRECO on 20 March 2017, and focused on preventing corruption and promoting integrity in central governments and law enforcement. At the moment there is no date for the start of the monitoring of the Italian action with respect to these issues.

XII. Group of Experts on Action against Violence against Women and Domestic Violence

The Group of Experts (GREVIO) is the body responsible for monitoring the implementation of the Council of Europe Convention on Preventing and Combating Violence against Women and Domestic Violence (Istanbul Convention) by the Parties which have ratified it.

> GREVIO's main purpose is to draw up and publish reports evaluating legislative and other measures taken by the Parties to give effect to the provisions of the Convention. If necessary, in the event of serious and persistent acts of violence covered by the Convention, GREVIO may initiate a special inquiry procedure. It can also adopt general recommendations on themes and concepts of the Convention.
>
> GREVIO currently has 10 members (with increases in the number of ratifications of the Istanbul Convention, this can go up to 15) with multidisciplinary expertise in the area of human rights, gender equality, violence against women and domestic violence or in the assistance to and protection of victims. The first ten members of GREVIO were elected by the Committee of the Parties at its first meeting of 4 May 2015. Among them is the Italian expert Simona Lanzoni.

In 2017, after receiving the respective national reports on the state of implementation of the Istanbul Conventions, the GREVIO published the first evaluation reports on the implementation of the Istanbul Convention in the following countries: Albania, Austria, Denmark, and Monaco. The monitoring process of the Group of Experts towards Italy will begin in February 2018 with the administration of the first questionnaire. The first evaluation visit of the GREVIO in the country is scheduled for February 2019.

XIII. Lanzarote Committee

The Committee of the Parties to the Convention on the Protection of Children from Sexual Exploitation and Abuse (or "Lanzarote Committee", named after the city in which this legal instrument was adopted), is the body established by the Council of Europe in order to monitor the implementation of this Convention.

The Committee is composed by the representatives of the current and potential States party to the Convention and has the function of assessing the situation for children's protection against sexual violence at national level on the basis of information provided by national authorities in response to two periodic questionnaires (a general questionnaire and a thematic questionnaire) and in other sources. The Italian member of the Committee is Tiziana Zannini of the Department for Equal Opportunities of the Presidency of the Council of Ministers.

The Committee also functions as the facilitator of the collection, analysis, and exchange of information, experiences and best practices to increase the capacity to prevent and combat sexual abuse and violence against children. In this context, the Committee organises capacity building activities aimed at the exchange of information and the organisation of hearings on specific challenges raised by the implementation of the Convention.

In 2017, the Committee adopted a special report on the protection of children affected by the refugee crisis (3 April) and an interpretative opinion on the applicability of the Lanzarote Convention to sexual offenses against children facilitated by the use of information technology and communication technology (12 May).

European Union*

I. European Parliament

The European Parliament (EP), together with the Commission and the Council of the European Union, exercises a fundamental role in the promotion and protection of human rights within the overall framework of EU activities.

Among the permanent EP Committees prominent in human rights issues the following are highlighted: the Subcommittee on Human Rights (Chair: Pier Antonio Panzeri; other Italian member: Ignazio Corrao) within the Committee on Foreign Affairs (Italian members: Goffredo Maria Bettini, Mario Borghezio, Fabio Massimo Castaldo, Lorenzo Cesa and Pier Antonio Panzeri).

Other Committees with significant involvement in human rights issues are the Committee on Civil Liberties, Justice and Home Affairs (Italian members: Caterina Chinnici, Laura Ferrara, Lorenzo Fontana, Cécile Kashetu Kyenge, Barbara Matera and Alessandra Mussolini); the Committee on Constitutional Affairs (Vice Chair: Barbara Spinelli; other Italian members: Mercedes Bresso and Fabio Massimo Castaldo); the Committee on Legal Affairs (Vice Chair Laura Ferrara; other Italian member Enrico Gasbarra); the Committee on Employment and Social Affairs (Italian members: Laura Agea, Tiziana Beghin, Brando Benifei, Mara Bizzotto and Elena Gentile); the Committee on the Environment, Public Health and Food Safety (Italian members: Marco Affronte, Simona Bonafè, Alberto Cirio, Elisabetta Gardini, Giovanni La Via, Massimo Paolucci, Piernicola Pedicini and Damiano Zoffoli); the Committee on Development (Italian members: Ignazio Corrao and Elly Schlein); the Committee on Women's Rights and Gender Equality (Vice-Chair: Barbara Matera; other Italian members: Daniela Aiuto and Pina Picierno and the Committee on Petitions, of which more below.

In 2017, the Sakharov Prize for Freedom of Thought was awarded to the democratic opposition in Venezuela, in particular to the National Assembly (Julio Borges) and to all political prisoners on the list of the Foro Penal Venezolano, represented by Leopoldo López, Antonio Ledezma, Daniel Ceballos, Yon Goicoechea, Lorent Saleh, Alfredo Ramos, and Andrea González.

---

* Claudia Pividori

Among the European Parliament's actions adopted in 2017 containing specific references to Italy, we recall the resolution of 13 September 2017 on the mobilisation of the European Union Solidarity Fund to provide assistance to Italy (P8_TA-PROV(2017)0335).

Commission for petitions

The task of the Commission is to examine the petitions submitted by citizens (a right enshrined in the CFREU under article 44, as well as articles 24 and 227 TFEU), and endeavor to resolve any breaches of their rights under EU law. Italian members of the Commission are Alberto Cirio, Andrea Cozzolino and Eleonora Evi.

II. European Commission

The European Commission plays a central role in the development and implementation of European Union policies on human rights both within the Union and as regards third countries.

Of the 28 Commissioners, particularly important are: Frans Timmermans, First Vice-President responsible for the quality of legislation, inter-institutional relations, the rule of law and the Charter of Fundamental Rights; Dimitris Avramopoulos, Commissioner for Migration, Home Affairs and Citizenship; Marianne Thyssen, Commissioner for Employment, Social Affairs, Skills and Labour Mobility; Christos Stylianides, Commissioner for Humanitarian Aid and Crisis Management; and Věra Jourová, Commissioner for Justice, Consumers and Gender Equality.

Further details on the Commission's action can be found in the section on EU Legislation in 2017 (see Part I, International Human Rights Law, III.B).

Among the actions undertaken in 2017 particularly relevant to Italy, on 4 July 2017, the Commission presented an Action Plan to guide Italy to reduce pressure along the Central Mediterranean route and increase solidarity. Within this Plan, the Commission proposes a series of measures to be taken to accelerate collective action by the European Union along the Central Mediterranean route. As regards the Commission, these measures include: further increasing the capacities of the Libyan authorities; increase funding for migration management in Italy; ensure full mobilisation of EU agencies; start and finance a new resettlement system, in particular from Libya, Egypt, Niger, Ethiopia and Sudan; collaborating with Libya to strengthen controls on the southern border; intensify the interventions to stipulate readmission agreements; intensifying cooperation with Niger and Mali; continue to work with the International Organization for Migration to accelerate voluntary returns assisted by Libya and Niger to their countries of origin; the EU-Africa Trust Fund. Member States should: contribute more substantially to the EU-Africa Trust Fund; accelerate relocation from Italy; contribute to the dialogue with Tunisia, Egypt and Algeria; accelerate discussions on the reform of the Dublin system; mobilise their skills to contribute to the repatriation of irregular migrants from Italy. In turn, Italy should: draw up a code of conduct for NGOs carrying out research and rescue activities in the Mediterranean; respect the commitments made on relocation; quickly implement the Minniti law and expedite the repatriation.

On 21 June 2017, the Commission proposed to allocate €1.2 billion from the EU Solidarity Fund to Italy following the four earthquakes that successively hit the peninsula (24 August 2016, 26 and 30 October 2016, and 18 January 2017). On 21 November 2017, the Commission announced the allocation of €28 million of cohesion policy funds to relaunch the economic activity of the Umbria region. Lastly, in August 2017, the Italian regions hit by the earthquake accepted the first volunteer quota of the European Solidarity Corps, a new initiative of the Union launched in December 2016.

III. Council of the European Union

Within the Council there are the Human Rights Working Group (COHOM), the Working Party on Fundamental Rights, Citizens' Rights and Free Movement of Persons (FREMP), the Working Group "Asylum" and the Working Group of Public International Law (COJUR), within which a sub-group devoted to the International Criminal Court operates (COJUR-ICC).

Among the decisions adopted in 2017 containing specific references to Italy, decision 2017/1599 of the European Parliament and of the Council of 13 September 2017 on the mobilisation of the European Union Solidarity Fund to provide assistance to Italy is noteworthy.

IV. Court of Justice of the European Union

Following the entry into force of the Treaty of Lisbon, which made the Charter of Nice legally binding, the Court of Justice plays an ever more vital role for the promotion of human rights within the scope of EU law.

Italian members of the Court are currently Antonio Tizzano, as a judge and Vice-President, and Paolo Mengozzi, as an advocate-general.

According to the data provided by the CJEU, in 2017, Italy ranked second in the number of preliminary rulings (article 267 TFEU) taken before the Court (57 out of 533), preceded only by Germany. From 24-28 May, a delegation from the Court of Justice visited Italy, meeting representatives of the Constitutional Court, the Superior Council of Magistracy, the Council of State, the Court of Cassation, as well as Sergio Mattarella, President of the Republic.

For a selection of the CJEU jurisprudence concerning Italy in 2017, see Part IV, Italy in the Case-law of the Court of Justice of the European Union.

V. European External Action Service

The European External Action Service (EEAS) assists the High Representative of the Union for Foreign Affairs and Security Policy in upholding the CFSP/CSDP and ensuring the consistency of EU external actions in their functions both as President of the Foreign Affairs Council and as Vice-President of the Commission. Since November 2014, Federica Mogherini has been the High Representative.

No significant actions concerning Italy took place in 2017.

VI. Special Representative for Human Rights

Appointed by EU Council decision 2012/440/CFSP of 25 July 2012, the mandate of the European Union Special Representative for Human Rights involves enhancing dialogue with all relevant stakeholders concerning EU human rights policy, including international organisations, States as well as civil society organisations. Stavros Lambrinidis was appointed on 1 September 2012 as the first incumbent. The first mandate has been extended until 28 February 2019.

No significant actions concerning Italy took place in 2017.

VII. Fundamental Rights Agency (FRA)

An advisory body established in 2007, the FRA is the main technical instrument available to the EU with the task of supporting European and national institutions in the promotion and protection of human rights. Since 16 December 2015, Michael O'Flaherty (Ireland) has been Director of the Agency. Since July 2015, Filippo di Robilant (vice president from

29 September 2017) has been on the FRA Management Board for Italy. The latter was also appointed to the Executive Board in May 2017.

The research element of FRA's work consists mainly of the gathering and comparative analysis of data concerning the fundamental rights situation in the various EU Member States, including Italy. In this area, a brief summary is given below of some of the reports drawn up by the FRA in 2017, followed by some comments on the most significant facts that emerged concerning Italy:

- *European legal and policy framework on immigration detention of children* (June 2017): According to the report, a significant number of children are detained in the European Union pending completion of asylum or repatriation procedures. Having as a reference point the rights of the child to the protection and care set forth in article 24 CFREU, the report outlines the main safeguards foreseen in the EU to prevent illegal and arbitrary detention, with the aim of assisting Member States in implementing asylum and migration policies in line with human rights standards.

As reported, in Italy the prevailing practice is to not detain minors who are seeking asylum or involved in repatriation procedures. Similarly, families with children are not normally detained due to lack of adequate facilities. Regarding the protection of family ties, the report notes that in Italy, national law provides that mothers whose children are less than six years old can benefit from the suspension of the sentence, except for women convicted of violent crimes. and access alternative forms of detention. Finally, the report notes that in Italy, due to the unavailability of structures for minors seeking asylum, the length of stay in the first reception centres can be considerably extended, to the detriment of, among others, the right to education.

Antisemitism – Overview of data available in the European Union 2006-2016 (November 2017): The report summarises data on anti-Semitic incidents occurring in EU Member States collected from international, governmental, and non-governmental sources.

As far as Italy is concerned, data on anti-Semitic criminal conduct are collected by the General Investigations and Special Operations Division (DIGOS). The number of anti-Semitic crimes registered in Italy has increased from 16 in 2010 to 58 in 2014, while they decreased slightly in 2015 (50). No data was available for 2016 when the report was completed.

Among the actions undertaken in 2017 with a particular relevance to Italy, the FRA organised a seminar on fundamental rights aimed at hotspot operators in Taranto on 11 May 2017, in collaboration with the Ministry of the Interior, the European Commission (migrants support team), UNHCR, and IOM. The FRA also participated in some training courses for voluntary guardians of unaccompanied foreign minors and asylum seekers on 20 October in Florence; on 24 November in Cagliari; on 1 December in Pescara.

The director of the FRA, Michael O'Flaherty, visited Italy from 14-18 September to assess the evolution of the migratory situation in the central Mediterranean and the need for further support from the Agency. The director visited the hotspot in Pozzallo (Sicily) and met representatives of EU agencies and Italian authorities managing crisis points, as well as border guard units carrying out search and rescue operations.

VIII. European Ombudsman

The European Ombudsman, an institution established in 1992 by the Treaty of Maastricht and provided for in articles 24 and 228 TFEU, examines the complaints lodged by European citizens about maladministration in the institutions and bodies of the European Union. The Ombudsperson is elected by the EP, and their duties are performed with complete independence. Emily O`Reilly, previously the National Ombudsperson of the Republic of Ireland, currently holds this position.

According to the report on the activities of the European Ombudsman concerning 2016 (published on 16 May 2017), over the period considered, the Office processed 1,880 complaints, of which 101 were from Italy. Again in 2016, it launched 245 investigations (of which 29 for complaints from Italy), completing a total of 291. In the same year, 10 investigations were initiated by the Ombudsperson on their own initiative.

IX. European Data Protection Supervisor

Established by Regulation 45/2001, the European Data Protection Supervisor is responsible for ensuring the right to the protection of individual privacy in the handling of personal data by EU institutions and bodies, as specified in articles 7-8 of the Nice Charter. It is an independent body elected by the Parliament and the Council of the EU and the current Supervisor is Giovanni Buttarelli, who was previously Secretary-General to the Italian Data Protection Authority.

No significant actions concerning Italy took place in 2017.

Organization for Security and Cooperation in Europe (OSCE)*

Through a multi-dimensional approach to security, the OSCE (57 participating States) deals with conflict prevention, crisis management and post-conflict rehabilitation. Among its specific mechanisms and bodies are the Office for Democratic Institutions and Human Rights (ODIHR), the High Commissioner on National Minorities, the Representative on Freedom of the Media and the Special Representative and Coordinator for Combating Trafficking in Human Beings. human. The Italian diplomat Lamberto Zannier was Secretary General of the OSCE until July 2017. He was succeeded by Thomas Greminger, Switzerland.

The Head of the Italian mission at the OSCE is currently Amb. Alessandro Azzoni. 13 members of the Chamber of Deputies and the Senate sit in the OSCE Parliamentary Assembly. The head of the Italian parliamentary delegation is Paolo Romani. The other 12 Italian parliamentarians are: Marietta Tidei (vice president of the OSCE Parliamentary Assembly), Ferdinando Aiello, Luigi Compagna, Cristina De Pietro, Sergio Divina, Emma Fattorini, Federico Fauttilli, Claudio Fava, Francesco Monaco, Guglielmo Picchi (Vice- President of the first committee), Emanuele Scagliusi and Francesco Scalia. From 1 January 2016, the Italian official Roberto Montella is the Secretary General of the OSCE Parliamentary Assembly.

Italy is one of the major contributors to this organisation. In 2016 (latest data available), the Italian contribution to the budget was around €14.5 million (about 10.4% of the total budget), equal to those of France and the United Kingdom, lower only to the contribution of Germany (11%). Italy also contributed 1.3% of the extra budgetary expenses with a commitment of €626,859, ranking in twelfth place. In 2016, Italy had the highest number of officials involved in the Secretariat, in OSCE institutions and in field missions (61).

---

* Pietro de Perini

I. Office for Democratic Institutions and Human Rights (ODIHR)

The ODIHR is the main institution of the OSCE which has been assisting Member States in the implementation of their commitments on the human dimension since 1991. On 19 July 2017, Michael Georg Link (Germany) ended his term as Director of the Office (started on 1 July 2014). Ingibjörg Sólrún Gísladóttir (Iceland) took over.

There are no specific activities of the Office having objected to Italy in 2017. Among the documents published by the ODIHR in the year in question we mark the report *"The Responsibility of States": Protection of Human Rights Defenders in the OSCE Region (2014-2016)* on the implementation of international standards presented in the ODIHR guidelines on the protection of human rights defenders. In this report, the ODIHR provides an overview of the most critical challenges faced by the human rights defenders in the OSCE region, together with a set of best practices developed in the States Parties to the Organisation for the protection of these people and various recommendations. Numerous references to this report concern Italy with reference to good practices (protection programs for human rights defenders, importance given to human rights education issues, the promotion of a culture of rights between Government officials, the system judiciary and law enforcement agencies, as well as between the media and the general public), and in relation to some critical issues (in the field of discrimination against human rights defenders belonging to minorities, especially Roma, of defamation in the press and failure to set up independent national human rights institutions). Specific mention is made for the adoption by the Foreign Affairs Committee of the Chamber of Deputies in February 2017 of a resolution on human rights defenders (No. 7-01051) which, as reported, has incorporated proposals presented by a network of organisations for human rights (the "In Difesa di" network, see Part II, National Bodies with Jurisdiction over Human Rights, VIII).

II. High Commissioner on National Minorities

The office of the High Commissioner on National Minorities is the institution responsible for identifying, and as far as possible addressing, situations of inter-ethnic tension in the OSCE area. As well as serving as a conflict-preventing mechanism, the High Commissioner can also support quick solutions which can defuse processes of escalating violence. On 19 July 2017, the Italian diplomat Lamberto Zannier, former Secretary-General of the OSCE from 2011 to 2017, became the new

High Commissioner on national minorities, taking over from Astrid Thors (Finland).

During the year in question, there were no activities with connections to or concerning Italy.

III. Representative on Freedom of the Media

Established in 1997 with a view to ensuring a high level of compliance with the rules and standards on freedom of expression and freedom of the media accepted by the States Parties to OSCE, the Representative on Freedom of the Media acts as an early warning instrument in cases of violation of the right to freedom of expression, with particular attention to any obstacles or impediments to the activities of journalists. From March 2010 to July 2017, this position was held by Dunja Mijatovic (Bosnia and Herzegovina). On 18 July 2017, Harlem Désir (France) was appointed as the new OSCE Representative on Freedom of the Media.

During the year in question, there were no activities with connections or concerning Italy.

IV. Special Representative and Coordinator for Combating Trafficking in Human Beings

The Office of the Special Representative and Coordinator for Combating Trafficking in Human Beings is responsible for assisting OSCE States to progressively meet their commitments in this area under the 2003 Action Plan. It also serves as the body co-coordinating all OSCE activities combating trafficking. From September 2014, Madina Jarbussynova (Kazakhstan) is the OSCE Special Representative and Coordinator.

As part of a series of fact-finding missions carried out at reception and temporary protection centres in the OSCE region countries most affected by large migration movements, the Special Representative visited Italy in July 2017. The visit examined the progress of competent authorities in identifying and assisting potential victims of trafficking in mixed migratory flows. It also generated data on how to effectively support the work of law enforcement and first responders to identify trafficking victims and perpetrators and informed tailored policy recommendations and initiatives to increase skills and awareness of these phenomena.

Humanitarian and Criminal Law*

I. Adaptation to International Humanitarian and Criminal Law

Italy is part of all the main international conventions concerning the law of armed conflicts and international criminal law. With the l. 4 December 2017, No. 200, Italy ratified and implemented an amendment to the Rome Statute establishing the International Criminal Court, adopted in 2015, concerning the elimination of article 124 of the same Statute. The latter provision, better known as "opting out clause", provisionally provided that each State may declare that it does not accept, for a period of seven years from the entry into force of the Statute against it, the jurisdiction of the Court with respect to war crimes committed by their own citizens or on their territory. Italy has not yet ratified the amendments to the Rome Statute adopted in 2010 during the Review Conference of Kampala (Uganda) and related to the statutory provisions on war crimes and crime of aggression. On 6 December 2017, the Assembly of States Parties elected Italian Judge of the International Criminal Court, Rosario Salvatore Aitala.

In connection with the armaments sector, the obligation to present periodic reports on the state of implementation of the provisions of the various conventions is particularly important. In this regard, in 2017, Italy presented four reports: the annual report foreseen by the Convention on the prohibition or limitation of the use of certain conventional weapons (20 April 2017); the annual report required pursuant to article 7 of the Anti-personnel mines Convention; the report required under the Protocol on Mines and Explosive Traps and the Protocol on War Remnants Required to the Convention on the Prohibition or Restriction of the Use of Certain Conventional Weapons; the annual report required by the Oslo Convention on the Closing of Cluster Munitions (March 2017).

On 7 July 2017, the Treaty on the Ban on Nuclear Weapons was adopted. It was opened for signature on 20 September 2017 and to date (February 2018) it has been signed by 56 countries and ratified by 5. Italy, having voted against the resolution by which the United Nations

---

* Claudia Pividori

General Assembly decided to convene the Conference of elaboration of the Treaty, has not participated in the work of drafting it and is not among the signatory countries.

II. Italian Contribution to the "Peacekeeping" Missions and other International Missions

With the entry into force of the l. 21 July 2016, No. 145 regarding the participation of Italy in international missions, the procedures for authorisation and financing of the missions follow two distinct procedures: the procedure for the launch of new missions pursuant to article 2 (resolution of the Council of Ministers, transmission to the Chambers, parliamentary authorisation by means of guidelines) and the procedure for the extension of the same for the following year, included in the so-called parliamentary session on the progress of the authorised missions (articles 3 and 4). Article 3 of the law also provides that, by 31 December of each year, the Government present to the Chambers, an analytical report on the missions in progress for discussion and subsequent parliamentary deliberations. This report was presented by the Government on 28 December 2017.

For 2017, all international missions (both under way or newly activated), were authorised by activating the procedure established by article 2 of l. 21 July 2016, No. 145. In this regard, the resolutions of the Chamber of Deputies (No. 6-00290 and No. 6-00292) and of the Senate of the Republic (Doc. XXN, No. 71), approved on 8 March 2017, intervened. These resolutions authorised international missions and development co-operation interventions to support the peace and stabilisation processes envisaged by the Council of Ministers resolution of 14 January 2017, as well as the resolutions of the Chamber of Deputies (No. 6-00338) and Senate of the Republic (Doc. XXN, No. 78 and No. 80), approved on 2 August 2017. The latter authorised the international mission in support of the Libyan Coast Guard referred to in the resolution of the Council of Ministers on 28 July 2017.

The following list shows the military and police missions to which Italy participated with its own personnel in 2017. The total annual average number of armed forces' contingents used in the theatres operating in 2017 is 6,698 units. For the performance of these missions, a total fund of €1,132,505,294 was allocated for 2017.

Country/geographical area of Intervention	Italian Mission and Actions
Asia	Deployment of military personnel to the Global Coalition against Daesh
Afghanistan	Military personnel deployed to Resolute Support Mission (RSM) (NATO)
Albania	Italian police in cooperation programmes in Albania and the Balkan states
Bosnia-Herzegovina	European Union Force named ALTHEA
Cyprus	United Nations Peacekeeping Force in Cyprus (UNFICYP)
United Arab Emirates/ Bahrain/ Qatar/Tampa, USA	Deployment of military personnel to the United Arab Emirates, Bahrain, Qatar and to Tampa in support of missions in the Middle East and Asia
Kosovo/Balkans	European Union Rule of Law Mission in Kosovo (EULEX Kosovo)
	United Nations Mission in Kosovo (UNMIK)
	Operation Joint Enterprise (NATO)
Lebanon	Military contingent for training the Lebanese armed forces
	United Nations Interim Force mission in Lebanon (UNIFIL)
Libya	Sanitary support mission in Libya "Operation Hippocrates"
	United Nations Support Mission in Libya (UNSMIL)
	Assistance mission for the Libyan Coast Guard
	European Union Border Assistance Mission in Libya (EUBAM Libya)
Mali	European Union Training Mission Mail (EUTM Mali)
	Participation of military personnel in the United Nations mission in Mali, called the United Nations Multidimensional Integrated Stabilization Mission in Mali (MINUSMA)
	EUCAP Sahel Mali
Mediterranean	Deployment of military personnel to the mission in the Mediterranean Operation Active Endeavour (NATO)
	Deployment of military personnel to the European Union military operation in the Southern Central Mediterranean EUNAVFOR MED operation SOPHIA
Niger	Participation in the European Union mission EUCAP Sahel Niger

Country/geographical area of Intervention	Italian Mission and Actions
Palestine	Participation of military personnel in the mission Temporary International Presence in Hebron (TIPH2)
	Deployment of military personnel to training activities for the Palestinian Security Forces
	Participation of police and judiciary personnel in the mission denominated European Union Police Mission for the Palestinian Territories (EUPOL COPPS)
Palestine/Egypt	European Union Border Assistance Mission in Rafah (EUBAM Rafah)
Somalia/Indian Ocean	EU Atalanta – Participation of military personnel in the European Union military operation "Atalanta" combating piracy
	European Union Training Mission Somalia (EUTM Somalia)
	EUCAP Somalia (ex EUCAP Nestor)
	for the extension of the use of military personnel in training activities for the Somali and Djibouti police forces
	Running the Italian military base in the Republic of Djibouti to the needs of international missions in the Horn of Africa and the western Indian Ocean

Part IV

National and International Case-Law

Human Rights in Italian Case-law*

This section presents an overview of the case-law of the Italian courts in 2017 and highlights the theme of human rights. The focus is on the case-law of the Constitutional Court and the Court of Cassation. The intent is not to provide an exhaustive examination, but rather to cite and note the guidance and the new paths that were recorded in 2017 within Italian judicial practice regarding human rights standards, with particular reference to those reflected in international law.

The case study is preceded by a brief analysis of some data extracted from the observation of the case-law of the Court of Cassation, Civil and Criminal Divisions, and of the rulings of the administrative courts, issued over the last five years (2013-2017) for the drafting of this section of the *Italian Yearbook*.

In particular, the question addressed was how often Italian judges have made use of international human rights law. A study based on the DeJure platform (Giuffrè publishers) (https://www.iusexplorer.it/Dejure/Home/Home) highlighted in how many cases the judgements issued by the Court of Cassation and by the Administrative Courts (TAR and Council of State) have referred to the following international legal instruments: European Convention for the Protection of Human Rights and Fundamental Freedoms (ECHR); Charter of Fundamental Rights of the EU (CFREU); International Covenant on Civil and Political Rights (ICCPR), International Covenant on Economic, Social and Cultural Rights (ICESCR); Convention on the Rights of the Child (CRC).

Regarding the ECHR, the Court of Cassation, Civil Division, used it in 1835 rulings in 2013, down to 943 in 2017; the Court of Cassation, Criminal Division, cited the ECHR in 697 cases in 2013, increased to 1362 in 2017 (the peak was 1541 recurrences in 2016); it was mentioned by the administrative judges (TAR and Council of State) 550 times in 2013 and 574 in 2017. Therefore, the decline in use in the Civil Division of the Court of Cassation and the increase in the criminal division stands out. This data must be integrated with a decisive element: the "Pinto" cases. The progressive "internalisation" of the proceeding to compensate those who are victims of excessive duration in proceedings has led to a strong incidence of rulings by the Court of Cassation, Civil Division, on

* Paolo De Stefani

this type of appeals, an incidence that has considerably decreased over the years.

In 2013, the "Pinto" rulings were 70% of the overall decisions of the Court of Cassation, Civil Division referring the ECHR, while in 2017, this percentage fell to 29%. "Purified" of this component, the recurrence of the ECHR in the case-law of the Court of Cassation, Civil Division, has not decreased by half, as indicated above, but significantly increased during the past five years: from 544 "non-Pinto" cases of 2013 it has in fact passed to 670 in 2017. The Court of Cassation, Criminal Division, used the ECHR in 697 recurrences in 2013, increased to 1025 the following year, 1183 in 2015, 1541 in 2016 and 1362 in 2017. In the last two years, therefore, the Court of Cassation, Criminal Division, has used the ECHR more often than the Civil Division. The administrative justice cited the ECHR in 550 cases in 2013, 626 in 2014, 476 in 2015, 256 in 2016, 574 in 2017 – more than half of the cases, between 2013 and 2015, were "Pinto" cases; in 2016, there were only 25 cases of this type and 154 (out of a total of 574) in 2017.

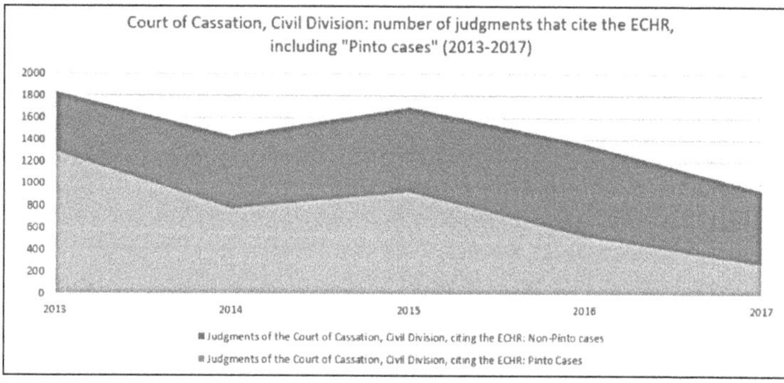

Source: elaboration by the *2018 Yearbook* research and editorial board

Overall, the decisions of the Italian jurisdictional instances above considered (i.e. Court of Cassation and Administrative Courts), which have in some way recalled the role of the ECHR (and directly or indirectly the case-law of the ECtHR) have remained around 4% over the past years, with a peak of 4.8% in 2015 and a decrease to 3.5% in 2017.

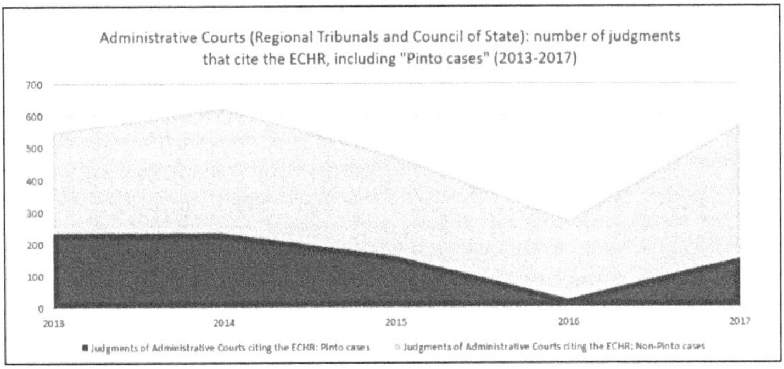

Source: elaboration by the *2018 Yearbook* research and editorial board

The numbers referring to the other international instruments considered are much more contained. The CFREU is often cited in conjunction with the ECHR. The Court of Cassation, Civil Division, has cited the ECHR and the CFREU together in 222 rulings in 2013, decreased to 56 in 2017; simultaneously, however, the autonomous relevance of the CFREU was increasing. It was cited separately from the ECHR 44 times in 2013 and 99 in 2017 (with a peak of 162 recurrences in 2016). The ratios are found to be inverted in the field of administrative justice, where in 2013 the rulings referring exclusively to the CFREU were clearly prevailing compared to those in which the CFREU and the CEDU were cited together; Almost equivalence was achieved in 2015, before moving back to a prevalence of the EU instrument in 2017 (80 decisions mentioning only the CFREU versus 49 that cite it together with the ECHR).

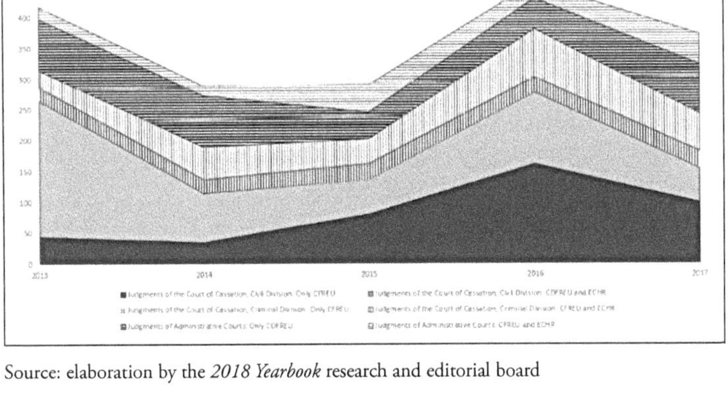

Source: elaboration by the *2018 Yearbook* research and editorial board

An international instrument that has remained relatively recalled in the Italian case-law is the CRC. The Convention on the Rights of the Child is referred to by the Court of Cassation, Civil Division, in 16 decisions in 2013, 22 in 2014 and 2015, 18 in 2016 and 20 in 2017. For the Court of Cassation, criminal division, cases are around 5 per year between 2013 and 2016, going up to 10 in 2017. Administrative justice has cited it in 6 cases in 2013, 5 in 2014, 4 in 2015, 2 in 2016 and 12 in 2017.

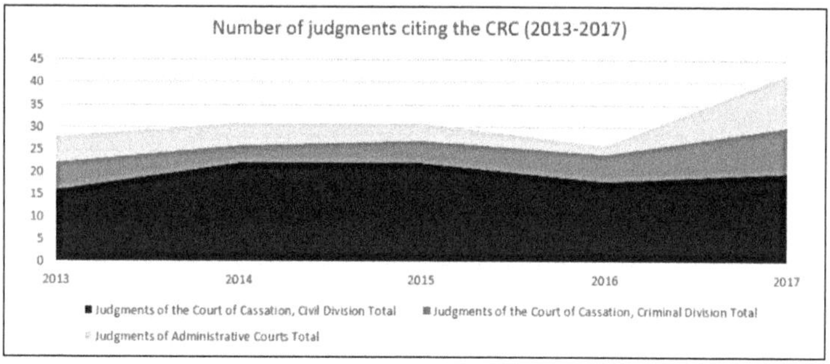

Source: elaboration by the *2018 Yearbook* research and editorial board

The Covenant on Civil and Political Rights (ICCPR) recurs in 4 decisions of the Court of Cassation, Civil Division, in 2013, 3 in 2014, 8 in 2015, 7 in 2016 and again 8 in 2017. The recurrences are higher at the Court of Cassation, criminal division: between 40 and 45 per year between 2013 and 2016, 28 in 2017. There were few recurrences per year in administrative cases.

The Covenant on Economic, Social and Cultural Rights is practically unknown to the Italian courts considered here.

By far the most significant presence among the instruments considered is therefore that of the ECHR (also including the jurisprudence of the ECtHR). In particular, it is important to point out the remarkable reduction of the "Pinto" cases, which highlighted the norms of the ECHR other than article 6(1) ECHR related to the excessive duration of proceedings. In fact, also articles 3, 8 and 13 of the ECHR are widely recalled. When it comes to criminal proceedings, the principles of fair trial – as enshrined in article 6 ECHR, but also in similar provisions of the ICCPR – are certainly those most cited.

I. Aspects of the Relationship between the Italian Justice System and European Case-law

A. Obligation to Abide by the Final Judgements of the ECtHR: Article 46 ECHR does not Impose the Revocability of Final Judgements in Civil and Administrative Matters

With judg. 26 May 2017, No. 123 the Constitutional Court examines the Italian legal system obligation to comply with the decisions adopted by the ECtHR, an obligation which nevertheless seems to find a limitation in the final nature of the judgements adopted in Italy on the subject addressed by the ECtHR. The question of constitutionality has been raised by the Council of State in relation to final Italian judgements which, although being recognised in conflict with the ECHR for procedural shortcomings, could not be revoked in the absence of a specific rule in the public administration code and in the code of civil procedure (see *Yearbook 2016*, p. 215). The judgements of the ECtHR held that, in dealing with some cases of doctors who would have been entitled to be hired indefinitely by the University of Naples, the Italian administrative justice had not respected, in particular, the fair trial standards of the article 6 CEDU.

The Constitutional Court recognises that in many cases the reopening of the trial, despite the existence of the *res judicata*, would be the most appropriate means to restore the situation to the state prior to the adoption of the ruling contrary to the ECHR. The reopening of the process is also the measure recommended by the Committee of Ministers of the Council of Europe (Recommendation R(2000) 19 January 2000, No. 2). In fact, practically all the States of the Council of Europe have adopted laws that allow this procedure in the case of criminal judgements, and more than half of them provide also for civil and administrative matters. In 2011, the Constitutional Court established that a constitutionally oriented approach, consistent with the ECtHR case-law, regarding article 630 Criminal Procedure Code, makes it necessary to include the execution of a judgement of the ECtHR that has found a violation of the ECHR among the legitimate bases for a retrial (see *Yearbook 2012*, p. 327-328). The question that is now proposed is whether the reopening of the process should be considered imposed by article 46 ECHR (obligation to comply with the judgements of the ECtHR), through article 117(1) Cost., also in civil and administrative litigations.

The Constitutional Court points out that while in the criminal process the State, in whose name the criminal action is conducted, is the only subject that is opposed to the applicant, in the matters subject to civil or administrative judgements the parties are mostly other private subjects or administrations different from the State central administration. In these cases, the value of legal certainty and therefore of the *res iudicata* is meant to guarantee all the parties in the judicial proceedings and the State, with its legislation, cannot curtail it to the sole advantage of those who filed an application with the ECtHR.

In the absence of an amendment to the ECtHR rules of procedure allowing adequate participation in the proceedings before the ECtHR of all parties involved in the original trial (according to current rules, the participation of parties other than the applicant and the respondent State takes place only at the discretion of the President of the ECtHR), the Constitutional Court considers that the established violation of the ECHR by the State does not create an obligation for the Italian State to reopen a trial that awarded a final judgement in matters different than criminal law.

Therefore, the absence of a law that foresees this reopening does not constitute a violation of article 46 ECHR and the question of constitutionality regarding article 117(1) of the Constitution is declared unfounded. On similar matters, see also the decision of the Constitutional Court 166/2017, referred to in paragraph VII.A.

B. The Limitation Regime for VAT Fraud: Relationship between Italian Law and EU Law

The Constitutional Court has ordered a preliminary reference to the ECJ on a particularly sensitive issue, namely the statute of limitations in the case of VAT fraud offenses. These offenses directly affect EU financial interests, protected by article 325 TFEU. In the *Taricco* judgement (8 September 2015, C-105/14), the ECJ ruled that if an Italian provision in relation to limitation periods for such frauds against the EU prevents the imposition of effective penalties in a significant number of cases of serious fraud affecting the financial interests of the EU, or disposes for longer limitation periods in respect of cases of fraud affecting the financial interests of the Italian State than in respect of those affecting the financial interests of the EU, then the national court must disapply the norms of national law regarding the statute of limitations and issue a judgement on the matter. Some courts have found that such ruling of the ECJ seems to modify the Italian legislation on the limitation period, applying EU law to the detriment of that of the State, and this with retroactive effect, since the obligation to disapply the rules on limitation is imposed in all the trials, even for offenses committed before the *Taricco* ruling. In this way, the violation of a series of articles of the Constitution is assumed, in particular article 25.2 of the Constitution, on the prohibition of retroactive application of the criminal law.

According to the prevailing Italian doctrine and the jurisprudence of the Constitutional Court, the limitation rules, since they lead to the punishment or otherwise of the offender, must be considered entirely equivalent to those that define a criminal offense. In the tradition of other European countries and also in the *Taricco* ruling of the ECJ, the idea prevails that the rules on limitation are procedural in nature, thus, their application to proceedings relating to crimes committed in the past, although they may have consequences on the punishment or not of the accused, do not pose problems of legality.

The doubts of the Constitutional Court are based precisely on this Italian peculiarity regarding the legal concept of the statute of limitations. The *Taricco* ruling seems to highlight a contrast between EU law (which of course provides for the principle of non-retroactivity of the criminal law in article 49 CFREU and article 7 ECHR, but does not consider the statute of limitation as part of substantive criminal law) and the supreme principles of the Italian legal system, which affirm the principle of legality (or non-retroactivity of the criminal law) also with regard to the statute of limitations. Furthermore, the criteria that according to the ECJ must guide the internal judge in disregarding the Italian rule on limitation (namely the existence of a serious financial damage to the EU resulting from the existence of a significant number of cases in which the statute of limitations bars a criminal trial) are not sufficiently determined and require an intense intervention of the subjective assessment of the judge, once again in violation of the principle of strict legality.

According to the Constitutional Court, however, this contrast is only apparent, as it is a common principle in EU law, also referred to in the *Taricco* judgement, that EU law must harmonise with the constitutional traditions of the Member States, and not simply impose on them. Therefore, when a ruling by the ECJ requires the judge to disapply a national provision that deals with constitutional principles of the concerned State aiming at protecting fundamental rights, the judge is required to disapply the domestic law only subject to verification of the fulfilment of the rights affected. In the case in question, the decision of the ECJ that requires not to apply the statute of limitations if in conflict with article 325 TFEU, can only produce effects if it is ascertained (and this assessment is a task of the Italian Constitutional Court) that the disapplication does not imply a violation of the Italian Constitution. According to the Constitutional Court, this reading is in line with EU law and does not invade the ECJ's jurisdiction, as that which the Constitutional Court should deal with is not the interpretation of a TFEU rule, but only the compatibility of the ECJ interpretation of article 325 with the Italian

Constitution. It should be added that, in the present case, the traditional position of the Italian jurisprudence and doctrine, namely that the statute of limitations is part of substantive rather than procedural law, carries out a more advanced protection of the defence's rights and therefore its prevalence would be in line with the general principle of favouring the national law which provides for greater protection of fundamental rights over international or EU law (see article 53 CFREU and article 53 ECHR). It is now up to the ECJ to uphold or reject this line of reasoning, which would establish, once for all, the applicability of the statute of limitations, as part of the principle of legality, even when this would result in damage to the EU budget.

C. Administrative Penalties Imposed on the Basis of Rules That Have Been Subsequently Declared Unconstitutional: Final Judgements Should Not Be Annulled

The Court of Cassation doubts the constitutionality of a provision of the law establishing the Constitutional Court (11 March 1953, article 30, para 4), which states that judgements that find unconstitutional a criminal law norm entail the cessation of the effects of any criminal judgements adopted on the basis of the rule recognised as illegal even if they are final judgements. The case concerns a decision of the Constitutional Court (judg. 153/2014) that had considered illegitimate the administrative pecuniary sanctions for employers, introduced by legislative decree in 2013, in some cases of exploitation of workers. The Constitutional Court found that the decree was in violation of delegation law, that did not permit harsher sanctions in respect to the previous regime. To the employer, subject of an administrative sanction for violation of the norms subsequently recognised unconstitutional, the provisions of l. 87/1953 cannot be applied, since the sanction applied in this regard is administrative and not penal in nature. However, based on the criteria developed by the ECtHR in the 1970s, this sanction would have all the characteristics of a penal sanction, since it is applied as a general rule, has a repressive/preventive character, and/or reaches a considerable punitive level, being likely to reach a huge amount of money. Article 30 of l. 87/1953 is therefore of doubtful constitutionality, since by expressly mentioning only criminal judgements and not administrative judgements comparable to those of criminal nature, it would introduce a discrimination and would not allow the retroactive application of the mitigating effects of the ruling on constitutionality, overcoming the obstacle posed by the final character of the judgement.

According to the Constitutional Court (24 February 2017, No. 43), the jurisprudence of the ECtHR does not impose as a general rule the principle that a declaration of invalidity *ex tunc (i.e.* retroactive*)* of a law on the quantification of a penalty substantially criminal according to the said criteria, necessarily involves the annulment of a final judgement that imposed that sanction. This effect on judgements that have become final (*res iudicata)* will only concern, according to article 30 l. 87/1953, criminal judgements in formal sense, as those that most profoundly affect the personality of the convicted individual, and does not extend to administrative judgements, even if they may be considered substantially criminal according to the parameters of the ECtHR. This choice was made by the Italian legislator and does not appear unreasonable; it does not conflict with the ECHR, nor with the ECtHR jurisprudence, and can therefore be considered constitutionally legitimate. According to the jurisprudence of the ECtHR, in fact, the principle of legality (article 7 ECHR) obliges not to apply retroactively the incriminating norms, nor those that establish higher penalties, and to apply retroactively the norms that repeal a crime or which establish lighter penalties, provided this does not conflict with the rules on the final character of a criminal judgement. The obligation to retroactively apply a declaration of unconstitutionality of a rule on the determination of the sanction, quashing any judgements including those that are final, does not appear to have been affirmed by the ECtHR. The rule, therefore, cannot be applied outside the specific cases in which the national law so provides.

D. Administrative Sanctions Replacing Criminal Penalties

The Constitutional Court has dealt with a number of questions of constitutionality raised by various local tribunals that claimed the possible illegitimacy of certain law provisions which, by decriminalising and bringing to the status of administrative offenses some financial crimes (in particular the abuse of privileged information), they provided as penalty the confiscation by equivalent (that is, the confiscation of assets of the offender not directly linked to the crime, including sums of cash). This measure is also applied to acts committed before the entry into force of the bill on decriminalisation, provided that the related criminal trial has not ended. It was deemed that in this way the legislator has retroactively introduced a sanction which, although nominally administrative, represents in substance a criminal penalty according to the jurisprudence of the ECtHR, since it applies in a general way, is punitive in nature and seriously affects the subject against which is imposed. A criminal penalty applied with retroactive effect is in contrast with article 25.2 of the Constitution and with article 7 ECHR (interposed norm), hence the question of constitutional legitimacy.

The Constitutional Court (judg. 7 April 2017, No. 68) eventually declared the claim inadmissible. In fact, it has not been established by the referring courts if in the specific circumstances the new administrative sanction appears to be more serious than the previous penal one. It is indeed true that its administrative character does not automatically make it milder; on the other hand, however, the mere prediction of the possibility of a confiscation by equivalent is not sufficient to qualify it as more serious. Since the point has not been clarified by the referring courts, the conclusion can only be the inadmissibility of the appeal. Later on, however, the Court of Cassation renewed the request for a ruling on the constitutionality of the law in question, noting that the new sanctioning regime, although no longer criminal in accordance with Italian law, is nevertheless more severe for the individual (see Civil Cassation sec. II, Order of 29 December 2017, No. 31143).

On a similar matter, it is worth mentioning the judgement of the Constitutional Court 11 May 2017, No. 109. In this case, the depenalisation affected the offense of failing to pay social security and welfare withholdings for an amount lower than €10,000 per year. In this case, the question of constitutionality is also considered inadmissible.

II. Dignity of the Person, Right to Identity

A. Anonymous Birth and the Right of the Child to Know the Identity of the Mother

The Court of Cassation (Civil Cassation, joint sections, judg. 25 January 2017, No. 1946) pronounces on the right of an individual to know his/her origins, even when the mother wanted to keep her identity hidden at the childbirth. The Constitutional Court, with judgement 278/2013 (an adding-principle judgement, see *Yearbook 2014*, p. 278) had requested the establishment by law of a procedure that will allow a court to ascertain the natural mother's enduring desire not to disclose her own identity to the child when the latter, having become an adult, asks to access this information. The point to clarify is if, in the absence of such a law, the request made by the son to the judicial authority (juvenile court: see Civil Cassation, sec. I, judg. 7 June 2017, No. 14162) to verify, with due respect for the privacy of the woman, the mother's persistent will to maintain anonymity, is admissible or not. The conclusion of the joint sections is that an ordinary judge, pending the adoption of a law, can proceed to verify the consent of the mother to come out of anonymity. In the absence of such consent, the child's request must be rejected. Rejecting the request of the child pending the intervention of the legislator, would place the Italian system in contrast with the ECHR, in light of the fact that the ECtHR, as from the *Godelli v. Italy 2012* (see *Yearbook 2013*, p. 371, see also *Yearbook 2017*, p. 273-274) has held that the legislation in force for anonymous birth is too rigid and does not fulfil the individual's right to private life (article 8 ECHR).

B. Gender correction in Civil Status Registries

Some judges doubt the constitutional legitimacy, for violation of articles 2, 3 and 32 of the Constitution and article 8 ECHR as an interposed rule, of article 1 of l. 164/1982 (rules on rectifying the attribution of sex), in so far as it requires that the rectification of personal documents with regard to the sex (and name) of a person may take place "following changes in his/her sexual characteristics". Despite what has been affirmed several times by the Italian Court of Cassation and the Constitutional Court (see *Yearbook 2016*, p. 219-221) case-law, the law seems to indicate that it is necessary to carry out highly invasive surgical operations, violating the individual's right to gender identity, as a necessary precondition for the Civil Status Registry. The Constitutional Court (judg. 13 July 2017, No. 180) confirms its own case-law and that of the Court of Cassation by declaring the question unfounded. Both courts had interpreted the contested provision as also including provisions on the "modification of sexual features" which do not involve any surgical intervention. However, this does not mean, according to the Constitutional Court, that in order to authorise the rectification of sex determination in the Civil Status Registries, verifying the wish for change expressed by the person concerned is enough. On the contrary, it is for the competent court to establish the existence of an objective transition of the gender identity, in addition to the willingness expressed by the person concerned to change sex. This latter may completely disregard surgical operations. This must take place by balancing the individual's right to gender identity and the public interest in the certainty of legal relations.

In this regard, the Court of Cassation, Civil Division, section I, judg. 14 December 2017, No. 30125 is also noted. Since surgery on the primary anatomical sexual characteristics is not to be considered indispensable to determine the unambiguous and definitive change of sex which gives the right to rectify personal data, the provision of l. 164/1982 no longer applies, a law that sets a deadline of one year from the entry into force of the law to require the rectification of personal data by those who underwent surgery adjustment before 1982.

The judgements of the Court of Bologna, sec. I, 7 June 2017, No. 966; 3 August 2017, No. 1753; of the Court of Rome, sec I, 20 January 2017; 13 April 2017, No. 7518; 7 June 2017, No. 80; 4 August 2017, No. 15902, are largely applicable to the principles identified above.

C. "Surrogate" Maternity

The Constitutional Court was called to judge on the legitimacy of article 263 of the Civil Code (previous version of the Civil Code, the controversial point of which was not clarified by the reform in 2013) which allows the recognition of natural offspring with lack of evidence for a genetic link to be contested without taking the interest of the child into account. The case presented to the Constitutional Court concerned a married Italian couple who had travelled to a foreign country for a "surrogate maternity" procedure through egg donation and had then arranged to recognise the child as their own, still in the foreign country. After registering the birth certificate in Italy, the Public Prosecutor at the Juvenile Court had launched an investigation, entrusting the child to a special administrator which challenged the mother's recognition of the child. The results of the DNA tests showed that the child was genetically related to registered the father but not the woman registered as the mother (therefore entailed a state of non-adoptability).

According to the referring court, the Civil Code clearly privileges verifying the truth about the child's origins and does not in any way consider the child's interest since the relationship with the to-be mother would be cut off (social parenting). This fact would constitute a violation of the principle of the best interests of the child sanctioned by the CRC (among others, see judgement 31/2012 of the same Constitutional Court, see *Yearbook 2013*, p. 333).

The provision is also contrary to article 8 ECHR, in particular in the light of the *Paradiso and Campanelli v. Italy* case in 2015 (see *Yearbook 2016*, p. 263 – see also below, Italy in the Case-law of the European Court of Human Rights, III) the 2017 Grand Chamber's ruling that overturned the Chamber's conclusions). Parties to the underlying proceedings, including the child's special curator, supported the non-constitutionality of the provision, stressing that the public interest in verifying the filiation status should not necessarily and automatically prevail over the interest of the child. The constitutional provisions allegedly infringed are articles 2, 3, 30, 31 and 117(1) of the Italian Constitution (this latter, through the interposed provisions of the ECHR, of the CRC and of the CFREU, article 24).

In judg. 18 December 2017, No. 272, the Constitutional Court dismissed the claim and considered the question of constitutionality as ill-founded. The Court firstly recalls that various law provisions, including the 2013 reform in the realm of family law, limit the possibility of challenging the recognition of the child for lack of proven genetic link, or prohibit the promotion of the act of paternal disowning. It therefore reaffirms the prevalence, under certain conditions, of the interest of the child over the need to prove a genetic link. Genetic links, however, form part of a person's identity and could not therefore be totally sacrificed if the child's best interest were to be fully pursued. In conclusion, the Court does not agree that article 263 of the Civil Code, although failing to mention the best interest of the child, gives exclusive importance to the child's biological status and notices that within the framework of Italian in-force legislation, there are ways to ensure parenthood even when the lack of genetic links is ascertained, as evidenced by the very case that gave rise to the referral. On the other hand, the importance to be given to the best interest of the child cannot outright cancel the strong disvalue that Italian law ascribes to the surrogate maternity, which is prohibited by unequivocal criminal law provisions.

D. Registration of foreign administrative acts and alleged incompatibility of same-sex marriage with public order

The Court of Cassation, Civil Division, has ruled on further cases in which the Italian civil status authorities rejected the request to register as the child of both members of a homosexual couple, legally married in a foreign country, the child born abroad as a result of assisted procreation methods. The case dealt with by the Court of Cassation, Civil Division, sec. I, judg. 15 June 2017, No. 14878 concerned a request to register in Italy the correction made to the foreign act acknowledging the baby as the child of both members of the couple, instead of just one. The application was rejected by the registrar of the municipality of Venice, who considered the request contrary to public order, since the inclusion as the second legitimate parent of the child of the other member of a same-sex couple would have implied recognition of the effects of same-sex marriage, which is not possible under Italian law. The Courts that subsequently intervened during 2015 had confirmed the validity of the rejection based on the concept of public order.

Section I of the Court of Cassation notes that, firstly, l. 76/2016 introduced into the Italian legal system a form of same-sex partnership which, although not fully equating the so-called "civil partnerships" with the marriage (in particular as regards the legislation on adoption), does not allow the same-sex marriage to be considered totally alien to Italian law. Above all, however, the Court dwells on the notion of public order relevant in that circumstance, namely, the registration in Italy of an administrative act issued abroad. The relevant notion is not that of national public order (a concept that determines the limits to private autonomy imposed by peremptory norms of the State), but of international public order, understood as setting limits on the application in the State of foreign laws, limits that ought to be assessed in the light of the legal principles characterising the current historical moment at both domestic and international levels. Following a broad analysis of national legislations in domains such as non-discrimination on grounds of sex, the right to marry and found a family, the right to private and family life and the rights of the child (to protection, family, personal identity, the principle of the best interests of the child, etc.), as well as the relevant provisions of the Constitution and recalling the numerous judgements of the ECHR on the subject, the Supreme Court finally concludes that the registration in Italy of a foreign document showing that a minor is the child of two persons of the same sex (in this case, two women) legally bound in marriage, is not contrary to (international) public order.

The judgement is fully compatible with that of the Joint Sections 20 September, 2016, No. 19599 (see *Yearbook 2017*, p. 252-253), which is in fact widely quoted.

In a similar vein, the Court of Trent (judg. 23 February 2017) points out that in recent years the notion of parental responsibility has also emerged in our legislation, so that it seems that the model of parenthood based solely on the biological bond between the parent and the child has been overcome. The Court therefore recognises the effects in Italy of the act issued by the Canadian authorities certifying that two children born with surrogacy are the children of both members of an Italian homosexual couple.

E. Access to Heterologous Fertilisation and Pre-implantation Diagnosis

In 2015, the Health Councillor of the Autonomous Province of Trent excluded heterologous insemination from the services provided by the provincial health service, with the consequence that couples who wanted to have access to this treatment in other Italian regions would have to do so at their own expenses. The reason given was that this procedure was not mentioned as an essential level of healthcare. A couple brought the matter before the Court of Trent, alleging that the position of the health administration was unlawful, because it prevented totally infertile couples, as the one in question, for whom no possibility of homologous fertilisation can be envisaged, to self-determine in such matter. While acknowledging the non-absolute nature of the right to health, which is, in particular, conditioned by the availability of financial resources allocated to the health services, the Court nevertheless considers that it is the responsibility of the health authority to reasonably guarantee equal treatment to all persons in a similar situation of need – namely infertile couples. Recalling the judgement of the Constitutional Court 162/2014 (see *Yearbook 2015*, p. 252), the Court observes that the impossibility of having their own child by resorting to heterologous fertilisation techniques can have a substantial negative impact on the health of the couple (the judgement speaks in this regard of disability). The persisting absence of the heterologous fertilisation methods among the health procedures included within the essential levels of healthcare does not justify, for an administration that is not in financial hardship, the denial of the right of couples with this disability to have access to the procedure, as an incompressible dimension of their right to health (Court of Trent, judg. 16 February 2017).

The Court of Milan has ruled on several occasions on the refusal by some hospitals in Lombardy to proceed with pre-implantation diagnosis on embryos produced through assisted procreation techniques and potentially affected by serious diseases, so as to select the healthy embryos to implant in the mother's uterus. Such diagnosis was in line with the decision of the Constitutional Court 96/2015 (see *Yearbook 2016*, p. 218), an adding-principle judgement, which had on this point recognised some flaws in l. 40/2004 on medically assisted procreation, calling for legislative amendments, but also endowing the courts with the authority to decide the pending cases on this matter. While recognising that the practices required for pre-implantation diagnosis on embryos are not yet included among the essential levels of assistance, the Court requires the health authorities to carry out the diagnosis requested, as per the ruling of the Constitutional Court, finding that there is a high risk for the embryos so produced to be carriers of serious diseases transmitted by parents and highlighting that the medical and technological resources to conduct such diagnosis are accessible in health facilities in Lombardy (Court of Milan, sec. I, judg. 18 April, 13 July and 21 July 2017).

F. Violence against Women

The Court of Cassation, criminal division, sec. VI, judg. 6 October 2017, No. 49997, the Supreme Court confirmed that in the crime of mistreatment in the family, the legal asset protected is not only the family, but also the physical and psychological safety of family members. In this particular case, the convicted person had mistreated his wife for years with repeated beatings, death threats, harassment and humiliation, including preventing her from working outside the home. In another case (Court of Cassation, Criminal Division, sec. III, judg. 21 February 2017, No. 16543), the husband had imposed the presence of his lover on his wife by using threats.

According to the Court of Cassation, criminal division, sec. VI, judg. 19 December 2017, No. 3087, the oppressive conduct against a spouse who is no longer a cohabitee constitutes the crime of mistreatment in the family (article 572 of the Criminal Code) and not that of stalking, since the bonds arising from the family relationship remain intact even after the termination of the cohabitation. The crime of stalking (*atti persecutori*: article 612-*bis* of the Criminal Code) may be applied when a divorce has taken place or a de facto relationship has ceased. (see also Court of Cassation, Criminal Division, sec. VI, judg. 13 December 2017, No. 3356; sec. III, judg. 14 November 2017, No. 6919). Similarly, the crime referred to in article 572 of the Criminal Code as well occurs when the cohabitation of persons who have lived *more uxorio* outside of marriage comes to an end, given that there is a stability of relations between the two, dependent on their duties with respect to their child (Court of Cassation, Criminal Division, sec. VI, judg. 20 April 2017, No. 25498).

Article 11 of l. 122/2016 regulated the right to compensation in favour of victims of violent intentional crimes, finally implementing Directive 2004/80/EC. The law provides that the State must provide compensation to victims of these crimes (as well as the crime of illicit intermediation and exploitation of labour) who find themselves in poor economic conditions, when the offender is insolvent or remains unknown or unenforceable. There is a difference of approach in the application of the relevant provisions of the law in question. The Court of Appeal of Milan, judg. 18 April 2017, No. 1653 found that the Italian provision requires the prior enforcement of the offender as a condition for access to compensation at the expense of the State. If this were the case, the provision should, according to the aforementioned judgement, be disapplied, as it would be clearly contrary to the aims of the Directive. It should facilitate the victim's access to compensation, in particular in cases where the person is the victim of a transnational crime, or suffered in a European country other than his or her own or by nationals of EU Member States other than his or her own. The Court of Turin instead (sec. IV, judg. 18 April 2017, No. 2067), ruling on the request made by a woman victim of sexual violence and other injuries, highlights the peculiarities of the Italian system, which distinguishes between victims of terrorist crimes and mafia, and victims of other intentional violent crimes: while for the former the State provides immediate and direct compensation, for the latter the protection of the State is just subsidiary. In order to have access to the subsidiary compensation, however, according to this adapting interpretation, it is not necessary to finalise the enforcement procedure on the individual, but it is sufficient to provide evidence of his incapability to pay any compensation. In the specific case, such evidence had not been provided, the applicant having merely indicated that the offender is still in detention and has never offered any compensation.

III. Political Rights and Freedom of Association; Citizenship; Freedom of the Press

A. Electoral Law

The Constitutional Court ruled (judg. 9 February 2017, No. 35) on the constitutionality of l. 52/2015, the so-called "Italicum" law, which amended the electoral laws for the Chamber of Deputies (d.p.r. 361/1957) and the Senate (lgs.d. 533/1993), an issue raised by the courts of Messina, Turin, Perugia and Genoa. The ruling was of considerable political importance, in particular because it forced the Parliament to legislate urgently on the matter, given the impending electoral deadline (in 2018). The decision was in line with judg. 1/2014 (see *Yearbook 2015*, p. 258), which found some of the provisions of the electoral law reform introduced by law 270/2005 (the so-called "Porcellum" law) constitutionally illegitimate. In its 2017 decision, the Constitutional Court once again found that the Parliament enacted a law that articulated the principles of parliamentary representation of the citizens entitled to vote, of freedom and equality of voting and of effective governance (all constitutionally protected principles) in a way that was disproportionate and unreasonable. The provisions of the electoral law that provided for a second ballot between the lists with the highest number of votes, in the event that no one had reached 40% and the norm that provided for the possibility for the candidate elected in more than one multi member district to choose in which district the actual election had taken place, were thus considered unconstitutional. The Court also specifies that the electoral law as reformed in 2005, although deprived of the censored rules, remains in force and suitable for possible use in the next elections (Parliament has however adopted a new electoral law: l. 3 November 2017, No. 165, so-called "*Rosatellum*").

B. Political Rights of Members of the Armed Forces

In 2010, a Carabinieri officer was sanctioned with disciplinary measures (warning and close arrest) for joining a political party (the *Lega Nord – Bossi*) as well as for assuming the position of regional secretary of a political party for Piedmont (the *Party for Defence and Security Workers*). The punitive measure was challenged before the courts on the ground that it was contrary to the fundamental right to freedom of association and participation in political life, protected inter alia by article 11 ECHR, article 12 CFREU and article 22 ICCPR. Article 49 of the Constitution recognises the right of every citizen to associate in political parties and contribute, with a democratic method, to the determination of the politics of the country; the subsequent article 98 of the Constitution adds that, by law, the State can set limits to the right to join political parties for certain categories of citizens, including members of the armed forces. Before the Council of State, competent in the dispute between the sanctioned military and the State, the government representative had argued that the rules of the Military Law Code, which establishes the principle according to which armed forces must stay outside the political arena, necessarily imply that the military cannot join political parties or take up positions within them. According to the Council of State, however, the ban on membership of political parties must be explicitly spelled in the law and cannot be inferred from a general provision of the Military Law Code. The sanction for enrolment in the *Lega Nord – Bossi* must therefore be annulled. As regards the occupation of leading positions within a political grouping, this is incompatible with military status. Accordingly, the Military Law Code provides for a special leave for military personnel participating in electoral campaigns and for extended leave of military personnel elected in political positions. The sanction issued for having taken a leadership position within a political group was therefore lawful (Council of State, sec. IV, judg. 12 December 2017, No. 5845).

The Veneto Regional Administrative Court (sec. I, order 3 November 2017, No. 981) raised the question of constitutionality in relation to a provision of the Military Law Code which prohibits the military from forming trade unions, allegedly in breach of articles 11 and 14 ECHR, and thus contrary to article 117(1) of the Constitution.

IV. Asylum and International Protection

A. Judicial Claims against the Rejection of International Protection Applications

The Joint Sections of the Court of Cassation (Civil Division, joint sections, judg. 28 February 2017, No. 5059) confirm that it is up to the ordinary judge and not the administrative courts, to hear the appeals against the denial of issuing a residence permit for humanitarian reasons decided by the head of the National Police Headquarters (*Questore*) in accordance with article 5(6) of the Consolidated Act on Immigration (lgs.d. 286/1998). In fact, the measure directly affects the fundamental rights of the concerned person, and not just its legitimate interests. Since the attribution of the humanitarian protection status is the task of the Territorial Commissions, the issuing of the residence permit for humanitarian protection should follow automatically and the Police does not have any discretionary power in it.

The Italian legislation on international protection (lgs.d. 19 November 2007, No. 251 and subsequent reforms) incorporates the principle prohibiting the repatriation of an individual to a State where he or she risks being subjected to inhuman or degrading treatment. This principle is also reiterated and emphasised in the Istanbul Convention of the Council of Europe on preventing and combating violence against women. A Moroccan woman who feared, in case of repatriation to her country, to suffer further harassment and violence from her ex-husband, such conduct being only mildly punished in that country, is theoretically entitled to international protection status, even if domestic violence is a private matter that does not depend on the particular socio-political context of Morocco (Civil Cassation, sec. VI, judg. 17 May 2017, No. 12333).

The Court of Cassation reiterated that the conditions of extreme poverty affecting a migrant landed in Italy, in particular the impairment of his/her right to food and health in his/her country of origin, do not justify the granting, alternatively to refugee status and/or subsidiary protection, of humanitarian protection under article 5(6) lgs.d. 286/1998. Humanitarian protection is accorded based on evidence of serious violations of human rights, such as the right to life, the right not to be subjected to torture, the right not to be reduced to slavery, etc., faced by the applicant due to the deeds of some specific entities, and does not lend itself to be granted to those who complain about the poor economic or health conditions of their country (Court of Cassation, Civil Division, sec. VI, judg. 23 November 2017, No. 28015). The Court of Bologna (sec. II, judg. 26 October 2017) considers that factors such as health needs, in particular if the claimant has started any medical treatment that could not be continued in the country of origin, the presence of minor children, the inclusion in professional and social programmes despite the condition of irregular migrant, assessed on a case-by-case basis, justify the recognition of humanitarian protection. The Court of Venice (sec. III, judg. 26 October 2017) identifies the vulnerability of the applicant for international protection (persecuted by family members in Mali, victim of genital mutilation, requested for marriage by a local nobleman despite being already married), along with the situation of widespread violation of human rights in the State in question, as a sufficient basis to grant her the humanitarian protection. The Court of Cassation, Civil Division, sec. VI, judg. 9 October 2017, No. 23604 concludes that it is legitimate to attribute humanitarian protection to a Pakistani woman of Christian religion, domestic worker, threatened at home with a blasphemy complaint filed by her employer. The circumstances of the case highlight the high vulnerability to which the person would be exposed if forced to return to her country of origin.

According to the Court of Cassation, Civil Division, sec. VI, judg. 17 January 2017, No. 1044, the socio-political situation in Bangladesh, according to information available on the website of the Ministry of Foreign Affairs, does not justify the recognition of humanitarian protection to

Bangladeshi citizens. According to the Court of Appeal of Bari (sec. I, judg. 6 December 2017, No. 2066), the same applies to the case of Guinea. In the same judgement, the Court of Bari states that subsidiary protection cannot be granted to potential victims of female genital mutilation and to those who engage in such practices almost professionally.

The Supreme Court finds that a territorial court's judgement that rejected the application for humanitarian protection made by a Nigerian citizen is illegitimate. The Nigerian citizen had reported that he had suffered murder attempts in various parts of the country by his uncle for reasons of inheritance. According to the Court of Appeal, the application had to be rejected because the fear for life or safety arose, in this case, from a relative, and not from a situation of widespread violence at the state level. However, according to the Supreme Court, exposure to danger can also be linked to the inability of state authorities to deal with the phenomenon of private violence resulting from family or clan traditional rules. Since this eventuality has not been adequately considered, the judgement on the request for subsidiary protection must be repeated, resorting to the power/duty to gather any relevant information, as provided by the law (Court of Cassation, Civil Division, sec. VI, judg. 10 January 2017, No. 319); Similarly, in relation to the appeal of a Nigerian citizen, see Court of Cassation, Civil Division, sec. VI, judg. 16 January 2017, No. 871, 3 July 2017, No. 16356 and sec. I, judg. 24 November 2017, No. 28152. In the latter case, the applicant had already been persecuted by the brother of her deceased husband who, in the name of traditional customs, claimed her as his wife; the Court had verified the inability of the local authorities to counteract the effectiveness of those customs).

The fact that the applicant comes from a territory of Nigeria in which, according to the information of the Italian Ministry of Foreign Affairs, there are no situations of conflict or endemic violence comparable to those affecting the north of the country, is sufficient to exclude the presence of the conditions to grant the applicant subsidiary or humanitarian protection (Court of Cassation, Civil Division, sec. VI, judg. 18 January 2017, No. 1268). The Supreme Court (Court of Cassation, Civil Division, sec. VI, judg. 11 September 2017, No. 21035) holds that the risk of death, if the repatriation were carried out, does not give entitlement to humanitarian protection if it derives from purely personal events (in this case the threats came from a paternal uncle who attributed the applicant, a citizen of Gambia, the loss of the livestock entrusted to him in custody) not linked to particular situations related to the socio-political background of Gambia. The Court of Rome (judg. 4 May 2017), on the other hand, recognises humanitarian protection to a young man from Gambia who had escaped police arrest while fearing harassment due to his father's position as a military officer who had deserted during the country's recent riots. While excluding the risk of torture, the Court observes that the possible imprisonment of the applicant would expose him to inhuman or degrading treatment, given the documented standards of detention and that his return could still place him in a situation of extreme vulnerability.

The assessment by the territorial commissions and the judiciary of the factual situation must be always carried out also on an autonomous basis (see, for example, Court of Cassation, Civil Division, sec. VI, judg. 14 November 2017, No. 2691). An exception is made for a case in which the territorial judge ascertained the radical unreliability of the applicant's testimony (Court of Cassation, Civil Division, sec. VI, judg. 29 December 2016, No. 27428). By applying indications from the ECJ, the Court of Cassation, Civil Division (sec. VI, judg. 21 July 2017, No. 18128) issued a judgement returning a decision to the lower court that had denied international protection to an individual. The individual had been denied protection as the reason for the persecution he feared in his country (being homosexual) had not been raised in a previous application. According to the approach also endorsed by the Court of Cassation, this circumstance is not *per se* sufficient to cast doubt on the applicant's credibility, since it is necessary to consider the particular characteristics of the individual in relation to the social context. The request for protection of a Pakistani national who feared persecution at home because of his homosexuality, rejected by the judges of merit, must be reviewed in the light of the interpretative guidelines of the Court of Cassation. According to these guidelines, the fact that homosexuality is considered a crime in the country of origin may justify the protection required (Court of Cassation, Civil Division, sec. VI, judg. 19 April 2017, No. 9946).

The alleged lack of a clear distinction in the practice of Nigerian law between intentional murder and manslaughter, with the result that the asylum seeker, a Nigerian citizen of Christian faith, responsible in his country for a road traffic accident which led to the death of a person, would be exposed, if sent back to Nigeria, to a possible death sentence or prison sentence to be served in inhuman conditions, was not properly assessed by the Italian court as a basis for granting humanitarian protection. According to Court of Cassation, Civil Division, sec. VI, judg. 13 June 2017, No. 14700, this justifies the referral of the case to the territorial judge for further consideration.

B. Application of the Dublin Regulation

Also in 2017, the Council of State ruled on several cases concerning the application of article 3(2) of the Regulation of the European Parliament and of the Council 604/2013 of 26 June 2013, which provides for the non-transfer of an asylum seeker to the authorities of the State that would be competent to treat him/her according to the general rules, when there are "substantial grounds for believing that there are systemic flaws in the asylum procedure and in the reception conditions for applicants in that Member State, resulting in a risk of inhuman or degrading treatment within the meaning of article 4 of the CFREU". In such circumstances, the transfer, to be lawful, requires prior verification that it does not amount to refoulement. Decisions to this effect were made with regard to Bulgaria

(Council of State, judg. 3 November 2017, No. 5085) and Hungary (judg. 27 September 2016, No. 4004).

V. Discrimination – General Issues

A. Discrimination Based on Nationality

The Court of Cassation, Civil Division, (employment section, judgements 8 May 2017, No. 11165 and No. 11166) considered an appeal brought by the INPS (the Italian National Social Security Institution) against a judgement of the Court of Appeal of Milan that had found a case of collective discrimination based on nationality and, indirectly, ethnicity, in the conduct of INPS that in 2013 had issued a circular in which it implicitly stated that the household allowance provided for by law. 448/1998, article 65 (in favour of low-income families with at least three under age children) was to be paid to foreign residents only from 2013 (according to the provisions of l. 97/2013, article 13), while instead the benefit was due starting from the entry into force of Directive 2003/109/EC, on equal treatment for third-country nationals who are long-term residents in Europe. The ruling of the Court of Cassation clarifies some interesting aspects of the dispute. First of all, it points out that collective claims (i.e. filed by associations such as, in the specific case, ASGI-*Associazione Studi Giuridici sull'Immigrazione* ("Association Judicial Studies on Immigration") and other similar associations) for discrimination, as originally introduced in the Consolidated Law on Immigration (articles 43 and 44) and then incorporated in lgs.d. 215/2003 (as amended, for procedural aspects, by lgs.d. 150/2011, article 28) although expressly referring only to racial and ethnic-based discriminations (as well as cultural and religious assimilated to the former), can also refer to discriminations based on nationality.

Since these rules are aimed at the effective protection of a right, it is not acceptable to exclude the possibility that a collective body representing a certain category of individuals at risk of discrimination – in this case immigrants – may ask the court to issue an anti-discrimination injunction only when discrimination is based on race and not when it is based on nationality. Indeed, some differences in employment and social security treatment based on nationality are lawful based on article 3.2 of Legislative Decree 215/2003. But when such differences appear to be discriminatory, it would be illogical, contrary to the principle of equality (article 3 of the Constitution) and in breach of the right to a fair trial (article 6 ECHR) to deny a collective body protecting the interests of immigrants the right to seek such remedy. The Court also emphasises the value of collective actions against discriminatory measures which potentially affect many individuals but which have not yet resulted in specific measures against anyone – and which therefore no individual would be entitled to challenge. With regard to the merits of the dispute, the Court of Cassation considers that l. 97/2013, which expressly extends the allowance to the family unit, besides Italian and EU citizens, also to non-EU citizens who are long-term residents, just adapt (belatedly) the Italian system of social allowances to the European directive of 2003 (and this also in order to avoid an infringement proceedings already brought against Italy).

The norm should therefore be applied as from 2003, not 2013, as maintained by INPS. The allowance, according to the Court of Cassation, is an essential social benefit, owed to poor families and aimed at supporting their social inclusion through income support. The judgement cites the cases *Dahbi v. Italy,* of the ECHR in 2014 (see *Yearbook 2015*, p. 320) and *Kamberaj* of the ECJ (judg. 24 April 2012, C-571/10 – see *Yearbook 2013*, p. 378-379).

On similar issues see also the section dedicated to the social rights of immigrant citizens: VIII.H.

B. Allowances in Favour of Victims of Racial Laws

The Council of State (sec. IV, judg. 7 February 2017, No. 532) clarifies that the payment of the life annuity provided for by l. 10 March 1955, No. 196 (measures in favour of persecuted anti-fascist politicians or victims of the 1938 racial laws and of their surviving relatives) in favour of persecuted Jews and their orphans, is a restorative measure, aimed at partially remedying the consequences of one of the worst tragedies in Italian history and ensures protection of an inviolable right. It is therefore up to the competent authorities to determine, by means of an appropriate investigation, whether the conditions for granting it have been met. The *ad hoc* Commission of the Presidency of the Council of Ministers, therefore, could not reject the application for the life annuity submitted by the daughter of persecuted individuals, simply on the grounds that the parents of the person concerned had never requested certain social security benefits provided for by the same law in favour of the direct victims of the 1938 racial laws (on these social security benefits see also *Yearbook 2017,* p. 264). The Council of State (judg. 6 February 2017, No. 490) also recognises to the applicant certain rights deriving from other laws adopted in favour of officials of public administrations who were affected by the racial laws, including those who had had the words 'Jewish race' written on their birth certificates and identity documents (see l. 16 January 1978, No. 17).

In 2011, the above-mentioned Commission considered that, having been born in Rome in January 1944 and having the city been liberated from Nazi occupation on 4 June of the same year, the applicant had not suffered any physical, economic or moral damage as a result of racial laws. In fact, two birth certificates were produced for the child, one – the one deposited with the city registry office – which did not contain a reference to the Jewish race, falsified for the obvious purpose of protecting the family from the risk of deportation; the other, obtained later, after the family had gone in hiding, with the annotation required by law. Regardless of which document should be considered, there is no doubt that birth under occupation and with the risk of deportation (present even after the liberation of Rome) represented for the new-born, despite her young age, a prejudice linked to racial discrimination of a serious and intolerable nature.

VI. Rights of Persons with Disabilities

A. Ability of Persons with Disabilities to Take an Oath in Order to Acquire Italian Citizenship

The law on the acquisition of Italian citizenship (l. 91/1992) provides that the person interested in the acquisition of citizenship takes an oath of loyalty to the Republic and to observe its Constitution and laws. The provision has been challenged (see *Yearbook 2017*, p. 265; the issue was also raised by the Court of Modena, sec. II, 7 February 2017, with extensive references to the Declaration and Convention on the Rights of Persons with Disabilities) for violation of articles 2 and 3 Cost., as well as article 18 of the Convention on the Rights of Persons with Disabilities, as it would not allow the acquisition of citizenship to persons with forms of disability that make it materially impossible for them to take such an oath.

The Constitutional Court (judg. 7 December 2017, No. 258) held the appeal to be well founded and recognised the unconstitutionality of the provision in question in so far as it does not provide for the exemption from the oath of a person who is incapable of fulfilling that obligation by reason of a serious and established disability.

B. Areas Reserved for Parking for People with Disabilities

The Court of Cassation, Criminal Division, has established that occupying a parking space reserved for the car of a person with disabilities (not a parking lot generically reserved for disabled people) throughout the day (until forced removal by the municipal police) constitutes a criminal offence of private violence and not a simple violation of traffic laws (Court of Cassation, Criminal Division, sec. V, judg. 23 February 2017, No. 17794).

C. Discrimination in Schools. Teacher Support

The failure to assign a special support teacher to a pupil certified as a child with disabilities and for whom an individualised educational project has been drawn up, constitutes discrimination and violates an individual's right, thus falling within the jurisdiction of an ordinary judge and not of the administrative tribunal (see *Yearbook 2015*, p. 265; see also Campania, Salerno TAR, sec. II, judg. 13 February 2017, No. 266). The school's failure to draw up the individualised educational project and the related dynamic-functional profile constitutes instead a failure on the part of the public administration, which can be reported by the affected person to the administrative tribunals as violation of a legitimate interest.

The Regional Administrative Tribunal (TAR) of Campania, Naples, (section IV, judgements 27 April 2017, No. 2250 and 12 December 2017, No. 5874) reiterates the importance of the two documents (the individualised educational project and dynamic-functional profile) just mentioned. Drafted by the local social, health and educational services, they determine the assignment of a support teacher for a number of hours corresponding to the needs of the pupil. In the absence of such documents, the granting of support by the school on the basis of a discretionary assessment must be considered unlawful. The TAR gives the school administration 15 days to prepare a draft individualised education project, specify the appropriate hours and appoint a support teacher; failing that, a special commissioner will be appointed.

> The temporary absence in a high school of the staff responsible for the assistance of an over 18-year-old student with serious psychophysical disability, who caused physical injury (a fall with a fracture) to a teacher through his uncontrolled behaviour, entails liability for damages of the student and also of the school administration, which could not prove that it had taken all appropriate informative, organisational and emergency measures to ensure the safe participation of the boy in school life. The Ministry of Education initially defended the administration by arguing that, in the absence of support staff, the teacher should not have let the student with disabilities in the classroom (Court of Rome, sec. XII, judg. 6 September 2017, No. 16632).

D. Assistance to Relatives with Disabilities

The Court of Cassation has established that permits provided for by l. 104/1992 to allow workers to care for relatives with disabilities – in this case a parent – must be counted as worked days in determining the duration of the worker's annual leave. This is in line both with the particular value attributed by laws, including international law (Directive 2000/78/

EC is cited, as well as the Convention on the Rights of Persons with Disabilities), to the protection and assistance of persons with disabilities and with article 36 of the Constitution (right to a weekly rest day and paid annual holidays). Indeed, workers need not only to regain the energy spent on work, but even more intensely need to get back the energy invested in assisting a person with disabilities (Court of Cassation, Civil Division, labour section, judg. 7 June 2017, No. 14187).

VII. Social Rights

A. Laws with Retroactive Effect on Pensions and the Case of "Swiss Pensions"

The Constitutional Court returns to the issue of constitutional legitimacy, also in the light of the jurisprudence of the ECtHR. Laws adopted in the past years have replaced the earning-based formula with a contribution-based scheme to calculate the value of pensions. In many cases this has entailed a reduction in the economic remuneration due by INPS (Italian Social Security Institute) to the worker, even when the latter has worked in countries other than Italy. The new Italian regulatory framework has also had consequences for Italian workers in Switzerland who, even if paying their pension contributions in that country, nevertheless expected to be able to redeem them, at the most favourable conditions foreseen until 2006 in Italy, once they had retired. However, with a retroactive provision of authentic interpretation inserted in the 2007 Budget Law, Parliament had put an end to a case-law orientation generally favourable to the recognition of the most favourable parameter (the earning-based scheme) for workers entitled to the so-called "Swiss pensions". Hence, a series of claims to the ECtHR, which, in its ruling of 2011, *Maggio and others v. Italy* (see *Yearbook 2012*, p. 347-348), recognised that Italy had violated article 6 ECHR for interfering with its legislation on the outcome of pending lawsuits. In the most recent case, *Stefanetti and Others v. Italy*, of 2014 (see *Yearbook 2015*, p. 319-320), the ECtHR also noted not only a problem of invasion by the Italian lawmakers of the prerogatives of the judiciary, but also a violation of article 1 protocol I ECHR (right to property), since the judgement "imposed" by the retroactive law had led to a reduction in pension treatment, compared to what the claimants expected, of almost 70 per cent.

In the light of that recent case-law, according to the referring judge, the dictum of the Constitutional Court 264/2012 (see *Yearbook 2013*, p. 320), which, while noting the judgement of the ECtHR in the *Maggio* case, confirmed the constitutional legitimacy of the regulatory framework created in Italy after 2007, arguing that the general interests protected by the laws reforming the pension system had to prevail over the individual interests protected by article 6 ECHR, no longer appears sufficient to guarantee the congruity of Italian legislation with respect to the case-law of the ECtHR.

However, with judg. 12 July 2017, No. 166, the Constitutional Court confirms the interpretative guidelines adopted in its decision 264/2012, ruling out the possibility that the *Stefanetti* judgement introduced substantial innovations. It acknowledges that the existence of cases such as those covered by the ECtHR decision, in which a great gap exists between what workers expected in terms of pension treatment and what they actually achieved (a pension below the minimum Italian pension level), requires an *ad hoc* legislative intervention. In its conclusions, the Court observes that "a further legislative inertia on the serious problem raised by the Strasbourg Court would not be tolerable."

B. Changes to the Pension System: Blocking the Revaluation of Medium-high Pensions

The Constitutional Court returned to a subject already dealt with in ruling 70/2015 (see *Yearbook 2016*, p. 233) and linked to the freeze of pensions' indexation for the years 2012 and 2013. An indiscriminate standstill, justified by budgetary reasons not adequately specified, had been acknowledged illegitimate by the Constitutional Court. A law enacted in 2015 reshaped the whole issue, providing for a total freeze only for pensions over six times higher than the minimum pension paid out by INPS. Some courts doubt however the constitutionality of this measure, due to its necessarily retroactive nature, contrary to the principle of protection of legitimate expectations and to the alleged unreasonableness of the measure. The Constitutional Court (judg. 1 December 2017, No. 250) finds the question of unconstitutionality to be unfounded. First, the Court considers that freezing the revaluation for only two years does not constitute a disproportionate sacrifice compared to the general interest of the Country, especially since it has a modest impact on the means of subsistence of pensioners of medium-high income. On the other hand, the measure was introduced by a law and on the basis of non-unreasonable arguments, indeed suggested to the Parliament by the previous ruling of the Constitutional Court itself.

VIII. Immigration

A. Issuing, Refusing to Issue or Withdrawing a Residence Permit

A foreign citizen had his residence permit for subordinate work withdrawn by the police, on the basis, among other things, of the fact that he was being investigated for facilitating illegal immigration. He was finally acquitted because the prosecution was time-barred. The applicant considers – without arguing on this point – that the revocation of a residence permit merely on the ground of being criminally investigated (and subsequently acquitted) is unlawful. According to the Basilicata TAR (sec. I, judg. 29 January 2017, No. 811), the fact that at the time the individual was accused of the above-mentioned crime was a sufficient reason to issue the contested revocation decree, even if the final outcome of the criminal proceeding was of acquittal.

According to the Rome TAR (sec. I, judg. 6 December 2017, No. 12064), convictions in the field of drugs are "automatically" an obstacle to the issuing of renewal of the residence permit of a non-EU citizen: such a conviction, for the particular negative social value it brings with it, leaves the administration no options.

The Council of State (sec. III, judg. 28 April 2017, No. 1971 and 22 December 2017, No. 6031) reiterates that the availability of sufficient means of subsistence for the duration of the stay, as assessed on a case-by-case basis, but never below the minimum amount of the INPS social allowance (i.e., €5,824.91 p.a. for 2016), is an essential condition for the renewal of the residence permit. The purpose of the rule is to avoid the inclusion of persons who are not able to "offer an adequate pay-off in terms of work and tax participation in public expenditure"; proving to have labour income is also a guarantee that non-EU citizens will not engage in irregular or criminal activities.

The Parma TAR (sec. I, judg. 18 December 2017, No. 404) states that a residence permit may be revoked (or its renewal denied) if the foreign citizen presented false documentation regarding one of the necessary conditions for its issuing, and this even before the judgement on the offence of forgery is final, since the competent administrative authority can carry out an independent assessment of the use of the suspect documents and this evaluation, if carried out in fair a reasonable fashion, is not subject to the judicial control of the TAR.

B. The Order Validating the Extension of Detention at an Identification and Deportation Centre Adopted without the Person Concerned Being Heard, on the Grounds of Anti-Scab Prophylaxis, Is Unlawful

A Justice of the Peace had ruled on the extension of the detention of an immigrant at an identification and expulsion centre without hearing the person concerned, who had asked to be heard. The justification given was that the immigrant was undergoing prophylaxis against scabies and his presence in the court's premises could have consequences on the health of the staff present. The Court of Cassation first found that normal prophylaxis does not constitute a danger to public health, then that the failure to hear the individual concerned constitutes a breach of the rights of the defence, with the consequence that the order adopted by the justice of the peace must be annulled (see, *inter alia*, Court of Cassation, sec. VI, order 13 November 2017, No. 26803).

C. Withdrawal of Reception Measures for Asylum Seekers

The Piedmont TAR (section I, judg. 7 August 2017, No. 949) upholds the appeal lodged by an asylum seeker, guest of a reception facility, against whom the Prefect had decided to revoke the reception measures for infringing the internal regulations of the structure. The withdrawal had been adopted as a matter of urgency, but the Prefect did not notify the person concerned of the initiation of the procedure, nor give it the reasons why it was so urgent. In this way, the measure failed to apply the minimum level of fairness of an administrative procedure and thus it is disproportionate. In a similar vein, see also Marche TAR, sec. I, judg. 7 August 2017, No. 676 (which refers to the obligation for the State to guarantee the reception of the asylum seeker until the completion of the procedure before the Territorial Commission for the recognition of international protection, with the consequence that the revocation of reception measures can only take place in particularly serious circumstances); Council of State, sec. III, judg. 10 February 2017, No. 536; Marche TAR, judg. 1 February 2017, No. 94 and 29 June 2017, No. 541; Veneto TAR, sec. III, judgements 15 May 2017, No. 478 and 30 January 2017, No. 102; Liguria TAR, II, judg. 13 February 2017, No. 110.

Committing the crime of unwary purchase of goods (of several mobile phones) by an asylum seeker, even if takes place outside the reception facility, nevertheless constitutes a serious violation of the rules of cohabitation of the hosting facility and justifies, according to the Valle d'Aosta TAR (sec. I, judg. 2 August 2017, No. 47), the revocation of reception measures to the seeker of humanitarian protection. The poor handling of the Italian language may justify an inaccurate understanding of the specific nature of the crime committed, but cannot be relied upon to argue that the conduct was not perceived as unlawful. According to the TAR, the care receiver must behave in an irreproachable manner both inside and outside the caregiving environment.

In the case presented in Alto Adige TAR, sec. I, judg. 24 June 2017, No. 165 and 19 June 2017, No. 191, the Court upholds the claim filed by some asylum seekers against the revocation of the already enjoyed reception measures, decided by the administrative authority on the basis of a hasty assessment of their possible involvement in a brawl. Indeed, their actual presence in the scene of crime and their personal liability were not proven facts. The Court observes that, reading between the lines the impugned measure, the sanction responded to the urgency to immediately respond to the social alarm echoed in the media around the episode; urgency prevailed over a careful ascertainment of the facts and a proportional repression. According to the Court, the duty incumbent on the Administration to investigate and give reasons for the measures adopted is all the more crucial due to the consequences of the revocation of reception measures. Indeed, the revocation affects not only the asylum seekers as individuals, whose prospects of integration are compromised, but also the larger society, since it places the recipients of the revocation measure in the need to fend for themselves in the absence of any reference points.

The opposite conclusion was reached by Lombardy – Brescia TAR, sec. II, judg. 30 January 2017, No. 109; in this case, the authorities were able to identify precisely the asylum seeker as the person who triggered a violent brawl.

D. Access to Legal Aid

A Nigerian woman had filed an action with the Juvenile Court in order to obtain the temporary residence permit provided for by article 31 of the Consolidated Law on Immigration, having just delivered a baby. She was admitted to legal aid (even if the procedure of article 31 does not necessarily require it) and was assisted by a lawyer of the Court of Naples. Subsequently, however, the court withdrew the legal aid, alleging that article 119 d.p.r. 115/2002 extended the right to legal aid to non-Italian citizens or stateless persons only if they are "legally resident". At the time of applying for a residence permit, the woman was evidently not a legal resident, hence the decision. Challenging the ruling before the Court of Cassation, the applicant pointed out that the Italian legislation was in breach of articles 2, 3, 24 and 117.1 of the Constitution, articles 7 and 8 UDHR, article 14 of the Covenant on Civil and Political Rights and article 6 ECHR along with article 47 CFREU. The Court of Cassation upholds the appeal, stating that "since legal aid represents a necessary implication of the right to defence as guaranteed by the Constitution (article 24), the concept of 'legally residing foreigner' must be interpreted in a broad sense, including also foreigners who have in place a procedure (either administrative or judicial) aimed at obtaining a residence permit". Legal aid also applies to all civil proceedings, even if the presence of the lawyer is not strictly required by law (Court of Cassation, Civil Division, sec. II, judg. 14 December 2017, No. 30069 and No. 30070).

E. Expulsions, Refoulement

According to the Court of Cassation, Criminal Division, sec. I, judg. 25 May 2017, No. 38041, the expulsion of a foreigner cannot be enforced – regardless of the occurrence of the cases specifically listed in the Consolidated Law on Immigration – when it would cause irreparable health damage. This circumstance must be assessed on a case-by-case basis and without strictly applying the legal notions of "illness" or "accident" referred to in other sectors of national legislation. The case concerned the expulsion of a one-legged foreigner, who had been in Italy for over thirty years, whose health would have been compromised by deporting him to his country of origin, due to the total lack of public assistance for persons with his form of disability. On this point, see also Court of Cassation, Civil Division, sec. VI, judg. 8 March 2017, No. 6000: foreign citizens suffering from HIV, chronic hepatitis following hepatitis C, and epilepsy, who could suffer irreparable harm from the immediate execution of a deportation order, cannot be expelled.

The Court of Cassation confirms that even the detained foreigner has the right – and the burden – to request the renewal of the residence permit, in the absence of which he exposes himself to the measure of expulsion (article 13 Consolidated Act on Immigration). It remains the task of the Justice of the Peace, when assessing the legitimacy of the order of expulsion issued by the Prefect, to verify the existence of factual circumstances which render the measure unenforceable, in particular the existence of personal and family ties in the territory of the State (Court of Cassation, Civil Division, sec. VI, judg. March 15, 2017, No. 6780).

According to the Court of Cassation, the existence in Italy of family ties, in particular of children under the age of 18, can render a deportation order unlawful, as in breach of article 8 ECHR. However, the protection of the right to private and family life is not unconditional, since article 8(2) ECHR allows for interferences by public authorities if provided for by law as a necessary measure for the purposes of national security, the economic well-being of the country, the prevention of disorder or crime, the protection of health or morals and the protection of the rights and freedoms of others (see, for example, Court of Cassation, Civil Division, sec. I, judg. 24 November 2017, No. 28157).

The Court of Cassation, Criminal Division, sec. I, judg. 18 May 2017, No. 49242, dealt with a peculiar case. The application concerns a foreign detainee, convicted for drug-related offences, who requested the order of expulsion as a security measure to be revoked. The applicant alleged a serious risk that the deportation, following his release from prison, would expose him to torture or inhuman treatment: this would therefore justify subsidiary protection. As he was close to the end of his penalty, the detainee asked for an urgent examination of his case, in order to avoid his protracted administrative detention in an expulsion centre, pending his application for protection was processed by the competent bodies. The request was rejected.

The Court of Cassation, having extensively set out the cornerstones of national, EU and international law on the protection of persons seeking international protection, concludes that the refusal to revoke an expulsion order, in the present case, is a clear violation of international standards and, in particular, of EU law, the ECHR and the Geneva Convention on the Status of Refugees. The Italian legislation also expressly provides that "the rejection or expulsion or extradition of a person to a State are not admitted if there are well-founded reasons to believe that he or she risks being subjected to torture" with l. 14 July 2017, No. 110 (introduction of the crime of torture). It follows that when assessing a request for revocation of a deportation order decided on grounds of security, or an application to suspend the enforcement of such measure, the supervision courts are required to examine all factual and legal aspects referred to by the applicant and to examine, where necessary, as an interim matter, any elements likely grant the detainee refugee status or subsidiary protection. Accordingly, the Italian legislation on refoulement or expulsion for reasons of public order and internal security does not apply when the person concerned runs a serious risk, if returned to his/her country of origin, of being subjected to death penalty, torture or other inhuman or degrading treatment or punishment.

F. "Deferred Refoulement"

Article 10(2) of lgs.d. 286/1998 (Consolidated Act on Immigration) enumerates some cases in which the refoulement of irregular immigrants, instead of being carried out instantly, can be deferred – for example, when it is necessary to temporarily admit them to the national territory to provide them with urgent assistance. In these cases, the *Questore* must then arrange for the deportation of the irregular immigrant with accompaniment to the border. The referring court considers this measure to be a form of restriction on personal freedom (article 13 of the Constitution) adopted by an administrative authority without judicial review and therefore unlawful. Even the provision according to which the deportation order can be taken upon the crossing of the border, or "immediately afterwards", leaves the police a margin of discretion (for example, defining "immediately after") that is not compatible with the guarantees of the right to personal freedom enshrined in the Constitution and in EU law.

The Constitutional Court (judg. 20 December 2017, No. 275), while recognising that the challenged provision requires a legislative intervention that aligns it with the right to personal freedom, concludes that the appeal is inadmissible, as it turned out that, in the specific case, the order of compulsory accompaniment had remained unexecuted and replaced by a subsequent order to leave the State within seven days, as provided for in article 14(5-*bis*) of lgs.d. 286/1998.

G. Monetary Sanction for the Crime of Facilitation of Illegal Immigration (Smuggling of Migrants)

The Court of Ragusa suspects a potential violation of the constitutional principles of reasonableness and equal treatment in the provision of the Consolidated Act on Immigration (article 12(3-*ter*), lgs.d. 286/1998 which punishes with a fixed fine (€15,000 or €25,000 for each person introduced into Italy) the crime of illegal entry of foreigners. According to the referring court, the fixed nature of the monetary penalty does not make it possible to adapt the sanction to the characteristics of the facts and of the perpetrator, which may vary considerably depending on the circumstances. According to the Constitutional Court (judg. 21 June 2017, No. 142), the question is unfounded, since the fine provided for is on top of the custodial penalty, this latter being determined based on the ordinary parameters of seriousness of the act and personality of the offender. Moreover, the fine is by no means "fixed", as it depends on the number of smuggled persons. Both the amount established for each person and the multiplier criterion (the number of migrants being smuggled) appear to be reasonable and not arbitrary criteria.

H. Social Rights of Immigrants

With several orders, some territorial courts (Court of Milan, order 12 December 2017; Court of Bergamo, sec. labour, judg. 30 November 2017, No. 6422) have found that the application of some INPS memorandums is discriminatory and therefore ineffective. These are those that exclude all non-EU citizen women who are not entitled to refugee status or beneficiaries of subsidiary protection and who do not hold a long-term EU residence permit or a residence card for family members of EU citizens from the "birth bonus" benefit (an allowance of €800,00 to be paid from 1 January 2017 to those born in the year, introduced by l. 232/2016, the budget law for 2017). Since the law establishing the benefit does not provide for any distinction on the grounds of nationality, the introduction of such restrictions by INPS, in a memorandum which certainly cannot contravene a primary source of law, reveals itself as discriminatory.

I. Unaccompanied Minors

The Council of State intervened in a situation that occurs quite often, namely the discrepancy in age classification between the data recorded by security agents at the time of the person's irregular entry in Italy and the age subsequently declared by the concerned person at the reception facilities and when applying for international protection. The individual in question had been registered as an adult when entering into the Italian territory, but had subsequently showed a birth certificate that qualified him as a minor at the time of arrival. Accordingly, as an unaccompanied foreign child, he was placed in a reception facility for minors. While applying for international protection (he would eventually be granted humanitarian protection), he sought a residence permit for minors, but the application was rejected by the competent police office (*Questura*), which relied on the statements he made on arrival (also in observance of the principle of self-responsibility) and considered the later clarifications as an attempt to circumvent the Italian immigration law; as regards the birth certificate he possessed, since it was neither translated into Italian nor legalised, it was given no legal value. The expert medical report, which proved the compatibility of the radiological assessment conducted on the person with his minor age, was also denied any probative value.

The Regional Administrative Tribunal (TAR), hearing the case against the rejection, confirmed the position of the police.

The Council of State (sec. III, judg. 29 December 2017, No. 6191) quashed the TAR's decision, acknowledging that, although the facts had occurred before the entry into force of l. 47/2017 (provisions on measures to protect unaccompanied foreign minors), the principle of the best interest of the child (article 12 CRC) had to be applied. Evidence which proved the applicant's minor age, although formally flawed, should have prompted a further investigation and, if appropriate, should have led to apply the presumption of minor age.

The Court adds that the principle of self-responsibility cannot apply to a minor, especially considering that he was not assisted by a cultural mediator when filling in forms at the first identification stage. The Council of State further states that numerous cases are documented of identification forms filled in by irregular migrants landed in Sicily flawed with errors and of forms filled out in a standardised fashion. It follows that, in the presence of sound supporting evidence, the police authorities and the TAR should have recognised the applicant's minor age and avoided jeopardising his rights.

The Court of Cassation (Civil Division, sec. VI, judg. 12 January 2017, No. 685; 26 April 2017, No. 10212) reiterates that the appointment of the legal guardian for the unaccompanied foreign minor within the shortest possible time is the responsibility of the court supervising the guardianship in the territory in which the minor was found. The case concerned a child who had irregularly landed in Sicily. It is not, therefore, the task of the Juvenile Court, whose competence may emerge in case of adoption, which is a completely different procedure.

IX. Right to Private and Family Life. Right to Property

A. *Interceptions and Privacy of Correspondence*

The Court of Appeal of Reggio Calabria asked the Constitutional Court to rule on the legitimacy of some provisions of the criminal code and of the criminal procedure code which, while allowing – under come precise conditions – the interception of telephone, telematic and electronic communications, as well as environmental communications, for the purposes of criminal investigations, do not affect the protection provided by article 15 of the Constitution regarding mail correspondence. In the specific case, it was found impossible to use in Court the content of information contained in letters between a detainee and people outside the prison, who had been intercepted unbeknownst to the person under investigation.

The current legislation, in fact, requires marking with a special stamp the correspondence that will be subjected to censorship. In general, the control over postal correspondence takes place after the seizure of the letter, thus rendering the interference in the communication known to the interested parties. According to the referring court, this legislation contrasts with the principle of equality (article 3 of the Constitution), as it unreasonably discriminates between subjects who use for their communications the sending of postal letters and those who use any other means. Moreover, it is also an obstacle to effective investigation (article 112 of the Constitution).

According to the Constitutional Court (judg. 24 January 2017, No. 20), instead, the diversity of the communication means – material in the case of postal correspondence, mainly immaterial in the other cases – justifies the different treatment. The legislator has calibrated the various degrees of privacy protection based on the means used for communications; the different treatment is neither unreasonable nor discriminatory and strikes a fair balance between the right to the secrecy of correspondence and the interest in the prosecution of crimes. The protection of privacy in postal communication applies all the more for the correspondence of detainees, whose secrecy, to the modest extent in which it is allowed by the law, does not lend itself to being further limited.

B. Right to Be Forgotten

In 2016, the Authority for the Protection of Personal Data had requested companies "Yahoo! Italy" and "Yahoo! Search", the latter being operated by the Irish company "Yahoo! EMEA", to remove data relating to a person, retrievable through their search service, which linked him to the bankruptcy of a company of which he had been manager and to delete as well the URLs that reported the data of the applicant and the cached copies thereof.

The Authority endorsed the request and ordered the deletion of data, admittedly no longer relevant for the purpose of the right to freedom of the press. The affected companies challenged the decision, claiming that only "Yahoo! EMEA" was responsible for the treatment of personal data and therefore the measure should have concerned only that company. Since, however, "Yahoo! EMEA" was located outside the jurisdiction of the Italian regulator, an application was to be addressed to the Irish data protection authority. The Court of Milan (sec. I, judg. 4 January 2017, No. 12623) recalls the settled European case-law according to which, in the event of complex or long-term illicit conducts, the petition may be filed, at the choice of the petitioner, either with the Court (or other competent authority: in this case the Authority for the Protection of Personal Data) of the place where the event giving rise to the damage occurred (action theory) or with the court in the place where the damage occurred (event theory), namely the place where the injured person resides. On the basis of these principles, therefore, the Italian authorities' jurisdiction is confirmed.

This conclusion is in line with the right to an effective remedy, recognised by article 13 ECHR and article 47 CFREU and is consistent with the provisions of Directive 95/46. Since the Irish company created a branch in Italy, the latter's activities, although limited to the sale of advertising space, are inseparable from those carried out by the search engine. "Yahoo! Italia" therefore operates as a "Yahoo! EMEA" branch. As to the merits of the case, the Court of Milan broadly repeats what was stated by the ECJ in the well-known case *Google Spain*, case C-131/12, Grand Chamber, 13 May 2014 and concludes by confirming the position of the Authority for the protection of personal data, namely: the person concerned has, in the case in question, exercised his right to demand that the disclosure of his personal data meet the criteria of proportionality, necessity, relevance and non-excessiveness in relation to the purpose, accuracy and consistency with the individual's current and actual personal or moral identity, as required article 11 of the privacy code (lgs.d. 196/2003). As for the complaint that deleting data, including the correspondent caching, is an excessive measure, the Court replies that the new General Regulation on the protection of personal data (regulation 2016/6790, which will come into force in May 2018) expressly provides for the cancellation of any link, copy or reproduction referring to personal data available on the Internet.

Still on the subject of the right to be forgotten, The Court of Cassation, Civil Division, sec. I, judg. 9 August 2017, No. 19761, ruled on the current existence in the Italian legal system of a right to obtain the cancellation of a record, kept in the register of companies, that the applicant had found to produce negative effects on his business activity. The applicant had in fact been the sole director of an enterprise declared bankrupt in 1992; the data was in turn reported in the databases of various rating agencies, with the result that years later that distant event still tainted the image of the applicant and of his ongoing business. The judicial authority to which the interested party had appealed had ordered the Chamber of Commerce, responsible for the management of the register of companies, to anonymise the data referred to the manager of the business that bankrupted in 1992; against this decision, however, an appeal is pending. The supreme court is therefore to establish whether the right to the protection of personal data imposes, upon request of a party, to cancel or keep confidential the data entered in the register of companies, a part from the cases namely enumerated by the law, also when the concerned person invokes his own interest in making any data concerning him no longer accessible after a certain time.

The Court of Cassation extensively cites judg. C-398/15 of the ECJ (which rules on a similar issue concerning the Directive 95/46/EC of the European Parliament and of the Council of 24 October 1995 on the protection of natural persons with regard to the treatment of personal data), and concludes that the Italian legal system does not provide for the right to obtain the cancellation or anonymisation of data entered in the register of companies limited to certain individuals or on individual requests not expressly provided for. In this matter, the legislator has made a non-unreasonable choice favouring the disclosure of information, aware of the negative consequences that this can have the reputation and the ability to operate in the economic sector.

C. *Crime of Interference in Private Life*

According to the Court of Cassation (sec. V, sentence 10 January 2017, No. 22221), the conduct of filming intimate scenes with one's partner in what was then classified as the private residence of both, does not integrate the crime of unlawful interference in private life (article 615-*bis* of the Criminal Code), which in fact punishes the action of a person unknown to the private life of the individual, not that of those who participate in it, although for a limited period. In this specific case, the shots had not been made public in any way. Instead it constitutes the punished crime of article 615-*bis* the fact of a person who placed a "chip" inside the private car of his wife, the device being able not only to geolocate the woman but also to spy on conversations inside the car (Court of Naples North, sec. II, judg. 1 December 2017, No. 2885). Stairs and corridors of a condominium building are not places intended for the conduct of private life: the taking of images in such places is not therefore an interference in the private life of the inhabitants of the building (Court of Cassation, Criminal Division, sec. VI, judg. 30 May 2017, No. 34151).

D. Private Life and Social Media

The Court of Rome has issued, on its own initiative, an order addressed to the mother of a minor to cease from posting on Facebook photos and news regarding the child (without the consent of the latter), as well as to remove content concerning the minor published so far. The judge in fact found that the parent's conduct, after the divorce, had seriously embarrassed his son, whose family and health vicissitudes were known to a vast network of people, prompting him to request (and obtain from the judge) the transfer to a high school in the United States (Court of Rome, sec. I, judg. 23 December 2017). The Court of Mantua, ruling on a similar case, considers that the frequent publication on social media of photos of the minor children by the mother, against the opinion of the separated father, contrasts with the right to one's own image (article 10 Civil Code), as well as the provisions of the privacy code (lgs.d. 196/2003) and the CRC. The mother is instructed to abstain from continuing with the practice and to remove the published images (Court of Mantua, judg. 19 September 2017).

X. Children's Rights

A. The Processual Role of the Foster Family

The Supreme Court (Court of Cassation, Civil Division, sec. I, judg. 9 October 2017, No. 23574) intervened on a judgement by the competent Court of Appeal. The Court had ordered the revocation of the state of abandonment previously pronounced in respect of a minor who had been seriously neglected by the mother and placed in foster care with a different family. The Court therefore disposed that the girl be placed with her father, who had been found fit to perform parental tasks. The decision was quashed as it had been adopted without giving effect to article 5(1) of l. 184/1983 (right of the child to a family), as amended by l. 173/2015. The law establishes that in civil proceedings concerning parental responsibility, custody or adoption, the foster parent or the foster family in which the minor is placed must be heard by the judge otherwise the decision should be void, and foster parents are allowed to submit written memories in the interest of the child. The disregarded rule is intended to guarantee the best interest of the child, given the crucial role that the foster family can assume in delicate moments in the life of a minor.

The Court of Cassation reached a similar conclusion on another case of declaration of abandonment state, despite the entry into force of the new text of the mentioned article 5(1) l. 184/1983. Notwithstanding the mother's willingness to resume her parental obligations after a period of suspension due to psychological problems, the decision was found to have been taken without having properly audited the children (who were interviewed without adequate contextualisation and follow-up) and having only cursorily verified the availability of other relatives and without the necessary involvement of the foster family.

B. *Family Mistreatments vs. Abuse of Means of Correction*

According to the Court of Cassation, Criminal Division, sec. VI, judg. 13 March 2017, No. 11956, the systematic recourse to violent means against minors by teachers at kindergartens constitutes a crime of mistreatment within the family (article 572 criminal code), and not of abuse of the means of correction (article 571 criminal code), even if the adult's actions are supported by an "educational" intent (see also Court of Cassation, Criminal Division, sec. VI, judgements 28 June 2017, No. 40959; 3 July 2017, No. 47299).

Similarly, the conduct of the mother who submits her daughter for almost two years to constant harassment, forcing her to run away from home twice, cannot be considered abuse of the means of correction, but family mistreatment (Court of Cassation, Criminal Division, sec. VI, judg. 7 November 2017, n. 50745).

According to the Court of Cassation, Criminal Division, sec. VI, judg. 18 October 2017, No. 55833, the aggravating circumstance of committing the crime of mistreatment in relation to the spouse in the presence of the under-age child applies without being necessary to ascertain that the child, exposed to the perception of violent conduct, has the psycho-physical maturity necessary to understand the offensive or damaging scope of the deeds (in the circumstance, the child was few months old). According to the judges, even very young children are able to perceive what is happening around them and to absorb the violence they witness, suffering psychological wounds that can affect the development of their personality. Similar considerations apply to the crime of defamation. It is considered realised even if the communication to more people of the outrageous expressions extends to a four-year-old who, although not fully understanding the meaning of what has been said, is fully able to grasp the harmful scale, so as to be disturbed and turn himself into a potential instrument of propagation (Court of Cassation, Criminal Division, sec. V, judg. 23 February 2017, No. 16108).

C. Foreign Minors and Residence Permit for Parents

The Court of Cassation reiterates its interpretative orientation on article 31 of the consolidated law on immigration (lgs.d. 286/1998) concerning the residence permit issued for "serious reasons" to the benefit of the parents of a non-expellable foreign minor. The Juvenile Court had found that the girl's early age justified the denial of the extraordinary residence permit to her parents, as it would have been an easy task to integrate her into the social context of the parents' country of origin. The judgement of the Court of Cassation goes in the opposite direction. Both the girl's preschool age and her rooting in Italy constitute "serious reasons" making article 31 of the consolidated law applicable (Court of Cassation, Civil Division, sec. I, judg. 3 August 2017, No. 19433).

Besides, according to the Supreme Court, the justification provided by a court to reject the application for temporary residence permit pursuant to article 31 of the immigration consolidated law, based on the fact that the injury caused to the child by the removal of the parent was not "irreparable", identifies a parameter (that of irreparable damage) that the law does not consider. What should be considered is the existence or not of an actual, concrete, perceivable and objectively serious harm to the psychophysical wellness of the child caused by the distance of the parents (Court of Cassation, Civil Division, sec. VI, judg. 19 July 2017, No. 17861).

XI. Due Process: the "Pinto" Act

A. Application of the "Pinto" Act

According to the Supreme Court, the remedy for excessive duration of the trial, provided by the l. 89/2001 ("Pinto" act), does not apply where the prejudice suffered by the claimant has not exceeded a minimum severity threshold. The prejudice must be assessed both in relation to what is at stake and to the extent of the delay with respect to the reasonable duration of the procedure. In the specific case, a "Pinto" remedy application for a trial that had exceeded the duration deemed to be reasonable by eight months, and concerning a €375 worth dispute, was correctly considered inadmissible (Court of Cassation, Civil Division, sec. II, judg. 29 December 2017, No. 31150).

Court of Cassation, Civil Division, sec. II, judg. 29 December 2017, No. 31149, confirms that, in application of the decision of the Constitutional Court 184/2015 (see *Yearbook 2016*, p. 244), the calculation of its excessive duration also includes the preliminary investigation phase, from the moment when the commencement of an investigation is notified to the accused.

The death of the defence attorney, replaced by another lawyer after more than one year, if it did not in itself entail the interruption of the trial, cannot affect the calculation of the reasonable duration of the trial (Court of Cassation, Civil Division, sec. VI, judg. 5 January 2017, No. 186).

Some decisions of the Supreme Court apply the principle, established by the Civil Sections with judg. 6 May 2016, No. 9142 (see *Yearbook 2017*, p. 288), according to which the enforcement procedure initiated within six months from the conclusion of the main trial is to be considered part of the trial as for the assessment of the unreasonable duration of the procedure; it is instead a separate procedure if it is activated after six months have passed. Among the decisions applying the same dictum adopted in 2017: Court of Cassation, Civil Division, sec. VI, judg. 9 January 2017, No. 227, No. 229; sec. II, orders 21 July 2017, No. 18011; 26 July 2017, No. 18570, No. 18571; 27 July 2017, No. 18612, No. 18613, No. 18614, No. 18615; 2 September 2017, No. 20837; 6 September 2017, No. 20837; 19 September 2017, No. 21626, No. 21627; 12 October 2017, No. 23992; 13 October 2017, No. 24186, No. 24187, No. 24188, No. 24189.

The right to just satisfaction rests exclusively within the person who is a party in the presupposed judicial procedure and it cannot be subrogated by anyone else (Court of Cassation, Civil Division, sec. II, judg. 2 October 2017, No. 22975). The heir of the applicant is entitled to compensation only for the delay subsequent to the moment in which he/she was constituted as a party in court; before that moment only the original applicant held the right to a reasonable duration of the proceedings in which it was a party (Court of Cassation, Civil Division, sec. VI, judg. 5 January 2017, No. 183; Court of Cassation, Civil Division, sec. VI, judg. 3 February 2017, No. 3001).

According to the Supreme Court, sec. VI, judg. 26 January 2017, No. 2028, the damage caused by the excessive duration of a procedure is an objective fact and occurs independently of the awareness of the affected individual. The compensation is, therefore, also due for the years in which the person concerned, still a child, had no knowledge of the judicial case (initiated in 1976 and not yet concluded in 2009).

Just satisfaction of less than the minimum threshold of €500 per year of delay in an administrative procedure may be ordered by the judge when the case was a collective one, of a modest value, and uncertain as to its outcome, and when the proceeding, although characterised by delays, has not caused significant worries to the applicants (in the circumstances the applicants – former non-commissioned officers of the armed forces who lamented a non-payment of arrears of remuneration – received a compensation of €3,000 for a trial – which ended with a rejection of their application – lasted from 1994-2010).

B. Issues of Constitutionality

The Court of Cassation, Civil Division, (sec. II, orders 3 November 2017, No. 26221 and 21 December 2017, No. 30734) raises the question of constitutional legitimacy in relation to article 54(2) of the lgs.d. 112/2008, which had modified the "Pinto" act, establishing the prompt submission of a special motion as a condition for applying for unreasonable duration of an administrative proceeding. In the *Olivieri and Others vs Italy* case of 2016 (see *Yearbook 2017*, p. 312), the ECtHR observed that this requirement was hindering the effectiveness of the guarantees offered by the Italian legal system. The Supreme Court also questions the compatibility between such provision and articles 6 and 13 of the ECHR – rules interposed in the judgement of constitutionality pursuant to article 117(1) Cost.

XII. Criminal Issues

A. Criminal Sentencing

With judg. 13 July 2017, No. 179, the Constitutional Court ruled on the legitimacy of article 73(1) of lgs.d. 9 October 1990, No. 309 (Consolidated Law on Drug Addiction), which, as the outcome of a complex succession of laws and constitutionality challenges, provides for a doubling of minimum penalties for "non-minor offences" of growing, sale, trade, etc. of "heavy" drugs, committed after 21 May 2014, while for "minor offences", irrespective of whether concerning "light" or "heavy" drugs, the penalties were reduced. It was submitted that these provisions amounted to a violation of articles 3, 25, and 27 of the Constitution, and also of article 3 ECHR, in relation to the predictable increased pressure on prisons and the disproportional nature of the sanctions, as well as of article 49 CRFUE.

The Constitutional Court carries out a wide examination of the parameters of constitutionality applicable to the legislation on penal sanctions. Mentioning, among others, its judg. 236/2016 (see *Yearbook 2017*, p. 254), the Court reiterates that it is its own task to verify proportionality and reasonableness of the sanctions established by law, indicating, if possible, which other sanction to apply in place of that found illegitimate, among those already provided for in the legislative system; if no suitable sanction can be found, the Court must call upon the Parliament to act. In the case of the contested law, the Court notes that the legal system does not lack instruments to mitigate the disproportion of the penalty for "minor" and "non-minor" offences and acknowledges that it is a legislator's prerogative to establish different forms of punishment between similar criminal conduct. The application is therefore declared inadmissible. The Court, however, expresses its "urgent desire" that the Parliament can quickly legislate to fix the rift that separates the penalties provided for the "minor" and "non-minor" criminal offences.

B. The Evidence Regime in Courts

The Court of Cassation, Criminal Division (sec. I, judg. 24 February 2017, No. 42802), in dealing with an application filed by a Tunisian citizen convicted of procuring illegal entry of migrants, deals with the evidentiary value of the pre-trial statements as a ground for verdict of guilty. The applicant had led 217 Syrians on a boat through the Sicily channel into Italy for profit in 2015.

The applicant had been convicted mainly on the basis of concordant testimonies of three Syrian asylum seekers, considered reliable but not subject to an adversarial process, who had recognised the applicant as the coxswain of the boat. The Supreme Court recalls the dictum of the ECtHR, to which all the sections of the Supreme Court have acceded, according to which the right of the accused to examine or cross-examine witnesses is an essential aspect of the right to defence.

A criminal conviction, therefore, cannot be based exclusively or decisively on statements collected in secret before the trial and not subject to cross-examination by the accused. However, an exception is permitted when the accused has been allowed to examine or cross-examine the witness in a sufficient and fair manner at the time of the statement or later. In the specific case, the Supreme Court found that the accused had had the opportunity to challenge the statements of the witnesses, but had renounced it by choosing a form of accelerated criminal procedure without asking for probative integrations.

The Court of Cassation (sec. V, judg. 24 February 2017, No. 29261) reiterates that the principle, often stated by the ECtHR, whereby an appeal court wishing to reform the trial court judgement is obliged to hear the witnesses again if their statements have to be interpreted differently from what was done in the previous instance, applies only if the decision of the trial court is to be reformed *in peius*. It is not mandatory to renew the examination of witnesses if the new interpretation of the probative content of their statements leads to the acquittal of the accused or to a lighter sentence. The principle set out in articles 6 ECHR and article 14 ICCPR must in fact be read in an exculpatory, not incriminating, perspective.

C. Torture and Inhuman Treatment

A superintending tribunal raises the question of constitutional legitimacy of article 35-*ter* of the Penitentiary Act, adopted in 2014 to introduce a compensation procedure in favour of prisoners who have been subjected to inhuman treatment. It is observed that the rule seems to refer only to the convicted detainee, and would not take into consideration the individuals subjected to security measures because of their social dangerousness, that entail restriction of personal freedom similar to criminal detention. In the case at the origin of the application to the Constitutional Court, the inmate complained that he had been detained, as a preventive measure, in a cell smaller than 3 square meters.

The Constitutional Court (judg. 13 April 2017, No. 83) agrees that if this were the correct interpretation, the provision would be contrary to the principle of non-discrimination, and a breach of article 3 ECHR. However, a comprehensive interpretation of the law that introduced article 35-*ter* of the Penitentiary Act and a constitutionally and conventionally oriented reading of the provision lead to conclude that the claim for inhuman detention can be filed also by inmates for security measure and that the parameters set by the law are sufficient to determine the compensation amount, although in the case of security measures the duration of the treatment cannot be determined at the beginning, since it depends on the continuing dangerousness of the individual. If early release is not possible, a reparation can be awarded in the form of a sum of money (similarly to what happens in the case of a prisoner sentenced to life – see *Yearbook 2017*, p. 297). For an application of this interpretative principle see Court of Cassation, Criminal Division, sec. I, judg. 14 June 2017, No. 35122.

> According to Court of Cassation, Criminal Division, sec. V, judg. 19 January 2017, No. 22203, the oppressive and degrading measures inflicted by some prison officers on detainees, although allegedly justified as disciplinary punishments, that worsen the conditions of detention by limiting the inmates' sphere of personal freedom, despite being *per se* not violent, integrate the crime of abuse of authority (article 608 of the Criminal Code). In the specific case, the agents forced an inmate who had refused to be transferred to another cell to kneel and crawl to the desk, where he was forced to sign the transfer request, while receiving punches and kicks.

According to the standards set by the ECtHR, three square meters is the minimum space available to the person detained in his/her cell, and below this standard the situation must be characterised as degrading treatment. The Court of Cassation reiterates that from the calculation of the square meters must be excluded, in addition to the toilets, the furnishings that are difficult to remove and which severely compress the person's freedom of movement (for example cabinets fixed to the wall). Therefore, the minimum is three square meters "walkable" (Court of Cassation, Criminal Division, sec. I, judg. 21 July 2017, No. 39584, No. 39585; see also sec. I, judg. 6 June 2017, No. 36238, No. 36239, No. 36240). In particular, while a normal bed does not prevent the prisoner's movement, a bunk bed does. The Supreme Court quashed a judgement that had not taken into account, in determining the amount of the compensation to be paid to a prisoner who had stayed in cells that offered a space of less than three square meters per person, the period spent in cells which, although abstractly exceeding the indicated size, were nevertheless under the minimum due to the presence of a bunk bed (Court of Cassation, Criminal Division, sec. III, judg. 7 December 2017, No. 29323).

D. Compensation for Unjust Detention

In 2017, the Court of Cassation, Criminal Division, has finally marked the end of a dramatic and painful judicial and human case, started in 1976. In a night of February 1976, two young *Carabinieri* (military police officers) were murdered while in their barracks in Alcamo Marina, province of Trapani. A suspect was arrested who named four other accomplices, including two minors. All were condemned to heavy sentences – three got a life sentence; the other two managed to escape to Brazil. The first arrested, the one who had accused the others, after repeatedly trying to recant his statements, died in prison, apparently committing suicide. In 2007 – after the passing away in 1998 of one of the accomplices, Giovanni Mandalà, sentenced to life and having spent 16 years in prison, first in pre-trial custody then as a convicted detainee – a *Carabiniere* who had participated in the investigations at the time of the event, provided some new evidence, which undoubtedly exonerated all the convicted person. He revealed that the evidence against the accused had been fabricated by the investigators, who had used torture to get the false confessions of those arrested. In 2012, the Court of Appeal of Reggio Calabria tasked to the review of the trial acquitted Giuseppe Gulotta, sentenced to life in 1989, while the juvenile section of the Court of Appeal of Catania did the same regarding the other two convicted who were minors at the time of the facts. In 2014, Giovanni Mandalà was acquitted *post mortem*. The next step was to determine a compensation for unjust detention in favour of Mr. Gulotta and of the children (and family) of Mr. Mandalà. In 2016, the Court of Appeal of Reggio Calabria, with a decision confirmed by the Court of Cassation, paid approximately €6.5 million to Mr. Gulotta (around €70 million requested). In 2017, the Court of Appeal of Catania pronounced on Mr. Mandalà's submission for reparation and attributed a total sum of over €6 million to his heirs, as opposed to more than €60 million requested.

The Supreme Court (Court of Cassation, Criminal Division, sec. IV, judg. 31 January 2017, No. 18168) upholds the decision on reparations. In fact, the request for damages submitted by the heirs of Mr. Mandalà for the material and non-material losses deriving from the unlawful facts (the investigations diverted, the torture, etc.) is groundless, since what the judge is called to award in the current procedure is only an equitable compensation for miscarriage of justice and the connected unjust detention of the person who was convicted and sentenced on the basis of false evidence, and then found innocent on all counts.

The Court of Cassation (Criminal Division, sec. IV, judg. 6 December 2017, No. 6194) has recognised that the compensation for unjust detention, including pre-trial detention (the claimant was subsequently fully acquitted "due to lack of evidence"), based on article 314 Code of Criminal Procedure, is not simply an amount mechanically calculated (i.e. over a ratio of about €235 per day of unjust deprivation of liberty), but may well incorporate any relevant elements that may increase such amount. Although it is not a form of damages, the just compensation must be commensurate with the pecuniary and non- pecuniary harm suffered, when this largely overrides the average value indicated by the standardised parameter. (On the compensation for unjust detention see also Court of Cassation, Civil Division, sec. IV, judg. 7 December 2017, No. 1283).

E. "Obstructive" Life Sentence

The Court of Cassation resumes its established jurisprudence (see *Yearbook 2015*, p. 302-303) on the compatibility with the constitutional norms and with international law of provisions that exclude from probation and other alleviating measures those sentenced to life who, having been recognized as belonging to mafia-type organisations, do not cooperate with justice (l. 354/1975, article 4-*bis*) (so-called "*ergastolo ostativo*" or "obstructive" life sentence). The circumstance of having committed the crime punished with the life sentence when below the age of 25 has no relevance in this regard (Court of Cassation, Criminal Division, sec. I, judg. 28 June 2017, No. 52017). Similarly, the "good behaviour" of the prisoner does not exclude the applicability of the special regime (Court of Cassation, Criminal Division, sec. I, judg. 21 February 2017, No. 28305). According to the case-law of the Court of Cassation, article 4-*bis* of the penitentiary act does not infringe the Constitution nor the ECHR, as it gives the convicted person the choice of whether to collaborate or not with the judiciary and the investigators (cooperation being a condition to enjoy ordinary benefits); moreover, the obstructive regime (in particular the denial of probation measures) does not apply when the collaboration with the investigators is impossible because it is objectively impossible or irrelevant.

On the topic see also Court of Cassation, Criminal Division, sec. I, judg. 4 July 2017, No. 53330. This last decision is worth mentioning because it clarifies that an application to the Supreme Court against the rejection by a superintending tribunal of a detainee's claim to home detention must be filed with the assistance of a lawyer and cannot be personally proposed. This is what articles 571(1) and 613 of the Code of Criminal Procedure provide, as amended by the l. 23 June 2017, No. 103, and this is found compatible with both the Constitution and the ECHR. (On rules that limit the possibility to submit a legal action to the Court of Cassation without the assistance of a qualified lawyer – a measure aimed at rationalizing, deflating and increasing the effectiveness of the Supreme Court's procedure, see also Court of Cassation, Criminal Division, sec. VI, judg. 13 September 2017, No. 42062).

F. Deadline for Filing the Depositing the Reasons for a Precautionary Custody Order

Article 311(5-*bis*) of the Code of Criminal Procedure provides that the grounds for a ruling on the pre-trial detention of an accused person must be filed by the competent judge within a deadline of thirty days. However, in some cases, a 15-day extension of the term was admitted in courts, when situations were particularly complex. The Joint Sections of the Supreme Court (Court of Cassation, criminal division, joint sections, judg. 20 July 2017, No. 47970) stand for a strict application of the deadline. The decision of the Supreme Court is based both on the case-law of the Constitutional Court, and on some principles emerging from the ECtHR jurisprudence, namely on the remark that "a quick settlement of appeals concerning precautionary measures is paramount; any provision that slows down the trial should be considered an exception".

G. The Condition of Prisoners in Special Detention Regime (Article 41-bis of the Prison System Act)

An inmate, subjected to the particular regime set forth in article 41-*bis*, l. 354/1975 (Prison System Act) for members of mafia-like organisations, had requested to receive books and magazines from outside the prison, including an encyclopaedic dictionary of mafias. When request was rejected, the inmate filed an appeal before the Court of Cassation, complaining that his right to information (article 10 ECHR) had been violated, since the prison administration is the sole entity to decide the sources of information that the detainees had access to. The Supreme Court considered the appeal unfounded, as the restrictions on the freedom of information are laid down in specific regulations issued by the government in relation to offenders linked to the mafia criminal networks, and aimed at preventing the person in prison from entering in possession of updated information about the criminal dynamics in which they have participated, so as to bypass, invoking the right to information, the specific features of a specifically designed detention regime (Court of Cassation, Criminal Division, sec. I, judg. 13 November 2017, No. 56362).

The Constitutional Court ruled in a similar matter in judg. 26 May 2017, No. 122. The referring court noted that a consolidated jurisprudence considered as lawful to limit the forms of access to information provided by the law in force for prisoners in the special detention regime. However, it found that the restrictive measures should not be applied directly by the prison administration, but rather on a case-by-case basis by the superintending courts tasked to supervise the application of the penalty, since such measures affect fundamental rights of detainees. The Constitutional Court considers the question unfounded. The contested norms do not preclude the prisoner from accessing information (article 21 Cost.), but only prevent him to receive books, newspapers, etc. by post or on the occasion of visits. No restrictions apply to books and newspapers available at the facilities of the penitentiary and dispatched through methods that allow the control by the prison authorities. Neither the right to correspondence (article 15 Cost) nor the right to private and family life (article 8 ECHR) are thus violated, because the limitation to their enjoyment is justified by the special dangerousness of inmates having links with mafia-like organisations.

The Constitutional Court (judg. 12 June 2017, No. 136) has also found that article 275(3) of the Code of Criminal Procedure, which provides that the mandatory precautionary measure applicable to persons suspected of the crime of being connected with the mafia is custody in prison, does not violate articles 3, 13 and 27 of the Constitution, nor is opposed to the jurisprudence of the ECtHR. According to the referring courts, also non-custodial measures should be ordered, namely in case of individuals suspected of minor forms of participation in the criminal association. The Constitutional Court, however, maintains that, in view of the goal of severing any connection with mafia networks, the position of the concerned person in the criminal hierarchy is not relevant.

H. European Arrest Warrant

Following the Directives 2013/48/EU of the Parliament and the Council, implemented in Italy by lgs.d. 15 September 2016, No. 184, and 2016/1919/EU, it is expressly recognised the right of every individual reached by a European arrest warrant to appoint a lawyer in the country in which the warrant was issued and in the one in which it is executed, benefiting of free legal aid if necessary, in order to guarantee the continuity of legal assistance and representation in courts. If the police fail to inform the arrested person of this right, and if the omission is raised at the hearing to validate the arrest, the arrest must be annulled. The point was clarified by the Court of Cassation

(Civil Division, sec. VI, judg. 9 May 2017, No. 24301), which also found that in the concrete case the nullity had not been raised, and, therefore, the appeal to the Supreme Court to annul the arrest was rejected.

I. Translation of Judicial Documents into the Language of the Accused

The Court of Cassation has been affected by an appeal filed by two non-Italian citizens, convicted of the crime of trafficking in human being, who complained about the violation of their right to a fair trial because the judgement of first instance had been notified to them in Italian and not translated into their own language. The Court of Cassation, holding what was also affirmed by the Court of appeal, confirms that, unless a prejudice is proved to be specifically derived from the communication of the document in a unknown language, the very fact that the judgement was immediately appealed by the defendants' lawyer is evidence that the lack of translation did not infringe the rights of the defence (Court of Cassation, criminal division, section I, judg. 13 September 2017, No. 56332).

The Supreme Court finds that the issuance by a prosecutor of a seizure order, written only in Italian, targeting a non-Italian textile manufacturer accused of possessing counterfeit garments is compatible with the principles of equal rights and fair trial. In fact, according to the Court, the seizure decree is not among the documents that must be provided in a language which can be understood by the accused in a prosecution. More generally, this limitation cannot be considered contrary to the right to a fair trial as established by the Constitution, the ECHR and other international norms, since the non-translation of an act of the prosecution is compensated by the provisions on free assistance of an interpreter: the latter can inform the party of the contents of documents written in Italian whose translation is not mandatory (Court of Cassation, Criminal Division, sec. V, judg. 30 March 2017, No. 41961).

J. Extradition and Risk of Mistreatment or an Unfair Procedure

The Court of Cassation held on several occasions during 2017 that the extradition of a person required to serve a prison sentence in Bulgaria involves the serious risk of inhuman treatment in the prisons of that state. In 2015, the ECtHR had in fact adopted a pilot judgement, noting a systematic situation of overcrowding and lack of services in Bulgarian prisons, with consequent cases of inhuman or degrading treatment of inmates. By 2017, the competent bodies of the Council of Europe have not changed their position. The conditions for granting extradition for execution of a European arrest warrant must be assessed on a case-by-case basis in the light of any measures taken by the requiring state. Therefore, the latter has to provide any information useful to exclude the concrete risk of degrading treatment (see Court of Cassation, Criminal Division, sec. VI, judg. 29 March 2017, No. 16175 and 10 November 2017, No. 52236). Similar considerations were held in connection with Romania, which was also the subject of an ECtHR pilot judgement on prison overcrowding in 2017 (Court of Cassation, Criminal Division, sec. VI, judg. 13 January 2017, No. 8529; 17 October 2017, No. 48433). The additional information provided by the State must also be subject to careful check by the competent Italian court, which can compare such data with the outcome of the Council of Europe's CPT inspections and also with any other reliable sources of information concerning both the State's prison system in general and the specific penitentiary in which the penalty is to be purged. For an application of these principles in cases of extradition to Albania, see Court of Cassation, Criminal Division, sec. VI, judg. 30 January 2017, No. 7845; 3 May 2017, No. 22249; 25 July 2017, No. 37496; 17 August 2017, No. 39207; 18 July 2017, No. 36220; 21 September 2017, No. 48635; 12 October 2017, No. 47893; urgent cases section, judg. 22 August 2017, No. 39400.

Following some legal reforms, introduced in particular since 2015, Kazakhstan is no longer in the list of States in which a relevant risk of torture or inhuman treatment in prison exists for extradited condemned persons. According to the Italian Supreme Court, in case of extradition to a foreign country, the detention conditions in the requesting State need not be particularly "advanced": what is essential is that there no systemic practices are reported of abuse and violations of fundamental rights of the prisoners. Measures such as probation and parole, aimed at re-socialising the convicted persons have been recently introduced in Kazakhstan. This makes possible extradition, unless it is ascertained, on a case-by-case basis, that a systematic practice exists in breach of the law (Court of Cassation, Criminal Division, sec. II, judg. 27 October 2017, No. 51657).

K. Crime of Private Violence – Improper Violence

The aforementioned jurisprudence of the Court of Cassation, sec. V, judg. 24 February 2017, No. 29261, rectifies a too strict interpretation of the crime foreseen in article 610 of the Criminal Code (private violence – harassment, threatening behaviour). In the specific case, a woman was forced, without physical constraints but by seizing her mobile phone as a "pawn", to get her on her ex partner's car; the man then accompanied her home at a very high speed, with the purpose, according to the woman, of making her disclose details of her private life. The Court, that recalls some precedents in which the notion of "indirect violence" was elaborated, finds that the offense of private violence does not require the utterance of an explicit menace, verbally or otherwise.

Instead, the offence may consist of any behaviour or attitude that causes fear or otherwise induces the victim to believe that she is going to suffer an unjust harm, in order to obtain from the victim a specific behaviour. Other examples of indirect violence may be padlocking a door that the person would have the right to open or, as in the case in question, seizing the mobile phone as a "pawn" to assure the victim's coming back to the perpetrator's car.

L. Propaganda and Incitement to Racial Hatred. Aggravating Factor of Racial, Ethnic and Religious Discrimination

The Court of Cassation (Criminal Division, sec. V, judg. 8 February 2017, No. 13530) intervened on a case where two women, mother and daughter, were convicted for assault causing personal injury on another woman of African descent. They were involved on car parking row. The conviction of the two women was for aggravated assault because the trial judge found it was a case of racial discrimination (l. 16 October 1975, No. 654 and subsequent amendments, and lgs.d. No. 122/1993, article 3, converted into l. 205/1993). The aggravating factor was contested by the applicants on the grounds that the dispute was not born in any way due to the ethnic characteristics of the victim and therefore could not be traced back to racial hatred. The Court of Cassation, recalling its consolidated jurisprudence, reiterates that the aggravating factor is applied when the perpetrator makes it perceptible to the outside and arouses in the others a feeling of hatred based on nationality, race, ethnicity or religion; or when the perpetrator's conduct gives rise to a concrete danger of discriminatory behaviour by others, based on the same prejudices; or also when the perpetrator's deeds objectively manifest a negative prejudice towards a single ethnic, racial, national, or religious group, irrespective of the perpetrator personally sharing such prejudice, and even if no third person is physically present. The women had used typically racist phrases, whose meaning was reinforced by the physical violence committed.

The same interpretative pattern was applied in Court of Cassation, Criminal Division, sec. V, judg. 10 July 2017, No. 38398. Some under-age young people had publicly addressed people as *zingari*, i.e. "gypsies" (actually Moroccan citizens). They were charged and convicted of the offence of harassment and threatening behaviour (private violence).

The Court of Cassation, Criminal Division, sec. V, judg. 19 July 2017, No. 49503 (a case of private violence resulting from a traffic dispute), after having repeated the principles outlined above, the Court rejects the applicant's defence that the type of insults used should not be understood as characterised by racial hatred, as they could have been addressed also towards an Italian citizen, although not ethnically so. However, the threat of "returning home in a case" addressed to the victim could only be seen as a way of stressing his non-Italian origins, thus confirming the objective discriminatory character of the expressions used. The Court also founds it not contradictory to apply contextually the aggravating factor of racial discrimination and the mitigating factor of provocation (as it would be to apply simultaneously the mitigating factor of provocation and the aggravating factor of futile reasons). Indeed, what counts in hate crimes is not the subjective motive that pushed the perpetrator, but the objective conduct likely to convey racial, ethnic or other hatred (Court of Cassation, Criminal Division, sec. V, judg. 28 November 2017, No. 2630).

The aggravating factor of racial hatred was correctly applied, according to the Court of Cassation (Criminal Division, sec. V, judg. 2 November 2017, No. 7859), by the judges who convicted a local politician who had criticised a minister of the Italian government of African origins, using defamatory terms on his Facebook profile. The Court reiterates that the right of criticism, even if it does not have to comply with the rules governing the freedom of the press, does not allow "gratuitous aggressions to the moral dimension of the offended person" and the use of expressions that "transmute into a mere verbal aggression of the criticised subject, whose person is denigrated as such". Therefore, inviting a person to "return to the jungle" cannot be considered a form of criticism of the technical-political competence of the addressee; moreover, it expresses a racist stereotype, that the norm against racial hatred aims at stigmatising.

Regarding the use of racist expressions on occasions of sport events, the Court of Cassation, Criminal Division, sec. III, judg. 4 May 2017, No. 31975 is worth mentioning. The Court had to decide whether the person responsible for organising, with other supporters, a football chant saying "*livornese ebreo*" ("Livorno Jew") against the team of the city of Livorno, accompanied by fascist salutes, could constitute the offence referred to in l. 654/1975 and subsequent amendments ("… the person is punished: a)… who makes propaganda of ideas based on the superiority of a race or on racial or ethnic hatred, or instigates to commit or commits acts of discrimination based on race, ethnicity, nationality or religion; b)… who, in any way, instigates to commit or commits violence or acts of provocation of violence for racial, ethnic, national or religious reasons (…). 3. Any organisation, association, movement or group that has among its purposes the incitement to discrimination or to violence based on race, ethnicity, nationality or religion is forbidden….").
The provincial head of the police (*Questore*) may impose a ban on access to sporting events to persons charged or convicted of these crimes. The Court of Cassation confirmed the interpretation given by the judge who had validated the measure of the *Questore*. It considered that by approaching the citizens of a town to the Jewish religion and recalling the policies of persecution of

which the Jews were victims during the fascist regime is indeed carrying out propaganda of racist ideas, namely it is a conduct likely to fuelling discriminatory attitudes in a large public, such as that reached during a sporting event, regardless of whether this propaganda reaches out.

The Emilia Romagna TAR (Bologna TAR, sec. I, judg. 19 December 2017, No. 851) rules on the *Divieto di Accesso ad eventi Sportivi* order ("prohibition of access to sporting events") issued by the police authority of Bologna and targeting a basketball fan who, together with other supporters of the team, had made the fascist salute during a match, provoking reactions from the opposing supporters and subsequent unrest. The TAR confirmed the legitimacy of the police measure. According to the judges, the fascist (or Roman) salute was intentionally used, in the circumstance, to provoke the violent reaction of the opposing fans and as signal that they were ready to a physical confrontation. Although in the specific case it did not carry any political meaning, the salute evoked nevertheless a criminal offence (apology of fascism) and was clearly an incitement to violence; the clash was avoided only thanks to the intervention of the police.

The offence of racist propaganda versus the freedom of press was also addressed by the Supreme Court (Court of Cassation, Civil Division, sec. I, judg. 30 May 2017, No. 13552). The Court found that an article published in the newspaper *La Repubblica* in which an investigation for racist and anti-Semitic propaganda via a website allegedly carried out by activists of a far right-wing political movement, which was accompanied by the photos of the founders and leader of that political movement, did not concretise libel of that political leader and the group. While admitting that from the perspective of the political group, its association with a criminal investigation was offensive, the Court states that an assessment of the defamatory nature (or not) of the text requires a comprehensive analysis of the article. In the latter, it was clearly indicated that the unnamed individuals being investigated were activists of a political movement and could not be confused with the persons portrayed, who were instead historical leaders of the same movement. Their pictures were featured just to stress the involvement of the political group. According to the Supreme Court, the conviction of the newspaper's editor-in-chief for libel must be revised and the defence based on freedom of press given application. It is worth pointing out that the controversial article was published in 2000 and that the Supreme Court quashed and sent back a judgement to the Court of Appeal of Rome for revision, which was pronounced by the latter in 2012.

Italy in the Case-law of the European Court of Human Rights*

I. Torture, Right to Liberty, Right to Life

On 3 March 2017, in the case of *Talpis v. Italy*, No. 41237/14, the European Court of Human Rights (ECtHR) found that the Italian authorities had failed to protect the applicant and her son against the acts of violence inflicted by her husband, by failing to take prompt action on the woman's requests for help, which led to the attempted murder of the applicant and the death of her son.

The ECtHR held, by 6 votes to 1, that there had been a violation of article 2 (right to life) of the ECHR on account of the murder of Ms. Talpis' son and her own attempted murder. It unanimously found that there had been a violation of article 3 (inhuman or degrading treatment) of the ECHR due to the failure of the authorities to fulfil their obligation to protect the applicant against the recurrent acts of domestic violence. Furthermore, it held, by 5 votes against 2, that there had been a violation of article 14 ECHR (prohibition of discrimination) in conjunction with articles 2 and 3 ECHR.

Particularly, the ECtHR held that by failing at intervening promptly on a previous complaint lodged by Ms. Talpis, the Italian authorities had deprived that complaint from any effect, creating a situation of impunity that propitiated the recurrence of the acts of violence which then lead to the attempted murder of the applicant and the death of her son. According to the Court of Strasburg, the authorities had not fulfilled their obligation to protect the lives of the persons involved.

Furthermore, according to the ECtHR, the severity of the climate of violence in which Ms. Talpis and her children lived, together with the judicial passivity demonstrated by the manner in which the authorities had conducted the criminal proceedings against Ms. Talpis' husband, are incompatible with article 3 of the ECHR.

Finally, the Strasbourg Court found that Ms. Talpis had been victim of discrimination as a woman on account of the inaction of the national

* Claudia Pividori

authorities, which had underestimated the violence suffered by the applicant, and therefore essentially endorsed it.

According to the ECtHR, the seriousness of the problem of domestic violence and discrimination against Italian women is reflected in the reports of the United Nations Special Rapporteur on Violence Against Women and the CEDAW Committee. The data show that domestic violence concerns mainly women and that, despite the implemented reforms, a significant number of women die at the hands of their current partner. It also shows that socio-cultural attitudes of tolerance towards domestic violence in Italy persist.

With three judgements issued during 2017, the ECtHR returns to deal with the violence that erupted in 2001 during the G8 in Genoa. This concerns the case of *Bartesaghi Gallo and others vs. Italy* (No. 12131/13 and No. 43390/13), *Blair and others vs. Italy* (No. 1442/14, No. 21319/14 and No. 21911/14) and *Azzolina and others vs. Italy* (No. 28923/09 and No. 67599/10). In all the referred cases, the applicants complained that they had been subjected to torture by police officers and health personnel within different places such as the Diaz-Pertini school, the Pascoli school and the Bolzaneto barracks. Furthermore, they complained about the ineffectiveness of the investigations carried out by national courts, in particular because the statute of limitations had been applied to practically all the acts committed and, overall, about to the inadequacy of the penalties imposed on those convicted. In all cases, the ECtHR asserts that there had been an infringement of article 3 ECHR (prohibition of torture, inhuman or degrading treatment), both at the substantive and procedural level. Regarding the first level, in the opinion of the judges of the Strasbourg Court, the acts of violence suffered by the applicants, expression of a punitive will and retaliation against them, fit the treaty definition of torture. Concerning the second profile, as already established in *Cestaro* (see *Yearbook 2016*, p. 255), the Court reiterates that the criminal legislation applied to the cases under discussion proved both inadequate as regards the need to punish acts of torture and devoid of the necessary deterrent effect to prevent other similar violations of article 3 ECHR. The Court granted the appellants amounts between €10,000 and €85,000 in respect for moral damage.

On 14 March 2017, *Alfarano* (No. 75895/13) and *Battista and others* (No. 22045/14) were removed from the register of the ECtHR, both relating to the violence committed in the "Bolzaneto" barracks, due to the agreement of an amicably settling between the parties.

The applicants in the *Cirino and Renne case v. Italy* (No. 2539/13 and No. 4705/13) are two detainees, of whom one has since died. The two applicants complained they were ill-treated by prison officers of the Asti Correctional Facility, where they were both detained at the time. Both applicants were subject to physical and verbal abuse, at all hours of the day and night for many consecutive days, along with the rationing of food and water and the deprivation of sleep and clothing. Moreover, the applicants had been separately placed in solitary confinement, without adequate access to sanitary facilities, appropriate heating or bed linen.

As in previous cases, the ECtHR finds a violation of article 3 ECHR both from the substantive and procedural point of view. Recalling the conclusions of the Italian criminal court, the ECtHR first concludes, that the treatment to which the applicants were subjected attained the level of severity required to bring the impugned conduct within the scope of the definition of torture. From a procedural point of view, it is once again the inadequacy of the Italian legal system and, in particular, the absence, at the time of the facts, of provisions penalising the practices referred to in article 3 ECHR, which lead to the finding of an infringement by the Court of Strasbourg. To each appellant the Court awards compensation of €80,000 for non-pecuniary damage.

In the *Pennino v. Italy* case (No. 21759/15), ruled on 12 October 2017, the applicant, invoking article 3 of the ECHR, claimed she had been ill-treated by the Italian police, and complained about the lack of adequate investigative measures concerning the events that she had reported. According to her reconstruction of the facts, during the time spent at a municipal police station where she had been taken for a minor offence (driving under the influence of alcohol), she had suffered ill-treatment that had caused her a fractured thumb and other bruises. Ms. Pennino lodged a criminal complaint, but the judge for preliminary investigations accepted the request of the prosecutor and ordered the dismissal of the case.

In ascertaining the violation of article 3 ECHR, the ECtHR holds that in cases where there are allegations of mistreatment when an individual is deprived of his or her personal liberty or, as in this case, is simply in contact with police authorities for an identity check or to give a statement, the State has the obligation to ensure that adequate and accurate investigations are carried out to verify facts. It is State responsibility to demonstrate the innocence of its agents by all possible means, preparing thorough and accurate investigations, and not relying on hasty or ill-founded conclusions. According to the ECtHR findings, these principles were disregarded by the Italian State in the present case. Although not denying the use of force, the Italian government justified these actions as a means to counteract the applicant's agitated and violent state, conducting incomplete and non-exhaustive investigations. In addition, the request and decision to close the investigation demonstrated a very succinct and standardised motive, as was the rejection of the judge to the victim's request for additional investigations.

In 2017, in 7 cases the ECtHR accepted the requests for temporary measures presented pursuant to article 39 of the Rules of Procedure of the Court. These measures were granted, in particular, within the framework of two cases concerning the condition of unaccompanied foreign minors placed in the centre for asylum seekers in Cona (Venice): *Darboe and Camara vs. Italy* (No. 5797/17, Government notified on 14 February 2017) and *Dansu and others vs. Italy* (No. 16030/17, Government notified on 20 March 2017). In both cases, pending the settlement of the appeal, the Court ordered the transfer of the applicants to suitable structures to guarantee the reception standards and the protection of the rights guaranteed to the minors.

II. Fair Trial, Right to Property

In the *Fasan and others v. Italy* case (No. 36974/11), decided on 13 April 2017, the applicants are the protagonists of a long trial case that took place before the appeals panel of the Chamber of Deputies and lasted 28 years, adding the proceedings at first instance and the appeal. After proposing an appeal under the "Pinto" law to obtain compensation for the damage caused on account of the excessive duration of the main proceedings, the claimants are recognised €4,000 as a relief for the second-degree proceedings only. Invoking article 6 ECHR, the applicants therefore turn to the ECtHR to claim for the recognition of compensation also in relation to the unreasonable duration of the first instance procedure (18 years), as well as to complain about the inadequacy of the amount of compensation obtained under the "Pinto" procedure.

In ascertaining the violation of article 6 of the ECHR, the Court of Strasbourg first of all rejects the Italian Government's objections to the applicants' lack of "victim" status. Observing that the duration of the proceedings must be considered a "continuous situation", the ECtHR points out that at the domestic level the applicants have not received any acknowledgment concerning the violation of article 6 ECHR within the first instance of judgement. In addition to this, the applicants can qualify as "victims" in account of the inconsistency of the sum granted to them by the Italian authorities as a compensation for the breach suffered (corresponding to about 21% of what the Court would have granted in the absence of any internal remedies).

In the *Bozza v. Italy* case (No. 17739/09), 14 September 2017, the ECtHR reiterates that the calculation of the length of a proceeding must also include the execution phase of a judgement that has finally recognised a certain right.

In this sense, considering the "final internal decision" (from which the six-month deadline set by the "Pinto" law must be calculated) the judgement of merit – and not the decision of the enforcement judge – constitutes a violation of article 6(1) ECHR (reasonable duration of the process).

In the *Arnoldi v. Italy* case (No. 35637/04), decided on 7 December 2017, the appellant Ms. Arnoldi lodged a criminal complaint against some of her neighbours for forgery. According to Ms. Arnoldi, they were guilty of having made false declarations in the context of a dispute concerning a chimney built illegally on her property. After more than seven years, the criminal proceeding, which was still in the preliminary investigation phase, was filed on the grounds that the offence was statute-barred. After turning to the national courts to complain of the excessive length of the criminal proceedings under the "Pinto" law, the appellant had seen her appeal dismissed for not having formally joined the proceedings as a civil party. In fact, although the national courts had acknowledged that the appellant had not been able to join the proceedings as a civil party precisely because of the unreasonable term of the preliminary investigations, they considered that the Ms. Arnoldi could not be considered a "part" of the proceedings and, therefore, could not complain of their excessive duration.

Rejecting the admissibility exceptions presented by the Italian Government regarding the applicability of article 6 ECHR in this case, the Court first of all points out the "civil" nature of the right of which the appellant sought protection by lodging the complaint, as well as the decisive nature of the phase of preliminary investigations for the protection of the right in question. According to the Court, in Italian law the position of the injured party who, awaiting the recognition of her status as a plaintiff, had exercised at least one of the rights and faculties in the criminal proceedings, does not differ from that of the civil party. Having noted this, in the absence of arguments capable of justifying such a length of preliminary enquiries, the ECtHR concludes that the latter have exceeded the "reasonable time" of duration in violation of article 6 ECHR

In the *Sante v. Italy* case (No. 32143/10), decided on 27 April 2017, the applicant alleged a violation of articles 6(1) ECHR (reasonable duration of the trial) and 13 ECHR (right to an effective remedy), complaining that the Court of Appeal, hearing a "Pinto" claim regarding the excessive length of a proceeding concerning Mr. Sante, did not consider the whole duration of the latter. Given the ten-year statute of limitation, in fact, the initial period of the procedure (1993-1998) had not been examined. By refusing the appellant's arguments concerning the alleged ineffectiveness of an appeal in cassation, the ECtHR rejects this part of the complaint due to the failure of exhaustion of internal remedies. On the other hand, the ground of appeal relating to the violation of article 6(1) ECHR was considered well founded, on account of the delay of more than six months in the payment of the compensation granted to the claimant under the "Pinto" procedure.

> The six-month deadline established by the ECtHR for the fulfilment of the "Pinto" decisions does not apply to the payment of the sums granted to the lawyers to cover the legal expenses, since they are not compensatory in nature. The *Izzo and other v. Italy* case (30 May 2017) is therefore inadmissible as manifestly unfounded.

With the judgement of 1 June 2017, the Court of Strasbourg has afforded a just satisfaction in the case *Stefanetti and others v. Italy*, decided on 15 April 2014 (see *Yearbook 2015*, p. 320). The case concerned the pension situation of some Italian citizens who had worked in Switzerland and had their monthly contributions reduced due to a law of authentic interpretation that negatively affected with retroactive effects a favourable judicial orientation in couts. This case was concluded verifying a double violation. A violation of article 6 ECHR to the extent that the contested legislative intervention was not justified by reasons of general interest, and a violation of article 1 protocol I ECHR, since a reduction of 67% of the pension allowance represented a disproportionate burden on the applicants. In this context, the Court found it reasonable to compensate them for material damage the difference between 55% of the sums that the applicants would have had if the law at issue had not been enacted and the sum they actually received, for a total of almost €900,000.

In the case *Lorefice v. Italy* (No. 63446/13), a judgement of 29 June 2017, the ECHR condemned Italy for violating article 6(1) ECHR (right to a fair trial) on account of the non-renewal of the preliminary investigation in a criminal appeal. In the present case, the applicant, acquitted at first instance because the statements made by two witnesses had been assessed as unreliable, had subsequently been convicted on appeal (condemnation then confirmed in cassation) on the basis of a reassessment of the credibility of those same testimonies, without however hearing the witnesses again.

> On 26 September 2017, the *Mazzarella v. Italy* (No. 24059/13) case was declared inadmissible. The case refers to an alleged violation of article 6 ECHR (right to a fair trial) in the context of a criminal proceeding – with abbreviated procedure – against the applicant and consisting in the refusal of the national courts to take into consideration a written statement filed by him. The Court concludes that the appellant has benefited from an adversarial procedure and has been able, at the various stages of the latter, to present the arguments he considered relevant for the purposes of the defence of his case. Pointing out that the appellant essentially contested the assessment of the elements of

the file by the national judges and the outcome of the procedure, the Court declared the appeal to be manifestly unfounded.

In *Cafagna v. Italy* (No. 26073/13), decided on 12 October 2017, the ECtHR finds a violation of article 6 ECHR, para. 1 and 3(d), on the ground that the applicant had not been able to have the main witness against him examined in the context of a criminal procedure for robbery, which ended in a conviction.

The ECtHR decision in the cases *Alpe Società Agricola Cooperativa con produzione e lavorazione propria and others* (19 October 2017, No. 8726/09 and other 38) and *Frubona Cooperativa frutticoltori Bolzano-Nalles s.c.a and others* (7 December 2017, No. 4180/08 and other 49) recall the established facts in the *Azienda Agricola Silverfunghi S.a.s. and others* case (see *Yearbook 2015*, p. 319). As with previous cases cited, the appeals in question featured agricultural companies that, on the basis of a constant domestic case-law, had the legitimate expectation of accumulating tax relief provided for by Italian law. The entry into force of a law of authentic interpretation, which prohibited the accumulation of such reductions with retroactive effect, however, had put an end to the applicants' claims, negatively affecting proceedings that were still pending.

In both cases, the ECtHR first denied the requests of removal of the appeals from the register on the basis of the unilateral declarations of the Italian Government, as the sums offered for the material damage and the expenses were considered insufficient compared to the sums granted in *Azienda Agricola Silverfunghi S.a.s. and others*. On the merits, the ECtHR found a violation of article 6 ECHR. Accepting that the legislative intervention was necessary to eliminate doubts about the scope and method of application of the benefits in question, the Court did not find that there were any overriding reasons of general interest that would be capable of prevailing over the inherent prejudice in the use of retrospective legislation that had the effect of determining the outcome of pending proceedings in favour of the State.

The same issue was dealt with in the case *Approvvigionamento Salorno s.a.c. and others v. Italy* (No. 8740/09 and 6 others), which was stricken out of the list by a decision of 17 October 2017 following a unilateral declaration by the Italian Government. The terms of this case, unlike previous cases, were deemed satisfactory by the Court of Strasbourg.

In *Mazzeo v. Italy* (No. 32269/09), decided on 5 October 2017, the ECtHR found a violation of article 6(1) ECHR and article 1 protocol I ECHR on the ground that it was impossible for the applicants to collect credits, recognised by a final decision of the Council of State, against a municipal administration. The Municipality in question, using a form of self-remedy, had annulled the administrative decision which constituted the legal basis of the applicant's' right to claim, depriving *de facto* the decision of the Council of State of its substance and of any prospect of execution. In the opinion of the ECtHR, this decision contravenes the principle of legal certainty, resulting in an infringement of the right of access of the interested parties to a court, as well as the right of the applicants to respect of their property. For the material and moral damages caused by the sense of powerlessness and frustration caused by the non-payment of their credits, the applicants are granted the total sum of €245,000.

The story of Mr. and Mrs. Messana is at the centre of four different appeals: *Messana v. Italy* (No. 26128/04), decided on 9 February 2017; *Messana v. Italy* (No. 37189/05), decided on 7 September 2017; *Messana v. Italy* (No. 30801/06) and *Messana v. Italy* (No. 37199/05), decided on 16 November 2017. In these appeals, the appellants complained of a violation of article 1 protocol I ECHR for losing possession of land due to the application of the mechanism of "indirect expropriation" in force at the time of the facts. Rejecting the Italian Government's requests for the removal of the appeal from the register and recalling its consolidated jurisprudence in the matter of indirect expropriation (see *Guiso-Gallisay v. Italy*, No. 58858/00, 22 December 2009), in all cases the ECtHR found a violation of the applicant's' right to respect for their property on account of the incompatibility of this procedure with the principle of legality.

The Court has also arrived to the same conclusion in the *Conti and Lori v. Italy* case (No. 17527/05) of 16 November 2017, concerning the same grievances of the Messana cases.

III. Private and Family Life

With a judgement issued on the 24 January 2017 in the *Paradiso and Campanelli* case (No. 25358/12), the Grand Chamber has overturned the judgement issued by the Chamber on 27 January 2015 in which Italy had been condemned for the violation of article 8 ECHR on the right to respect for private and family life (see *Yearbook 2016*, p. 263). The case concerned the refusal of the Italian authorities to register the birth certificate of a nine-month-old child and its decision to entrust him to the custody of social services. In the present case, the child was born in Russia following a surrogacy contract between a Russian woman and an Italian couple who did not have biological links with the child.

Section II of the ECtHR had originally declared admissible the complaint of the applicants, Ms. Paradiso and Mr. Campanelli, recognizing the existence of a de facto family falling within the notion of family life protected by article 8 ECHR. The Court had therefore established that article 8 ECHR had been infringed by the national authorities to the extent that, by resorting to the extreme measure of removing the child on the basis of the lack of biological links between the latter and the applicants, they had not reached the right balance between the child's best interests and public interest.

With the judgement of 24 January 2017, adopted with 11 votes in favour and 6 against, the Grand Chamber overturned the previous decision.

First of all, the Court considered that in the light of the short duration of the relationship between the child and the applicants, the complaint was to be considered under the notion of "private life" and not "family life" provided for by article 8 ECHR. Moreover, according to the Grand Chamber, the national authorities, having established that the child would not suffer serious and irreparable damage as a result of the separation, they had reached a fair balance between the different interests at stake. Finally, the Court considered that the measures contested by the applicants had as legitimate aims the prevention of legal uncertainty of minors in similar situations and the protection of rights and liberties of others, recognising Italy's legitimate desire to reaffirm the exclusive competence of the State in relation to the recognition of parenting links, in this case those supported by biological ties or regulated adoption procedures, with the aim of protecting the minors involved.

With the ruling of 9 February 2017 in the *Solarino v. Italy* case (No. 76171/13), the ECtHR has ascertained a violation of article 8 ECHR by Italy for not protecting the development and maintenance of a family bond between the applicant and his minor daughter. The Court of Strasbourg had considered legitimate the decision of the national court to suspend the parental rights of the applicant pending the conclusion of the criminal investigation for sexual abuse initiated following a complaint lodged by the mother of the minor. However, since the above-mentioned complaint had been dismissed and an expert report had excluded sexual abuse, the decision to limit the applicant's right of access to his daughter for the period September 2009 – November 2013 resulted in an excess of the margin of appreciation national authorities have when attempting to balance the interests at stake. The applicant was granted the sum of €7,000 for moral damages.

The ECtHR provides similar conclusions in the *D'Alconzo v. Italy* case (No. 64297/12), decided on 23 February 2017. In the present case, the ECtHR holds that Italian authorities did not undertake all the necessary measures that could reasonably be required from them in order to rebuild the family ties of the applicant with his children. According to the ECtHR, the unreasonable delays in the criminal proceedings brought against the applicant for alleged sexual abuse of his children, which concluded with a full acquittal, had a direct and decisive impact on the right to family life of the applicant.

However, the applicant's second complaint was not accepted. According to Mr. D'Alconzo, the decisions of the national courts had failed to favour bringing him and his children back together. Recognising that the authorities faced a difficult situation, stemming from the parents' serious misunderstandings between themselves and from the complaints lodged against one other, the Court considered that the authorities did all that could reasonably be expected to ensure compliance with the applicant's right of access, by adopting measures aimed at establishing effective contacts and by elaborating a project intended to bring the applicant closer to his children.

In the case of *Endrizzi v. Italy* (No. 71660/14), the applicant is a separated father who, despite both the Court and of the Court of Appeal granting him extensive rights of access, for many years had not been able to see his son due to the opposition of the mother and of the complaints for sexual violence presented by the latter (all of which have been proven unfounded).

While acknowledging that the authorities were facing a very difficult situation, due specifically to the tensions between the applicant and his ex-wife, the ECtHR considers that the authorities were not as diligent as the present case required and remained below what could reasonably be expected of them. In particular, the internal judges did not take the appropriate measures to create the necessary conditions to fully realise the right of access of the child's father. Since the beginning of the separation, the judges did not adopt useful measures to establish effective contacts. The Court observes that the national authorities allowed the mother for seven years to prevent the establishment of a real relationship between the applicant and his son. This failure to comply with judicial decisions in violation of article 8 ECHR created a de facto situation, for which the applicant was granted the sum of €15,000 for moral damages.

A violation of article 8 ECHR was also found in the *Improta v. Italy* (No. 66396/14) decided with a ruling of 4 May 2017. As in previous cases, the applicant is a separated father who complains of a violation of article 8 due to difficulties in exercising his right of access to his youngest daughter. In the present case, the procedure for establishing the applicant's access rights lasted about a year, during which the internal judges tolerated the mother unilaterally deciding how the father could see their daughter, effectively preventing the establishment of a true relationship between them. In view of the irreversible consequences that amount of time may have on the relationship between a young child and a non-cohabiting parent, the

Court of Strasbourg considers that an unjustifiable delay by the national authorities took place.

In the case of *Beccarini and Ridolfi v. Italy* (No. 63190/16), ruled on 7 December 2017, the applicants are the maternal grandparents of three minors, entrusted to them following a decision establishing that the mother was unable to take care of them. Following a report by the social services attesting to the applicants' difficult situation in managing their grandchildren, the latter were placed in a foster home and subsequently returned to their mother. Despite two decisions by the Juvenile Court ordering social services to arrange periodic meetings between the grandparents and the three children, the applicants did not see their grandchildren for five years.

Accepting the complaints presented by the applicants on the basis of article 8 ECHR, the Court of Strasbourg condemns Italy for not making adequate and sufficient efforts to preserve the family bond between the applicants and their grandchildren. In this sense, it was clear that social services had not implemented the Court's decisions authorising the meetings or had not prepared any project to bring the family closer together in order to restore still potentially positive relationships between grandparents and grandchildren.

At the centre of the *Barnea and Caldararu v. Italy* case (No. 37931/15), decided on 22 June 2017, there is the story of a Roma minor and her family. After a removal from her parents in 2009 at the age of two, a declaration of adoptability and a provision of foster care, in 2012, the Court of Appeal decided that it was in the child's best interest to return to her family of origin. However, since social services had not implemented a plan to rebuild the relationship between the applicants and the child, according to the provisions of the Court of Appeal, the child's stay in a foster family was extended and the number of meetings with the parents reduced. In accordance with the national courts, these measures were necessary given the passage of time and the child's integration in the foster family. Following the rejection of the application for special adoption presented by the latter, in September 2016, at the age of nine, the child returned to live with her birth family.

Accepting the applicants' complaints, the ECtHR finds a violation of article 8 ECHR. Firstly, the Court of Strasbourg noted that the reasons for which the child had been removed from her family and declared eligible for adoption did not constitute "very exceptional circumstances" capable of justifying the severing of family ties. In fact, the applicants were mainly criticised for not offering appropriate conditions to the minor while at no stage of the proceedings were allegations made of ill-treatment, sexual abuse or emotional deficiencies. Secondly, the Court observes that the same authorities had not properly implemented the Court of Appeal's 2012 judgement providing for the child's return to her family of origin. The passage of time, consequence of the social services' inertia in beginning the family rebuilding process, and the grounds alleged by the first-instance court for extending the child's temporary placement had been decisive factors in preventing the parents' reunion with their daughter, thus breaching the applicants' right to respect for their family life.

Recalling the decision of the *Oliari and others* case (see *Yearbook 2016*, p. 264), in the *Orlandi and others v. Italy* case (No. 26431/12, No. 26742/12, No. 44057/12 and No. 60088/12), ruled on 14 December 2017, the ECtHR condemns Italy for violating the right to respect for the private and family life of the applicants, a number of same-sex couples, by rendering impossible the registration of foreign marriages in Italy, as well as for the legal void that existed at the time (i.e. in the period preceding the adoption of the 76/2016 act on civil unions) regarding the recognition and the protection of same-sex unions.

IV. Freedom of Expression, Freedom of Movement

In the case of the *Petrie v. Italy* (No. 25322/12), 18 May 2017, the applicant complained about a breach of article 8 ECHR on account of the dismissal of an action for defamation brought by him against two people who, during a university conference, claimed that he had "accused Italy of being a country run by the Mafia". The case was handed down in favour of the applicant by the Court of first instance. On appeal, the national court however reversed the trial court's conclusion, noting a substantive identity between the statements attributed to him and those actually made, consisting in having denounced, in a debate at the European Parliament, the system of "recommendations" that would govern the Italian university.

In rejecting the applicant's complaint, the ECtHR first of all doubts whether the appellant's reputation could have been discredited by the disputed claims. Apart from this, the Court observes that the national courts carried out a detailed assessment of the balance to be guaranteed between the applicant's right to respect for his private life and the right to freedom of expression of his interlocutors. In assessing the divergent interests at stake, therefore, the national authorities did not exceed the margin of appreciation to them attributed and did not elude their positive obligations towards the applicant pursuant to article 8 ECHR.

The complaint *Travaglio v. Italy* (No. 64746/14) is inadmissible as manifestly unfounded. The applicant was a journalist, who complained of a violation of article 10 ECHR (freedom of expression) by reason of a conviction for defamation imposed on him for the contents of an article he wrote and published on a well-known Italian newspaper. The article dealt with an alleged relationship between an Italian political party of primary importance and the Sicilian mafia, the role played in such events by certain leading members of the party, and the involvement of *Carabinieri* officers. Considering the fact that domestic courts had found both the defamatory nature of the disputed article and the fraudulent conduct of the applicant, the ECtHR considered that a fair balance was struck at the national level between the rights at stake. As to the nature and severity of the penalty imposed, the ECtHR observes that the suspended prison sentence at first imposed was subsequently replaced with the payment of a fine of a modest amount (€1,000), as modest as the amount the journalist had been sentenced to pay in compensation to the injured party, jointly with the publisher (€20,000).

The case *Scozzafava and others v. Italy* (No. 20014/13) is inadmissible *ratione personae.* The applicants complained under article 10 ECHR (right to receive information) because the national authorities had failed to broadcast in radio and TV on a regular basis political talk shows as provided for by l. 14 April, 1975, No. 103. According to the ECtHR, the applicants formulated their grievance *in abstracto* and did not demonstrate to have been directly affected by the omission in question.

The Grand Chamber judgement of 23 February 2017, in the case *de Tommaso v. Italy* (No. 43395/09), established that there has been a violation of article 2 protocol IV to the ECHR (freedom of movement) on the basis of the lack of foreseeability of the Italian Act on preventive measures (then in force), as well as a violation of article 6(1) of the ECHR on account of the lack of a public hearing before the Court of Appeal. In the present case, the applicant had been placed under special supervision with a compulsory residence order for two years, as provided for by l. No. 1423/1956 on preventive measures against persons presenting a danger for security and public morality.

Proceeding with the examination of the case, the Court found, firstly, that the obligations imposed on Mr. de Tommaso had not amounted to a deprivation of liberty pursuant to article 5 ECHR, as claimed by the appellant, but merely to restrictions on his freedom of movement and therefore frameable pursuant to article 2 protocol IV ECHR. On the merits of the appeal, the Grand Chamber, unanimously, noted that although the 1423/1956 act satisfied the requirement of accessibility and effectiveness, being worded in vague and excessively broad terms, it had not met the foreseeability requirements. In particular, according to the judges of the Grand Chamber, the act left a wide discretionary power to the national courts, without clear detailed provisions as to the types of behaviour deemed dangerous to society and which could give rise to preventive measures. In doing so, this legislation was not adequate to offer protection against arbitrary interferences and to enable interested parties to regulate their conduct and foresee to a sufficiently certain degree the imposition of the preventive measures.

Regarding the complaint based on article 6 ECHR (right to a fair trial), the ECtHR considered (14 votes to 3) that the proceeding as a whole had been conducted in accordance with the conventional rules on the matter. However, as recognised by the Government and already held by a ruling by the Constitutional Court, the Grand Chamber unanimously found a violation of the fair trial rules due to the lack of publicity of the hearings before the Court of Appeal. Finally, with 12 votes against 5, the Grand Chamber concludes that there has been no violation of article 13 ECHR (right to an effective remedy) to the extent that the applicant had been able to lodge an appeal against the special supervision measures at the Court of Appeal, which had then effectively annulled them.

Italy in the Case-law of the Court of Justice of the European Union*

I. Equal Treatment in Family Services

In the case C-449/16, decided on 21 June 2017, the ECJ answers to a reference for a preliminary ruling submitted by the Appeal Court of Genoa in the context of a dispute involving Mrs. Kerly Del Rosario Martinez Silva, a third country citizen in possession of a "single work permit", against the National Institute of Social Security (INPS) and the Municipality of Genoa concerning the rejection of an application for a benefit for households having at least three minor children (ANF).

The request for a preliminary ruling essentially concerned two aspects. The first related to the nature of the ANF or whether it should be considered a family benefit within the meaning of article 3(1)(j) of regulation (EC) No. 883/2004 on the coordination of social security systems. To this question, the ECJ responds positively. In the light of its objectives (alleviate family's financial burdens) and the conditions for its allocation, (on the basis of a situation defined by law, regardless of any individual and discretionary assessment of the applicant's personal needs), according to the Luxembourg Court, the ANF falls within the definition of social security benefit.

The second aspect concerned the interpretation of Directive No. 2011/98 on a single application procedure for a single permit. In particular, if this were to be interpreted in the sense of precluding legislation, such as the Italian legislation at issue, that limits the ANF benefit only in the case of third-country nationals, to holders of a long-term residence permit and to families of EU citizens. In this case, the ECJ response is positive. Although the Directive No. 2011/98 provides for the possibility for States to introduce certain exceptions to the equal treatment of workers coming from third countries in terms of social security, Italy has never taken advantage of this possibility. It follows that a third-country national holding a single permit, may not be excluded from receiving benefits such as ANF.

---

* Claudia Pividori

II. Age-based Discrimination on Employment and Working Conditions

In the case C-143/16, decided on 19 July 2017, the ECJ answers to a reference for a preliminary ruling submitted by the Court of Cassation in the context of a dispute between the company Abercrombie & Fitch Italia Srl and Mr. Antonino Bordonaro concerning the termination of his on-call employment contract on the sole ground that he had reached 25 years of age.

The question raised by the referring court concerned the interpretation of Council Directive 27 November 2000, No. 2000/78/EC establishing a general framework for equal treatment in employment and occupation, and of article 21 Charter of Fundamental Rights of the European Union. In particular, the Court of Cassation questions if these should be interpreted in the sense of precluding Italian legislation (article 34, lgs.d. No. 276/2003) which authorises an employer to conclude an on-call employment contract with a worker under 25 years of age, whatever the nature of the services to be performed, and to dismiss that worker as soon as they reach the age of 25 years.

The ECJ answer was negative. According to the Luxembourg judges, in fact, the Italian legislation, although introducing a disparity based on age, pursues a legitimate aim of employment policy or the enhancement of flexibility in the labour market, as a tool to increase the employment of young people. The means to achieve these objectives, such as flexible and temporary employment contracts, are also appropriate and necessary.

III. Right to be Heard in a Case of Denied International Protection

In the case C-348/16, decided on 26 July 2017, the ECJ responds to a reference for a preliminary ruling made by the Court of Milan in the context of a dispute between Moussa Sacko, a Malian citizen, and the Milan Territorial Commission for the recognition of international protection. The case concerns the latter's rejection of Mr. Sacko's application for international protection within the meaning of article 2(b) of Directive 2013/32 (the so-called "Procedures Directive").

Upon his arrival in Italy, Mr. Sacko applied for international protection. After the rejection of his application by the Territorial Commission, he lodged an appeal to annul that decision before the Court of Milan. The Court indicated its intention to dismiss Mr. Sacko's appeal as manifestly unfounded, without first giving him the opportunity to be heard.

However, having doubts as to whether that approach was compatible with EU law, the Court of Milan suspended the procedure and asked the ECJ if the Directive 2013/32 should be interpreted as admitting a procedure such as the Italian one (based on article 19(9), lgs.d. No. 150/2011) whereby a judicial authority filed by an asylum-seeker whose application, being fully assessed including with an interview, was rejected by the Territorial Commission, is allowed to reject the judicial claim *de plano*, without being required to afford the applicant a further opportunity to be heard, in cases where the application for judicial review is manifestly unfounded.

The ECJ response is positive, subject to certain conditions. The first condition is that, during the judicial proceedings at first instance, the applicant was given the opportunity of a personal interview to illustrate his or her claim for international protection, and the report or transcript of the interview, has been made available to the court competent for the judicial review. The second condition is that, in case of appeal, when the court of second instance considers that the information collected in the personal interview conducted during the first instance is insufficient, may order a new hearing for the purpose of ensuring that there is a full examination of both facts and points of law.

IV. *Ne Bis in Idem* and Double-track Sanctions (Administrative and Penal) for the Omitted Payment of the VAT

In the case C-217/15, decided on 5 April 2017, the ECJ replies to a reference for a preliminary ruling made by the Court of Santa Maria Capua Vetere in the context of two criminal proceedings brought, respectively, against Mr. Massimo Orsi and Mr. Luciano Baldetti, as a result of offences relating to value added tax (VAT). The same facts had previously been subject to an assessment by the tax authorities, which ended with the application of a tax penalty to the detriment of the companies of which the two defendants were legal representatives at the time.

The question raised by the referring court concerns the interpretation of article 50 CFREU on the right not to be tried or punished twice in criminal proceedings for the same criminal offence. In particular, the referring court asks whether these provisions should be interpreted as impeding the application of Italian legislation (article 10-*ter*, lgs.d. No. 74/2000) which allows criminal proceedings to be initiated for the omission to pay VAT even if a tax penalty has been already imposed on account of the same facts.

The ECJ's reply is negative due to the fact that the application of the *ne bis in idem* principle enshrined in article 50 CFREU presupposes that it is the same person who is the subject of the penalties or criminal proceedings at issue. In the case in question, however, the tax penalty and the criminal proceedings concerned separate persons: the first was imposed on companies with legal personality; the second were brought against natural persons.

Index

D

E

J

K

L

M

O

P

Q

R

Table of Cases

Constitutional Court

Court of Cassation, Civil Division

Court of Cassation, Criminal Division

Administrative Courts

Ordinary Tribunals

European Court of Human Rights (in alphabetical order)

Court of Justice of the European Union (in chronological order)

European Committe of Social Rights, decisions on collective complaints

Research and Editorial Board

Peter Lang – Italian Yearbook of Human Rights Series

The legal and political significance of human rights has increased enormously at the international and European levels. Awareness has risen that the respect and the promotion of human rights must be at the centre of States and local communities' public policies and that human rights are at the basis of civil society initiatives and movements. There is a large machinery monitoring, at all the levels of governance, the way in which States implement the obligations assumed toward each person under their sovereignty.

The **Italian Yearbook of Human Rights Series** provides year by year, a dynamic and up-to date overview of the measures Italy has taken to adapt its legislation and policies to international human rights law and to comply with commitments voluntarily assumed by the Italian Government at the international level. The Series thus intends to contribute to the continuous monitoring activity on the situation of human rights in Italy undertaken at the local, national and international levels by relevant intergovernmental and civil society actors.

Each volume of this series surveys the activities carried out, during the year of reference, by the relevant national and local Italian actors, including governmental bodies, civil society organisations and universities. It also presents reports and recommendations that have been addressed to Italy by international monitoring bodies within the framework of the United Nations, the Council of Europe and the European Union. Finally, each Yearbook provides a selection of examples from international and national case-law which cast light on Italy's position vis-a-vis internationally recognised human rights.

The Yearbook is edited by the Human Rights Centre of the University of Padova, in cooperation with the UNESCO Chair in Human Rights, Democracy and Peace of the same University, and with the support of the Region of Veneto. The Centre, established in 1982, carries out research and education following a global and interdisciplinary approach. It hosts the Jean Monnet Centre of Excellence on intercultural dialogue, human rights and multi-level governance.

www.peterlang.com

www.ingramcontent.com/pod-product-compliance
Ingram Content Group UK Ltd.
Pitfield, Milton Keynes, MK11 3LW, UK
UKHW021848100926
8556IPUK00020B/1113

9 782807 60981